Comics, Culture, and Religion

Also Available from Bloomsbury

Dreams, Vampires and Ghosts, Louise Child
Religious Diversity in Europe, edited by Riho Altnurme, Elena Arigita, and Patrick Pasture
Spiritual Sensations, Sarah K. Balstrup

Comics, Culture, and Religion

Faith Imagined

Edited by
Kees de Groot

BLOOMSBURY ACADEMIC
LONDON • NEW YORK • OXFORD • NEW DELHI • SYDNEY

BLOOMSBURY ACADEMIC
Bloomsbury Publishing Plc, 50 Bedford Square, London, WC1B 3DP, UK
Bloomsbury Publishing Inc, 1385 Broadway, New York, NY 10018, USA
Bloomsbury Publishing Ireland, 29 Earlsfort Terrace, Dublin 2, D02 AY28, Ireland

BLOOMSBURY, BLOOMSBURY ACADEMIC and the Diana logo are trademarks of Bloomsbury Publishing Plc

First published in Great Britain 2024
Paperback edition published 2025

Cover image: *Time after time* by Kaisa Maria Krisangi Leka

A catalogue record for this book is available from the British Library.

A catalog record for this book is available from the Library of Congress.

ISBN: HB: 978-1-3503-2158-8
PB: 978-1-3503-2162-5
ePDF: 978-1-3503-2159-5
eBook: 978-1-3503-2160-1

Typeset by Newgen KnowledgeWorks Pvt. Ltd., Chennai, India

Contents

Illustrations

Figures

Tables

Contributors

Ilaria Biano is a scholar in religious and cultural studies. Her main research interests revolve around issues of secularization and postsecularity in contemporary society and culture. She has published in international journals and edited collections on non/religion and popular culture, religion and posthumanities, trauma, memory, and history.

Line Reichelt Føreland is an assistant professor at the University of Agder in the Department of Nordic and Media Studies. Her research interests focus on comics, indigenous and minority perspectives, and game-based learning. She coordinates the international research and development project "Minecraft as a teaching tool in Sámi and Norwegian classrooms" and has published on comics and education.

Kees de Groot is the KSGV Professor of Sociology of Worldviews and Public Mental Health at Tilburg University in The Netherlands and an associated member of the research group Religious Minorities and Religious Diversity at the University of Agder. His research is on religion in liquid modernity and has covered Catholicism, spiritual care, religion in the public domain, theater, events, and Tintin. His latest monograph in the English language is *The Liquidation of the Church* (2018).

Kambiz GhaneaBassiri is the Thomas Lamb Eliot Professor of Religion and Humanities at Reed College in Portland, Oregon. He specializes in the study of Islamic intellectual and social history in the classical and modern period and in the history of Islam in America. He is the author of *A History of Islam in America: From the New World to the New World Order* (2010).

Andreas Häger is an associate professor in sociology at Åbo Akademi University, Turku, Finland. His main research interest lies within the sociology of religion, particularly religion and popular culture. Publications include *Religion and Popular Music: Artist, Fans, and Cultures* (2018).

Ralf Kauranen is a researcher at the Department of Comparative Literature, University of Turku, Finland. He currently works on the project "The Novel's Knowledge: The Changing Roles of Book and Author in Society" (2022–4), funded by the Kone Foundation. A sociologist and comics scholar, Kauranen has shown a longtime interest in Finnish and transnational comics culture.

Evelina Lundmark is a postdoctoral researcher at the University of Agder in the Faculty of Humanities and Education. Her research focuses on atheism and secularism. She has published on atheist identity and community formation and the intersection between cultural Christianity and nationalism in Scandinavia. Her recent book is *Performing Atheist Selves in Digital Publics: U.S. Women and Non-Religious Identity Online* (2023).

Mark MacWilliams is a professor of East Asian Religions at St. Lawrence University. His areas of research are Japanese pilgrimage, popular culture, Shinto intellectual history, and method and theory in the study of religion. Recent publications include (with Okuyama Michiaki) *Defining Shinto* (2019) and *Japanese Visual Culture: Explorations in Manga and Anime* (2008).

Christophe Monnot is an associate professor of sociology of religions at the University of Strasbourg (France), and a researcher at the University of Lausanne (Switzerland). His research interests focus on local religious communities (congregations) and the settlement of religious groups with a migrant background. He has published on religious diversity and congregations. His most recent book in English is *Congregations in Europe* (edited with Jörg Stolz, 2018).

Paulina Niechciał is an assistant professor in the Center for Comparative Civilization Studies at Jagiellonian University, Poland. Her academic interests cover the anthropology and sociology of religion and contemporary cultures of Persianate societies of Iran, Afghanistan, and Tajikistan. She authored academic journal articles and book chapters on minority and identity studies and a monograph in Polish titled *Mniejszość zaratusztriańska we współczesnym Teheranie: o tożsamości zbiorowej w kontekście dominacji szyickiej* (Zoroastrian Minority in Modern Tehran: On Collective Identity in the Context of Shi'a Domination) (2013). Her most recent research project focuses on modern Zoroastrianism within a gender studies framework.

Michael J. Prince is a professor of American Literature and Culture at the University of Agder in the Department of Foreign Languages and Translation. His research interests focus on the beat poets, popular music, film, and comics. He has also published on science fiction and film adaptations. His most recent book is *Adapting the Beat Poets: Burroughs, Ginsberg, and Kerouac on Screen* (2016).

Sofia Sjö is a research librarian at the Donner Institute for Research into Religion and Culture (Åbo, Finland). Her research interests focus on religion, media and popular culture, youth and religion, and religion and gender. She has recently coedited the volume *The Diversity of Worldviews among Young Adults: Contemporary (Non)Religiosity and Spirituality through the Lens of an International Mixed Method Study* (2022).

Irene Trysnes is an associate professor at the University of Agder in the Department of Sociology and Social work. Her research has focused on gender and inequality, youth and religion, and social science didactics. She has co-authored "Hot Case-workers and Squint-eyed Whores—Sexual Harassment of Norwegian Social—and Health Care Students in Practical Training" (2022) and "The Role of Religion in Young Muslims' and Christians' Self-presentation on Social Media" (2021).

Sissel Undheim is a professor in Religious Studies at the University of Bergen, Norway. Her teaching and research interests cover ancient as well as contemporary religion. She has published books and articles on Roman religion, gender, reception, New Age, and popular culture, particularly Lego. Her most recent monograph, *Borderline Virginities* (2018), is a study of sacred virgins in fourth century Rome.

Acknowledgments

This volume was envisioned while talking with the Norwegian humor scholar Pål Ketil Botvar at the conference of the International Society for the Sociology of Religion in Lausanne (2017). Together with the sociologist of religion Ida Marie Høeg he invited me as a guest researcher at the University of Agder in the spring semester of 2021, which created a stimulating atmosphere to write the book proposal, invite authors, and contact the right publisher. Early versions of most chapters were discussed at following conferences in Barcelona (2019), online (2021), in Gothenburg (Nordic Conference in the Sociology of Religion 2022), and at seminars of the research group Religious Minorities and Religious Diversity. Anonymous external experts in comics studies further enhanced the quality of individual chapters by writing sharp and helpful reviews. Sonia Pavlenko assisted in preparing the manuscript. Leonie Jetten had faith in the project from the outset, followed the process closely, and compiled the index. Her commitment is beyond imagination. The publication in open access has been funded by the Faculty for Humanities and Education and the University Library of the University of Agder.

Introduction

1

Comics and Religion in Liquid Modernity

Kees de Groot

Comics offer us a particular perspective on society, culture, and religion. The study of visual art from medieval Europe has almost automatically focused on the church actors who commissioned art, on representations of religious motives derived from the Scriptures, and on the use of artistic work in religious contexts. Similarly, the European history of printing is intrinsically linked with the printing of Bibles. In the 1450s, the illuminated Gutenberg Bible was the first book to be printed using metal type and the first book to be distributed on a wide scale—some six hundred years after the illustrated Buddhist Diamond Sutra was printed by woodblock in China. The Diamond Sutra was the first printed book with a publishing date we can pinpoint (May 11, 868), and it contained both characters and drawings. Historically, it was hardly exceptional for images and texts intended for a popular audience to have a religious motif. Since the late nineteenth century, printing techniques have advanced to such a level that drawings in color can be reproduced on a mass scale and sold at affordable prices in journals, magazines, and albums. This circumstance enabled the production and distribution of stories told in images and text, such as *comics* in the United States, *bandes dessinées* in Europe, and *manga* in Japan. In this instance, the medium seems much less intertwined with religion. But is this impression correct?

Studying Comics and Religion

At first sight, it does not seem obvious to assume a connection between comics and religion. The study of religion has paid scant attention to comics, and the study of comics similarly has been largely uninterested in religion. Yet, comics and religion are related in ways that pertain to the core interests of both disciplines.

The present volume systematically explores the relationship between religion, comics, and culture in a global context (cf. Coody 2017). The first connection is that religions interact with comics. Comics are often used to convey religious content, such as in the *Comics Bible* (Silverstein 2021). Conversely, the portrayal of religion in comics and cartoons is sometimes met with vehement protest. In this case, religion and comics are entangled in an adversarial relationship. The second connection is that comics interact with religion. Religious elements occur even in mainstream comics; examples are the presence of Catholic moral tropes and imagery in the European *bande dessinée Tintin* (de Groot 2017), of Muslim identity markers in the *Ms. Marvel* series that features the superheroine Kamala Khan (Arjana 2018), and of a religious vocation in Craig Thompson's graphic novel *Blankets* (Kraemer 2016). The third connection is that comics sometimes function like a religion for their devotees. The readership's strong commitment to reading, discussing, and studying comics, both individually and collectively, is striking. This commitment also has strong material and physical aspects, as it is particularly apparent at megaevents such as Comic-Cons, where some of the visitors dress up as characters from comics, games, and movies (*cosplay*). In Japan and elsewhere, there are pilgrimages to places that feature in manga and anime (Sabre 2016; Sugawa-Shimada 2015). The worlds of comics and religion interact and overlap.

This book discusses comics in their relationship to religion from the perspective of culture. We regard the human condition that people give meaning to the world of which they are part as key to our understanding of society. We take a pragmatic stance regarding the definition of both religion and comics, but the following reflections should help to demarcate the subject.

We will not attempt to define what religion *really* is. We rather observe what people regard as religion and what not, leaving aside academic discussions on functional and substantive definitions. Substantive definitions are often regarded as stricter, but it could be argued that a substantive definition of religion requires that all comics that include an active role for the supernatural and the superhuman (Jeffery 2016) should be considered religious—at least if they invite some kind of faith in readers' imaginations. The chapters collected here usually reserve the concept of religion for institutions and aspects of culture that are generally regarded as religious. They follow the cultural construction of what counts as religion. Some authors use the concepts of *liquid religion*, *implicit religion*, or *invented religion* when tracing the sacred in the context of the secular.

More often, concepts such as *meaning making*, *sacralization*, and *ritualization* are used to address aspects that are often associated with religion but can also be observed outside the religious sphere.

We use "comics" as a general term, although humor is not the medium's defining characteristic. The cultural phenomenon of comics can be subsumed under the broader concept of visual narratives: those sequential images that tell a story with pictures, usually accompanied by text (Cohn 2021, 1). The narrative aspect excludes, for example, graphic instructions for assembling cabinets. Still, children's picture books are also visual narratives. Our focus, however, is on a cluster of specific cultural artifacts known as comics, *bandes dessinées*, graphic novels, and manga, that are published in journals, magazines, albums, or in digital form such as webcomics or hybrid editions. The distinction between the different formats is a matter of fierce debate, especially that between comics and graphic novels. This debate cannot be solved outside historical contexts and, indeed, it involves the politics of demarcation. Calling books "graphic novels" means granting them a higher status than if they are categorized as "comics." Comics are related to, but differ from cartoons, illustrated novels, animated films, and videogames. Cartoons originally consist of one panel but today are often subdivided into multiple scenes and are then called comic strips (Kannenberg 2021). Comics are sometimes turned into animated films, which invites researchers to explore the universes produced by various media.

The prehistory of comics, and of religion in comics in particular, could be said to go as far back as the Lascaux cave paintings or as medieval altarpieces depicting the life of the Virgin Mary in pictures and text. But its history proper should probably start with the combining of text and image in the Swiss pedagogue Rodolphe Töpffer's children's books of the 1830s, or with the comic strips published in the early-twentieth-century American newspapers (Baetens and Surdiacourt 2015; Banasiak and Wyeld 2018; Williams 2020). In the early 1900s, newspapers in the United States started to publish "funnies": *Yellow Kid*, *Katzenjammer Kids*, and the intellectually intriguing *Krazy Kat* (Barker 1994). European artists, such as Hergé (Georges Remi), began to copy some of their graphic features, including the use of balloons, and created stories of their own, turning these daily short adventures into elements of a longer story. The publication of these stories in books (*Les aventures de Tintin au pays des Soviets* [1930]) gradually transformed strips into pre-publications of the future full album. In later decades, these high-quality albums in softcover or hardcover with thirty-two, forty-eight, or sixty-four pages in A4 format were increasingly given inventive scenarios, a rich vocabulary, masterly artwork, and, especially since the late 1960s, page designs that transcended the boundaries of three or four strips per page.

In the United States, artists such as Will Eisner (*A Contract with God* [1978]) also began to cross the boundaries of the traditional comics format and promoted the technique of telling stories with pictures and text beyond the genre confinements of humor and adventure. They transgressed the cultural distinctions between commercial production and art and reached out to an adult audience. Like Töpffer, who had explained the pedagogical considerations that guided his artistic production, Eisner elaborated his view on the work he produced and named it *sequential art*. The specific literary ambitions of this type of visual art were expressed by the term *graphic novel*, as the term "comics" in the American context usually referred to genre fiction, such as stories on superheroes published in cheap stapled brochures. These beginnings were followed by internationally acclaimed works such as *Maus* (1986–7) by Art Spiegelman, an autobiographical approach to narrating the Shoah, and *Persepolis* (2000) by Marjane Satrapi, an autobiographical account of life in Iran. The world of comics has become artistically diverse.

An alternative historical narrative might start in Asia with various versions of manga (Chiu 2015; Johnson-Woods 2010). There are many histories of comics. This genealogy reflects a European perspective and pays homage to individual artists who in fact represent broader tendencies. Through the interplay of artistic strategies and propitious circumstances, their names have come to symbolize trends and innovations. Both comics and the study of comics are embedded in a social dynamic.

Comics and Religion in Contemporary Culture

Whereas the study of religion in films (e.g., Downing 2016) is well-established and includes sociological approaches (Cipriani and Del Re 2012), the social study of religion in comics is relatively underdeveloped. The study of religion in comic books, manga, and graphic novels has taken off since the early twenty-first century (Lewis and Kraemer 2010) after earlier "one-shots" such as Umberto Eco's essay on Superman, which was first published in Italian in 1962 (Eco 2004) and *The Gospel According to Peanuts* (Short 1965). The current volume gives impetus to the study of religion in comics from a sociological perspective. It aims to further our understanding of comics as an important and transformative part of popular culture and of religion as a social phenomenon in all its variety.

It is high time for the sociology of religion to be brought to bear upon the field of comics. For too long, the study of religion has been largely confined to the specifically religious sphere: churches, religious movements, or the spiritual milieu. This reflects a solid-modern perspective, which assumes that there are sharp boundaries between the various sectors in society. But it is becoming clear, especially under the postindustrial condition, that boundaries between the institutional spheres are more fluid. The sociologist Zygmunt Bauman has called this condition "liquid modernity" (Bauman 2000), the current phase of modernization. After the rise of hierarchical organizations that were founded to pursue particular purposes, such as industrial production or representation in Parliament, we are now witnessing the rise of networks, short-lived cultural trends, and virtual communities. Often, it is not clear whether these social phenomena are economic, political, cultural, or something else. The boundaries between the institutional spheres have become fluid.

What Bauman did not recognize, however, was that religion is also affected by this condition (de Groot 2018). Religion is not only a bastion against change, the agony of choice and flexibility, but it also contributes to cultural transformation and diversification, and is capable of devising playful ways of dealing with multiple conceptions of the world. It is in this context that religious actors and institutions use comics. Furthermore, in liquid modernity, religion is also present outside its own sphere. While specialized institutions are losing control over the way religion is lived and represented, religion is popping up in other spheres, such as that of visual arts and popular culture, including comics. Finally, it can be argued that the social world in which comics feature shows similarities with the religious field, such as when comics or sites that appear in comics are sacralized, or when tendencies to replace religion are apparent, for example, when comics are experienced as a functional alternative to religion with respect to making sense of the world. The intellectual equipment of the sociology of religion could be useful to research comics readerships.

This results in the following questions on the three connections between religion and comics mentioned earlier. (1) How do comics appear and function in the context of religion? (2) How do religions appear and function in comics? (3) How does the social role of comics relate to the social role of religion? These questions have dictated the structure (cf. Forbes and Mahan 2017) of this volume. The first part, Comics in Religion, starts with religions. How do religious communities and institutions use comics to communicate with their audience and why and when do they protest against them? The second part, Religion in Comics, starts with comics. How are religious beliefs, rituals, symbols, leaders, stories, and practices represented, criticized, and discussed in comics? The third part, Comics as Religion?, discusses the cultural role of comics in cultivating a sense of the sacred and making meaning.

In these three parts we learn *about* the world of comics. An additional part four shifts the perspective (cf. Kuttner, Weaver-Hightower, and Sousanis 2020). In Learning from Comics the question is asked: (4) What and how do comics teach about culture, about religion, and about the intertwinement of the religious and the social? Comics and their various relationships with religion are not only the subject of scholarly research but they are also a means of knowledge production themselves. Comics are used in teaching religious studies, demonstrate sociological insights in religion and society, and signify a broader trend of fictive story worlds providing means for engagement and social bonds. How do comics participate in the endeavor to expand our knowledge about religion and society?

A concluding chapter collects and systematizes the results and suggests paths for further research. How does the study of comics question and inform our understanding of religion in contemporary society and culture?

Attentive readers will have noticed that this is not a collection of essays on religious themes in comics. The focus on religion and comics is guided by an interest in society, culture, and media. Thus, sociology, cultural studies, and media studies are employed to understand the complex relations between religion and comics. The chapters address the context of production, the relationship between representations and social context, and reader responses to comics. The authors of the contributions to this volume deploy a variety of methods: literary analysis, surveys, interviews, ethnographic fieldwork, digital ethnography, and content analysis of media. The subject material treated is diverse and includes comics and readers from Europe, India, Japan, and the United States. The comics that are discussed range from accessible children's comics to multilayered graphic novels such as *Habibi*. Whereas literary studies tend to prioritize innovative and complex graphic novels (Ebdrup 2013), widely read comics are at least as interesting from a sociological perspective. Themes such as nationalism, trauma, memorialization, and "othering" appear across various chapters. A variety of religions (Christianity, Islam, Judaism, Hinduism, Japanese religions, and Zoroastrianism), religious themes, and concepts related to religion receive attention. We have attempted to promote diversity—all within the frames of the format described earlier. Yet some parts stick out, some panels are blurred, and other panels are merged. Just like in comics.

References

Arjana, Sophia Rose. (2018), *Veiled Superheroes: Islam, Feminism, and Popular Culture*, Lanham, MD: Lexington Books.

Baetens, Jan, and Steven Surdiacourt. (2015), "European Graphic Narratives: Toward a Cultural and Mediological History," in Daniel Stein and J. Tohn (eds.), *From Comic Strips to Graphic Novels: Contributions to the Theory and History of Graphic Narrative*, 347–62, Berlin: De Gruyter.

Banasiak, Rafal, and Theodor Wyeld. (2018), "A Brief History of the Graphic Novel," 22nd International Conference Information Visualisation (IV), Fisciano, Italy.

Barker, Kenneth. (1994), "A Theological Reflection on Krazy Kat," *Inks* 1 (2): 6–15.

Bauman, Zygmunt. (2000), *Liquid Modernity*, Cambridge: Polity Press.

Chiu, Monica. (2015), *Drawing New Color Lines: Transnational Asian American Graphic Narratives*, Hong Kong: Hong Kong University Press.

Cipriani, Roberto, and Emanuela C. Del Re. (2012). "Imagination and Society: The Role of Visual Sociology," *Cognitive processing* 13 (Suppl 2): 455–63.

Cohn, Neil. (2021), *Who Understands Comics? Questioning the Universality of Visual Language Comprehension*, London: Bloomsbury Academic.

Coody, Elizabeth. (2017), "The Tangled Relationship between Religion and Comics." Last modified March 17, 2021. Available online: http://www.sacredandsequential.org/2017/09/22/the-tangled-relationship-between-religion-and-comics/ (accessed April 14, 2023).

de Groot, Kees. (2017), "Tintin as a Catholic Comic: How Catholic Values Went Underground," *Implicit Religion* 19 (3): 371–400.

de Groot, Kees. (2018), *The Liquidation of the Church, Routledge New Critical Thinking in Religion, Theology and Biblical Studies*, London: Routledge.

Downing, Crystal. (2016), *Salvation from Cinema: The Medium Is the Message*, London: Routledge.

Ebdrup, Niels. (2013), Nordic Researchers Flock around Comics. *Science Nordic.* Available online: https://sciencenordic.com/denmark-history-media/nordic-researchers-flock-around-comics/1381437 (accessed March 22, 2023).

Eco, Umberto. (2004), "The Myth of Superman," in Jeet Heer and Kent Worcester (eds.), *Arguing Comics: Literary Masters on a Popular Medium*, 134–47, Jackson: University Press of Mississippi.

Forbes, Bruce David, and Jeffrey H. Mahan. (2017), *Religion and Popular Culture in America*, Berkeley: University of California Press.

Hoff Kraemer, Christine. (2016), "The Authority of the Image: Sex, Religion, and the Text/Image Conflict in Craig Thompson's *Blankets*," in Stewart M. Hoover (ed.), *The Media and Religious Authority*, 228–52, University Park, PA: Pennsylvania State University Press.

Jeffery, Scott. (2016), *Posthuman Body in Superhero Comics: Human, Superhuman, Transhuman, Post/Human, Palgrave Studies in Comics and Graphic Novels*, New York: Palgrave Macmillan.

Johnson-Woods, Toni. (2010), *Manga: An Anthology of Global and Cultural Perspectives*, New York: Continuum.

Kannenberg, Gene. (2021), "Cartoon," in Erin La Cour, Simom Grennan, and Rik Spanjers (eds.), *Key Terms in Comics Studies*, 44–5. Cham, Switzerland: Springer.

Kuttner, Paul J., Marcus B. Weaver-Hightower, and Nick Sousanis (2020). "Comics-Based Research: The Affordances of Comics for Research Across Disciplines." Qualitative Research (20200605). https://doi.org/10.1177/1468794120918845.

Lewis, A. David, and Christine Hoff Kraemer (eds.) (2010), *Graven Images: Religion in Comic Books and Graphic Novels*, New York: Continuum.

Sabre, Clothilde. (2016), "French Anime and Manga Fans in Japan: Pop Culture Tourism, Media Pilgrimage, Imaginary," *International Journal of Contents Tourism* 1: 1–19. Available online: http://hdl.handel.net/2115/64796 (accessed April 14, 2023).

Short, Robert L. (1965), *The Gospel according to Peanuts*. 16 print ed., Richmond: Knox Press.

Silverstein, Stanley. (2021), *Classic Bible Comics*, Manchester, New Hampshire: Sophia Institute Press.

Sugawa-Shimada, Akiko. (2015), "Rekijo, Pilgrimage and 'Pop-Spiritualism': Pop-Culture-Induced Heritage Tourism of/for Young Women," *Japan Forum* 27 (1): 37–58. doi: 10.1080/09555803.2014.962566.

Williams, Paul. (2020), *Dreaming the Graphic Novel: The Novelization of Comics*, New Brunswick, NJ: Rutgers University Press.

Part 1

Comics in Religion

2

From Subordinates to Superheroes? Comics in Christian Magazines for Children and Youth in Norway

Irene Trysnes

How do religious organizations use comics to communicate religion to children and youth? This chapter examines comics in two different Norwegian religious magazines for children: *Blåveisen* (Hepatica) and *Barnas* (*The Children's*). These magazines contribute to religious education in the form of Bible teaching, storytelling, and entertainment, and both have existed for about 150 years. The magazines use popular cultural elements, such as comics, in their religious education. The form of the comics, either a short story or a single strip, shapes the religious message and the way the religious narratives are presented.

For a long time, religious journals for children and adolescents have served as an important part of religious socializing. These journals covered topics like central stories from the Bible, communication of the values of children's upbringing, entertaining articles, often told stories about life in the mission fields, and encouraging the young readers to be obedient to their parents and to God. I will analyze two religious journals for children and adolescents from Norway focusing on how the use of comics has developed over time in these magazines and further contributed to a mediatization process. The following research questions are answered in this chapter: *What is the function of comics in two Norwegian religious magazines for children and what do the comics communicate?* The methodological entrance to the field is document analysis, which is a "systematic procedure for reviewing or evaluating documents" (Bowen 2009). In this study I have used content analysis to organize the comics into different categories.

Christian Children's Magazines in Norway: A Historical Overview

From the 1500s to 2012, Norway had a Lutheran state church and therefore, as the other Scandinavian countries, has strong "collective cultural–religious traditions, with majority churches encompassing between two-thirds and three-quarters of the population" (Lundby and Repstad 2018, 20). In later years, the Norwegian religious landscape has become more diverse with greater focus on aesthetization and sensual expressions (Repstad and Trysnes 2013). In the 1800s, Norway was characterized by the formation and growth of many organizations, both religious and non-religious, for various purposes (Gundersen 1996, 64–5). Many of these were mission organizations, several of which were organized into local associations focused on "the others" both in regard to inner and outer missions: "Missionary Unions became a place where laymen, both men and women, could express religious commitment" (Stensvold 2005, 317, author's translation). The Christian organizations quickly grew, and over time, several of these organizations developed extensive outreach networks aimed at children and adolescents, in which the focus was mainly teaching of the Christian faith.

The creation of organizations and associations, especially for children and adolescents, created a need for adapted teaching materials, which were very limited at that time. In fact, it was not until the 1800s that Norwegian authors started writing books for children, which was relatively late in comparison to the rest of Europe. In Germany, for example, there were picture books for teaching the alphabet to children as early as the 1500s, and the first children's magazines were published during the 1700s. Around the mid-1800s, several children's magazines were published in Norway, both of a religious and non-religious nature. The *Billed-Magazin for Børn* (*Picture Magazine for Children*) from 1838 to 1839 is considered to be one of the first, and in 1847, the *Missionsblad for Børn* (*Mission Magazine for Children*) was first published in Stavanger, Norway. Toward the end of the 1800s, ten different children's and adolescents' magazines were published (Helleve 2012, 11). Most Christian children's magazines have their background in Christian associations and mission organizations. Many of the magazines originating from the 1800s had an extensive use of imported texts and illustrations, often from the United States or Great Britain.

While children's books consisted mostly of a continuous story written by one author, children's magazines were periodical publications with several authors and a varied genre of storytelling, fiction, and entertainment content. Økland

(1981, 90) points out that the magazines also differed from the book format by forming a greater intimacy with the reader. The intimacy with the readers is also underlined by Dilliane (2016), who further argues that the periodical format has a relational character for a variety of affects and emotions.

For example, the reader received the magazine in the mail and had the opportunity to correspond with the editorial staff. The nonreligious children's magazines not only focused on entertainment and exciting stories but also on socially oriented stories with clear value sharing. Many contained a mixture of religious and secular narratives in their early years. The Christian children's magazines, however, differed from these, in that they had a clear focus on the dissemination of religious content.

The main role of the Christian children's magazines was religious socialization. The material in the children's magazines also followed a relatively "regular pattern." The front pages had an appealing illustration, sometimes with a theme. Inside the magazines, the exhorting and serious articles were often printed first, while the entertainment pieces were added toward the end, often on the last page (Økland 1981, 92). The comics were used both for entertainment purposes and to mediate religious content. Økland points out that the children's magazines "played against the two power poles in the child's life, home/family on one side and school/church on the other" (Økland 1981, 129, author's translation).

Understanding Comics in Religious Magazines: Theoretical Perspectives

The interaction between religion and popular culture has been described by multiple concepts. De Groot (2008, 2017) uses the metaphor "liquid religion" to describe how religious organizations adapt to the secular sphere and become more fluid. The notion "liquid religion" mainly refers to how religion becomes visible in new and more "liquid" ways outside the different congregations. In this chapter I use the metaphor to understand how "liquid modernity" influence the aforementioned religious magazines.

Hjarvard (2012) uses the term *mediatization of religion* and describes this as a "general process through which a variety of social fields become dependent on the media" (Hjarvard 2012, 24). Lundby (2018) points out how the terms mediatization and mediation both are interconnected but at the same time also refers to different processes. The concept of mediatization is more concerned with historical changes and "the mediatized conditions for social interaction following these historical changes," while the concept of mediation "concerns the ways in which the use of particular media in communication practices may influence the form and content of the message and its reception" (Lundby 2018, 5–6).

Hjarvard (2012) developed a three-point typology that describes the relationship between media and religious life:

1. Religious media. These media are owned and operated by religious organizations, and they have the option to control the content in the magazines.
2. Religion in the media. These are journalistic representations of religion in various media. Here, the religious actors have less control over the message.
3. Banal religion. This refers to the use of religious representations, symbols, and narratives used in new contexts and often for entertainment purposes. Banal religion has been criticized for being a negatively charged term. In this chapter, the term is referred to in relation to representations of religiosity that have a popular cultural character. These may be images or symbols that have a religious undertone and may be open to a multitude of interpretations.

It is especially concepts of religious media and banal religion that are of interest regarding how religious organizations use comics. Wessley (2017) has conducted an overview of the history and development of comics. He argues that comics have various functions that work together. They seek to entertain an audience; several comics were created for moral purposes, comics may have a propagandistic function and finally they may function as system-criticism (Wessley 2017, 32–9). Khoja-Moolji and Niccolini (2015) argue that comics may have a transformative function by reframing religion in popular cultural productions (36).

Furthermore, it is important to contextualize the comics in the religious magazines by looking at changes in the views toward children and childhood over the past years. The tendency has been to move away from focusing on the child as a subordinate who must show respect for authority and to consider the child as more of an equal deserving of respect. The actual magazine content around childhood has also changed. Allison James, the English researcher in the field of childhood, claims that the views toward children and childhood have changed from seeing children as "human becomings" to "human beings," thus focusing more on children as full-fledged people with their own wills and needs (James, Jenks, and Prout 1999). Childhood researchers point out that the perception of children has changed in Western societies, viewing them as subjects with their own wills and needs, who are adapted and shaped by the environment (Sommer, Samuelsson, and Hundeide 2010). Karin Hake's (2006) study on children's television programs in Norway from 1960 to 2005 points to the same tendency. While children's television shows in the 1960s and 1970s were designed on adults' terms, often with a clear training and educational focus, an important change took place following the 1980s, when the child increasingly became the focus and emerged as the protagonist of the stories. Hake points out that today's television has changed from a strong focus on education and learning to more of an entertainment focus, and the term "edutainment" is often used nowadays to refer to children's programs. Thus, the sharp distinction between learning and entertainment is eliminated, and learning is presented within an entertainment context. Religious education, and further religious comics, can be characterized as part of this edutainment trend, that is, a mixture of entertainment and the dissemination of faith (Lövheim 2007; Mikkola, Niemelä, and Petterson 2007).

Research on comics in the Nordic countries is relatively new, but it is an emerging field. Strømberg (2016) has made an overview of studies of comics in the Nordic countries and finds that over half of the studies are conducted within the field of language or literature studies, and that there are few studies from the field of sociology and theology (149). In the Norwegian context, there are also few studies on religious literature for children, and even less concerning periodicals. Religious literature has often been regarded as inferior and has generally had a low status in the research communities (Birkeland and Storås 1993, 11). Christian children's magazines thus became an additional low-status category (11). These were magazines with high-publication numbers (*Barnas* had 122,000 subscribers at its highest in 1979) that were read by many, and therefore their content was also of great sociological and historical interest.

One of the relevant works in this field is Ying Toijer Nilsson's study titled *Christianity in Children's and Youth's Literature* (1976). Astrid Ramsfjell (2005) wrote a doctoral dissertation on children's bibles. She also conducted a study of *Church books* for four-year-olds (Fireårsbøkene) in the Church of Norway from 1972 to 1997 and points to two main trends. First, there has been a toning down of adults as authority figures, which has led to the view of children's independence. Second, there has been a shift from focusing on sin and salvation to creation theology, which is linked to a more optimistic human perspective (142). Trysnes (2013) studied Christian songbooks for children, in which she focused on the changes in song lyrics, song themes, song styles, and musical genres. One finding was that songs thematizing the kind and obedient child had been abandoned. The child portrayed in the new Christian songs for children is active and independent. Also, the more negative aspects of Christianity, such as the devil, sin, and perdition, are no longer present in the new songs.

Åse Marie Ommundsen (1998) wrote a master's thesis about the views on children in Christian children's magazines from 1875 to 1910, which was later published in the report series "The Establishment of Norwegian Childhood" (1996, author's translation). Ommundsen studied a period in which many of the magazines were established, and her findings are interesting to compare with the later development of Christian children's magazines. One of the magazines she analyzed from this period was *Blåveisen*, which makes her study highly relevant to this chapter. Ommundsen (1998) points out that during the period she was studying, few changes occurred. *Blåveisen* did not develop to any significant extent; it remained dominated by moral narratives in which there was a continuation of stories, songs, devotional letters, Bible verses, and prize assignments (36). In the period she studied, the magazine had a clearly dualistic understanding of reality: "Everything that does not belong to God belongs to the devil, either on the side of the good or the wicked. Either one is a complete, unhappy, sinful and evil pagan, or happily saved on the way to heaven" (53). This clear division of the world also corresponds with Ramsfjell's (2005) findings in the moral narratives, which she divides into two categories: "the disobedient who will be punished" and "the pious who will be rewarded" (138). Einar Økland (1981) did a historical study of Norwegian children's magazines, in which he points out that the ideals of religious and secular upbringing generally go hand in hand with the various magazines. The aforementioned studies and theoretical perspectives form the backdrop for the following presentation of comics in Christian children's magazines.

Christian Children's Magazines: Selection and Development

I have chosen two journals adapted to children and adolescents for the purpose of obtaining a certain theological spread and also due to the number of copies in circulation. *Barnas*, formerly known as *Barnas søndagsskoleblad* (Children's Sunday School Magazine), is the oldest Christian children's magazine that still ezxists in Norway. It was started by the Lutheran priest Honoratius Halling in 1854 under the name of the *Børnebiblioteket* (Children's Library) and was often distributed free of charge at Sunday schools "as a prize for the most diligent students" (Hagen 1974, 73). In 1875, the magazine had a print run of 15,000. From 1865 to 1882, it was edited by H. E. Hansen. The magazine changed its name to *Barnas søndagsskoleblad* in 1935 (Harberg 1989, 46–7). Today, *Barnas* has a circulation of approximately twenty-three thousand and is the largest Christian children's magazine in Norway. It is distributed free of charge at many Sunday schools, but children can also subscribe to it and have it mailed to their home.

The other magazine is *Blåveisen*, which started in 1882, with Jens Marius Giverholt as editor. Giverholt, a theologian, was born in Bergen in 1848, and he wrote for children and taught Sunday school. In the beginning, the *Blåveisen* magazine had the subtitle: "A magazine for Sunday school and the home." Giverholt was the editor of *Blåveisen* until his death in 1916 (Ommundsen 1998, 35). In 1917, the magazine was taken over by the Norwegian Lutheran Mission, which ran it by that name until 2001. In 2001, the name changed to *Blink* (Flash), and in 2006, it once again changed to *Superblink* (Superflash). There was also a profile change, and the magazine became part of a larger club concept consisting of three elements: website, magazine, and CDs, with a target group of children aged five to thirteen. It has recently been replaced by a new platform called *Intro*.

Both magazines are part of the periodical genre, which is a mixed genre. It is characterized by multimodal texts, diverse voices, and different authors. Therefore, it is difficult to define. Furthermore, each number of a periodical functions both as part of a series and as a free-standing unit. "It is both open-ended and end-stopped" (Beetham 1989, 99). The periodicals also invite the reader to make his or her selection of texts as it is unusual to read a periodical "from cover to cover." Instead, readers can "construct their own texts" (Beetham 1989, 98).

Both magazines started out with a focus on religious education. In the earliest years, the focus was on raising well-behaved and obedient Christian children who would do the right thing, follow Jesus, and actively proclaim the gospel to others. Punishment and reward appear as a clear dichotomy in the religious dissemination, in which the punishment as an extreme consequence of disobedience was portrayed as eternal destruction, but mostly it was linked to something unpleasant for the child in this life if he or she lied, stole, and so on. In contrast, reward was linked to the promise of eternal life and a more subjective experience of happiness when the child chose the acceptable and right action. Up until the 1960s, the magazines were dominated by moral narratives with a clear religious didactic message. *Blåveisen* turned out to be focusing more on missionary stories and was also the most conservative one being part of a mission organization, which in 2007, broke its ties with the Church of Norway due to their acceptance of gay and lesbian priests. *Barnas* has a more liberal profile and is part of the Norwegian Sunday Association, with members from different Lutheran churches and organizations.

Due to the extent of this work, I chose to concentrate my reading on only one complete year of issues from every decade, focusing on content analysis. I have taken a "sampling" of the magazines from other years and read some single editions from the period. I have created an overview of the types of comics topics I found in the magazines and divided them into the following five categories. The categories are inspired by Wessely's (2017) different function of comics:

1. Moral comics—focus on obedience and the religious socialization of the child.
2. Mission comics—emphasize stories of missionaries spreading Christianity, often to the countries in Africa and Asia.
3. Bible comics—different Bible stories presented as comics.
4. Comics with animals—feature animals as the main characters, focusing on taking care of animals or nature.
5. Entertainment comics—without a specific religious content, with the purpose of being funny, entertaining children, and so on.

This categorization is a result of the analysis of all the comics present in the magazines and emphasize on how the comics communicate various themes in the magazines. However, the categories will sometimes overlap. For instance, comics with animals may also function as animals telling Bible stories. Other times they focus on taking care of animals. Some themes also disappear and are replaced with others during time. One may also argue that the overall function of comics is to entertain. Even so, the use of Bible and moral stories in comics is quite different from telling jokes through a comic strip.

Comics in the Magazines

Moral Comics

Moral narratives are generally dominant in the early editions of both magazines. In the 1930s, the magazine *Blåveisen* had only four pages, and moral narratives made up two or three of these. Many of these narratives are very dramatic and harsh, for instance that disobedience can lead to death, but some of the stories feature typical storytelling that addresses everyday events. Some of those stories can be characterized as a precursor to comics, combining pictures with a text line underneath. One such example is the short piece "What Will Mom Say," from 1933.

Here, we find the picture of a girl cutting her little brother's hair. The text addresses the reader, asking: "What will Mom say when she sees stairs and streets in her little boy's beautiful locks of hair? Poor mother! Poor little boy! Else (the girl's name, author) will probably regret what she has done when she sees the result. What will Mom say? Shh, here she comes."

The text is aimed at the youngest readers and is concerned with teaching them to do the right thing. It clearly encourages children to put themselves in the mother's place and to imagine themselves as the little girl who will regret what she has done. It depicts a familiar situation that many people can recognize and has a somewhat humorous undertone. This story is less serious than most others from this period, probably because it is intended for very young readers, as stated in its headline.

Many similar examples of "early comics" are tragic and, for instance, concern children who die. They are also characterized by exhorting words at the end. One example is the little story "The Last Tear":

> There was a little girl who laid on her bed and fighting death. In her hand, she held a handkerchief with which she wiped her sweat and tears away. Suddenly, she gave her mother the handkerchief and said, "Take it mother." The mother replied, "Do you not want it anymore?" The child answered, "No, mother, I do not need it anymore because I have cried my last tear." Then she closed her eyes and died. Her mother wiped away her little girl's last tear. It has been a long time since the first teardrop fell, and since then there has been a flood of tears. But there is a country without tears! Can you grasp it? In that country everyone is happy. To that country everyone is invited. We can all join the big party in heaven! (*Blåveisen* 1933, author's translation)

Such stories are very different from today's narratives for children, and thus they might appear brutal and oppressive. Their basis is obedience ideology, and they are written from a pronounced religious perspective that Hjarvard refers to collectively as *religious media*.

The most "dramatic" moral comics disappeared in the 1960s. Some of the reasons for this may be that child mortality was falling, living standards were increasing, and the perception of children was changing in Western society. These types of comics were replaced by mission comics, also dramatic and with similar themes, but more distant and about "the others out there." One example is how the front matter has a picture of a sun and a hepatica shining over a white boy standing and a white girl kneeling. On the other side, there are pictures of the "heathen children" who are not (yet) under the same protection. In the 1980s, there were also moral comics, but often of a more positive characteristic. They were about doing the right thing, with less focus on punishment and more on forgiveness. During this period, there was more focus on the child, and seemingly, the authoritarian parenting was softening. In the 1990s, the moral narratives in the comics were replaced with more open narratives lacking of a moralizing end.

The themes of the narratives also changed their character in the 1980s and 1990s. The magazines contained more dramatic Bible stories, fairy tales, and stories from other countries that portray good values and no element of punishment. The new comics of the past twenty years that feature the theme of upbringing focus on positive values, and they often also concern children who teach adults something. The stories are short, often with an open ending that invites the reader to reflect on different solutions to the problem. They also allow for a wider range of emotional expression for children; while the previous focus was on children being good and gentle, they are now allowed to express anger and frustration. The children are often portrayed with friends and shown as active, happy children talking about a religious theme. The aforementioned notion of *mediatization* may be one way to describe how religious content is presented using popular cultural elements (Hjarvard 2012).

The comic below is one example of how the Bible story of the "Man Healed at the Pool of Bethesda" is told, with children in a swimming pool as the context. This comic strip is called "The Thomas Church Tower Agent Club" and has appeared as a serial since 2010 in *Barnas* (Figure 2.1). The tower agent club is a theme in the magazine, and "tower agents" are also part of the Church of Norway's Christian faith education. It focuses on active children solving different mysteries and codes, wrapped in the narrative of being "special agents" searching for "secret divine powers" and "secret symbols," with the Christian message as the underlying framework. The tower agents' comics are one of many examples of how Bible stories are "recreated" and told through young children as main characters. As the example above illustrates, the comic has a subordinated function. Telling the biblical story is the main focus.

In the comic we meet the children Lukas, Martin, Linnea, and Sukai and it starts with Lukas saying:

"Yoho!" Jumping into the pool.

"So nice," says Sukai.

Figure 2.1 The Tower Agent Club. *The Norwegian Sunday School,* The Tower Agent Club. *2022, Barnas* no. 1, p. 14.

"Agreed," replies Martin.

"Do you remember the story of Bethesda?" says Linnea.

"The one where Jesus healed the paralyzed man?" replies Lukas.

Linnea: "Yes, and how the water sometimes got stirred?"

Martin: "Just like this!"

Linnea: "For a long time there were no traces of the pond, so a lot of people doubted that the history was true. But as late at the 19th Century some archeologists found it! In the middle of Jerusalem just like the evangelist John writes.

Lukas: That´s so cool! It says in the Bible those who seek will find."

The stirring in the water is symbolized with the boy Lucas stirring in the swimming pool. The comic function as the medium for telling an old bible story. The context is western and modern, but the comic only function as a tool to spread the biblical message, and can also be interpreted in terms of religious media (Hjarvard 2012).

Mission Comics

As mentioned earlier, *Blåveisen* was a mission magazine published by an organization that conducted extensive missionary activities abroad. The purpose was two-sided. The magazine was part of sharing the organization's missionary activities and was also aimed at influencing the religious beliefs of Norwegian boys and girls. The magazine was an important vehicle for children and young people to get involved in missionary work outside of the country. In the earliest magazines, only the mission stories had illustrations. These were often dramatic, portraying idolatry, fighting wild animals, and so on, and characterized by exoticism and focusing on differences between the "heathens" and the Christians.

One typical mission comic is called "The Savage Kid," a serial in *Blåveisen* (1959). It is about a little boy called Gbesimi and describes how he seeks help from a missionary after he hears him preaching the gospel of Jesus. The story follows the traditional path of a conversion story and focuses on how the stray, little, naked African boy gets help from the white missionary.

The same types of comics are also found in *Barnas* during the same period, and when there are illustrations or comics in the magazines, it is the mission stories that are featured. The reason these stories are often illustrated may have to do with their exotic character. We meet "Indian tribes," "snake tamers in India," "African slaves and wizards in the jungle," "Eskimo children," and so on. While *Blåveisen's* missionary material was taken from the organization's actual missionaries, *Barnas* collected narratives from various continents and mission organizations, stories that are thrilling and at times frightening, and are related to the adventure genre where the missionaries function as "superheroes" (Ahmed and Lund 2016) The stories often play on the differences between people, where the white missionaries are great heroes, but some also have elements of mutual identification and understanding. For example, a story is about how children from all countries play the same games, illustrated by Inuit children playing ball: "Those who are the most serious and best at playing games are often the best disciples and the best children" (*Børnevennen* 7, 1869). We can find examples of such attempts to engender cultural understanding even in the nineteenth century.

Both magazines present different mission comics that deal with children in other countries. In the early missionary tales, the male missionary is the protagonist. The native people of Africa or Asia are often presented as a group, and a few are mentioned by name. Those who are named are those who are converted, as well as the chiefs or sorcerers who oppose the missionary. In the 1960s, there are examples of missionary stories in which the child is at the center and teaches the adults, and these stories are even more common in the 1970s and 1980s. During this period, the focus flipped from adults to children both "out there" and back home.

Images of other cultures as dangerous or uncivilized largely have disappeared by the 1990s. In the 1980s, there were some comics focusing on non-Christian children who were in pain and suffering, but this appears less and less. In the 2000s, the magazines are more concerned with how culture is understood, and they present children as equal to adults. Today, the child is at the center of the story, while in the former comics, the focus was on the adult missionaries. There is also less of an emphasis on mission in the latest magazines. The communication of the Christian message to Norwegian children in a positive and appealing way is clearly the main focus.

Bible Comics

Bible comics focus on narrating bible stories through comics and have a central role in both magazines, often as regular slots. In the early magazines of the nineteenth century, they are often featured prominently, for example, on the first page. They rarely fill the entire magazine, and as mentioned, the moral stories take up much more space until the 1960s. Devotionals are gradually reduced to a smaller slot, while the recounting of Bible stories generally takes up more space. The Sunday schools' traditional "word for the day" is also found in the early editions of both magazines. These appeared in the late 1800s as more or less fixed elements. The words for the day are Bible verses that the children are expected to learn by heart. In the early issues, illustrated Bible verses are found in several issues. One example is Jesus and the children from No. 5 1868.

In the 1950s, more Bible stories and devotional material appeared in *Barnas*. The front page often had a picture from a Bible story from the New Testament with headings such as "Jesus as a role model," "Jesus as the Lord victorious," and so on. The magazine also had Bible reading plans and a review of the famous Bible stories. From the 1970s, some of the Bible stories were presented as comics, and the number of Bible stories presented as comics has continued to grow to the present. In the last ten years, almost every Bible story in *Barnas* is presented as a comic. The Bible stories often focus on stories about children, with Jesus performing miracles or focusing on other "superheroes" from the Bible.

The comic below is the story of God calling Samuel (Figure 2.2). It combines old and new interpretations, focusing on Samuel's mother Hannah and the high

Figure 2.2 The calling of Samuel. *The Norwegian Sunday School*, The calling of Samuel. *2022, Barnas* no. 1, p. 5.

priest Eli, wearing traditional clothes, while Samuel wears pajamas and has a cat in his bed. The text says that Hannah gave Samuel to the temple "when he was older," not when she had "stopped breastfeeding him," as is written in the Bible (1. Sam. 22–23).

The Bible comics in both magazines can be interpreted as religious media, using media to convey religious texts. The content of the stories becomes more "freely" interpreted as we move toward the present time.

Animal Comics

The *Børnevennen* No. 10 of 1869 features a story about the "animal tormenter." Narratives that deal with nature and the care of all living beings, both humans and animals, are common in this time and quite prevalent until the 1950s. Also, in the early magazines, there are illustrations of animals both for entertainment and information. In the 1960s, however, there are fewer of these types of stories. Eventually, they are replaced by more realistic stories that thematize the environment or pertain to factual matters, but especially by stories about poverty and charity toward people. The story of the animal tormenter follows the previously mentioned example narrative pattern. It is about little Edmund, who "was cruel enough to torment and afflict all the animals he could get his hands on." His father catches him attacking the bird and tells the boy that his cruel treatment will cause him to face the consequence on God's Day of Judgment. The father will also punish him if he finds him doing this again. However, Edmund does not stop his cruelty toward animals. One time, he torments some little puppies and must climb up a ladder to escape an attack from the puppies' mother. The ladder is in bad condition and Edmund clings helplessly to it. He fears for his life in this state and imagines all the animals he has tormented and killed, finally crying out to God for forgiveness, and is finally rescued from the ladder by a farm boy. After this, Edmund never hurts animals again. The story ends with a Bible verse: "There shall be no merciful judgment upon those who do not show mercy" (Jas 2:13). However, tales of kindness to animals and nature do not have a large role in the magazines; we find them mostly around 1900 up until the Second World War, after which they resurface with an environmental protection profile or a focus on friendship and God's love in the 1990s. In 2022, there is a fixed comic column in *Barnas* called "Gulliver in Paradise Bay" (Figure 2.3). The comic tries to explain the story of Hannah giving Samuel to the temple. The mother fish tells Gulliver that Hannah did not give Samuel to the priest, but to God.

Figure 2.3 Gulliver in a paradise bay. *The Norwegian Sunday School*, Gulliver in paradise bay. *2022, Barnas* no. 1, p. 2.

- Would you give me away? asks Gulliver.
- I don't need to, replies the mother fish.
- What do you mean? says Gulliver.
- The earth and every living creature already belong to God. It is God that created us, and we are his creatures, the mother fish says.
- Good, because I'd rather be with you, says Gulliver.

The conversation with Gulliver and his mother is an interesting example of how the former Bible comic with "Bible figures" is "explained" by animal figures in another comic with a moral message (Wessely 2017). As the Bible stories, mentioned before, it both can be interpreted as mediatization of religion (Hjarvard 2012) and what is suggested as a "liquidizing comic" (de Groot 2016) that attempts to transfer and adjust the Bible stories in our current context.

Humorous Comics

Entertaining materials and contests were early features in the magazines; however, these were mainly featured in the Christmas or other holiday editions. In the beginning, humorous comics were primarily comprised of Biblical riddles or questions, but later we also find, comics telling jokes without biblical references.

In the oldest magazines, we can also find examples of questions and contests, but to a much lesser extent. These types of segments were always placed on the magazine's final page, and as early as in *Blåveisen* no. 3 in 1883, there appears a "prize-winning riddle." The entertainment content increased after the Second World War, and in 2014, it accounted for over one-third of Blåveisen's slots and almost half of *Barnas*. One example of humorous comics is "The fury league" from *Blåveisen* in 2001, which is about sheep telling jokes. This might be an example of "banal religion" (Hjarvard 2012). The only biblical reference here is to the sheep (e.g., Jesus as the shepherd and his followers as sheep).

From Subordination to Superchildren with "Superpowers"

Initially, I briefly described how the view of children and childhood has changed over the years and how this has been reflected in religious comics. For example, the kind and obedient child has been replaced by the independent and active child. As in society in general, there has been a development from the view of children from human "becomings" to human beings in the comics. This corresponds with the gradual change over the years in the religious landscape of Norway (Repstad 2005, 2013; Trysnes 2012). Especially the animal comics and entertainment comics can be interpreted as examples of a religious liquidation process within the religious magazines (de Groot 2008, 2017) in which religious comics are influenced and shaped by secular environments.

The focus on religion has changed in its characterization through edutainment, that is, a mixture of entertainment and dissemination of faith. (Lövheim 2007; Mikkola, Niemelä, and Petterson 2007). These changes can also be observed in Christian children's songs (Trysnes 2013). The magazine comics have also changed from the thematizing of moral education to a general focus on edutainment. The content of the comics is chosen both to convey the Christian message, while, at the same time, serving an entertainment purpose (Wessely 2017) that is mediaized in the "liquid religious" comic book universe (de Groot 2008; Hjarvard 2012). The comics in the magazines, and those in general, now adapt to the secular culture and downplay the typical "religions of difference" (Woodhead and Heelas 2000) elements, such as sinfulness, missionary stories of other cultures, God's judgment, and try to reframe religious messages using elements of popular culture (Khoja-Moolji and Niccolini 2015). The comics are mediaized; shaped and influenced by popular culture, but they also have a focus on communication moral values (Wessely 2017) and a religious message as *religious media* (Hjarvard 2012). The comics present religion in a form that does not appear offensive and that is wrapped in popular cultural symbols. In this context, the comics can also be linked to how children now are placed at the center, not as sinners or subordinates, but more as secret agents connected to divine superpowers or as superheroes (Ahmed and Lund 2016).

References

Ahmed, M., and Lund, M. (2016), "'We're *All* Avengers Now': Community Building, Civil Religion and Nominal Multiculturalism in Marvel Comics' Fear Itself," *European Journal of American Culture* 35 (2): 77–95.

Aukrust, K. (1991), *Menighetsblad og andre religiøse og kirkelige tidsskrift i Norge. En foreløpig oversikt*. Oslo: Universitetet i Oslo, Arkiv for kirkehistoriske tradisjoner.

Beetham, M. (1989), "Open and Closed: The Periodical as a Publishing Genre," *Victorian Periodicals Review* 22 (3): 96–100.

Birkeland, T., and Storås, F. (1993), *Den norske biletboka*. Oslo: J. W. Cappelens forlag.

Bowen, G. A. (2009), "Document Analysis as a Qualitative Research Method," *Qualitative Data Journal* 9 (2): 27–40.

de Groot, C. N. (2008), "Three Types of Liquid Religion," *Implicit Religion* 11: 277–96.

de Groot, C. N. (2016), "Tintin as a Catholic Comic: How Catholic Values Went Underground," *Implicit Religion* 19 (3): 371–400. https://doi.org/10.1558/imre.v19i3.31123.

de Groot, C. N. (2017), *The Liquidation of the Church*, New York: Routledge.

Dillane, F. (2016), "Forms of Affect, Relationality, and Periodical Encounters, or 'Pine-Apple for the Million,'" *Journal of European Periodical Studies* 1 (1): 4–24. https://doi.org/10.21825/jeps.v1i1.2574

Eckert, G. (2001), *Wasting Time or Having Fun? Cultural Meanings of Children and Childhood,* Linköping: Studies in Art and Science.

Gundersen, K. (1996), *Visjon og vekst: framveksten av de frivillige kristelige organisasjoner 1816–1940*, Volda: Møreforsking.

Hagen, I. (1974), *Barnet i norsk kristenliv Oslo*. Oslo: Norsk søndagsskoleforbunds forlag.

Hake, K. (2006), *Historien om Barne-TV: Barndomsbilder 1960–2005*, Oslo: Universitetsforlaget.

Harberg, L. (1989), *Hundre år for barnet Oslo*, Oslo: Norsk søndagsskoleforbunds forlag.

Helleve, E. (2012), *Skrinet med det rare i: Norsk barneblad 125 år*, Oslo: Norsk barneblads forlag.

Hjarvard, S. (2012), "Three Forms of Mediatized Religion. Changing the Public Face of Religion," in S. Hjarvard and M. Lövheim (eds.), *Mediatization and Religion. Nordic Perspectives*, 21–44, Gothenburg: Nordicom.

James, A., Jenks, C., and Prout, A. (1999), *Den teoretiske barndom*, Oslo: Gyldendal.

Khoja-Moolji, S. S., and Niccolini, A. D. (2015), "Comics as Public Pedagogy Reading Muslim Masculinities through Muslim Femininities in Ms. Marvel," *Girlhood Studies* 8 (3): 23–39. https://doi.org/10.3167/ghs.2015.080304

Lundby, K. (2018), "Introduction: Religion and Media in Cultural Conflicts," in K. Lundby (ed.), *Contesting Religion: The Media Dynamics of Cultural Conflicts in Scandinavia*, 3–13, Berlin: Walter de Gruyter.

Lundby, K., and Repstad, P. (2018), "Scandinavia: Traits, Trends and Tensions," in K. Lundby (ed.), *Contesting Religion. The Media Dynamics of Cultural Conflicts in Scandinavia*, 13–32, Berlin: Walter de Gruyter.

Lövheim, M. (2007), *Sökare i cyberspace: ungdomar och religion i ett modernt mediesamhälle*, Stockholm: Cordia.

Mikkola, Teija, Niemelä Kati, and Petterson Juha. (eds.) (2007), *The Questioning Mind*, Tampere: Church Research Institute.

Nilsson, Y. T. (1976), *Tro och utro i modern barnlitteratur*, Oslo:Verbum.

Ommundsen, Å. M. (1998), *Djelvelfrø og englebarn: synet på barn i kristne barneblader i perioden 1875–1910*, Oslo: Institutt for nordistikk og litteraturvitenskap, Seksjon for nordisk språk og litteratur, Universitetet i Oslo.

Ramsfjell, A. (2005), "Barndomskonstruksjon i Den norske kirkes firårsbøker," in O. Davidsen, K. Nielsen, S. Klint, and R. N. Jakobsen (eds.), *Litteraturen og det hellige*, 132–43, Århus: Århus Universitetsforlag.

Repstad, P. (2005), "Fra forskjellsreligion til humanitetsreligion. En introduksjon," in P. Repstad and J. O. Henriksen (eds.), *Mykere kristendom. Sørlandsreligion i endring*, 9–33, Bergen: Fagbokforlaget.

Repstad, P. (2013), "Fra ordet alene til sanselig populærkultur?," in P. Repstad and I. Trysnes (eds.), *Fra forsakelse til feelgood: Musikk, sang og dans i religiøst liv*, 11–40, Oslo: Cappelen Damm Akademisk.

Rudvin, O. (1947), *Den kristelige presse i Norge. En historisk oversikt*, Oslo: Lutherstiftelsen forlag.

Seim, S. (1964), *Norsk søndagsskoleforbund 1889–1964*, Oslo: Norsk søndagsskoleforbund.

Ski, M., Voksø, P., and Aardal, E. (1961), *Kristenliv i Norge*. Oslo: Norsk kunstforlag.

Sommer, D., Samuelsson, I. P., and Hundeide, K. (2010), *Child Perspectives and Children's Perspectives in Theory and Practice*, Berlin: Springer Science.

Stensvold, A. (2005), *Nasjonal enhet—religiøst mangfold*. Oslo: Universitetsforlaget.

Strømberg, F. (2016), "Comics Studies in the Nordic Countries—Field or Discipline?," *Journal of Graphic Novels and Comics* 7 (2): 134–55. DOI: 10.1080/21504857.2016.1141574.

Trysnes, I. (2012), *Å campe med Gud. En studie av kristne sommerstevner på Sørlandet*, Oslo: Prismet bok.

Trysnes, I. (2013), "Fra 'Vær forsiktig lille øyne' til 'Takk, min Gud for hele meg': endringer i kristne barnesanger. Fra forsakelse til feelgood. Musikk, sang og dans i religiøst liv," in P. Repstad and I. Trysnes (eds.), *Fra forsakelse til feelgood: Musikk, sang og dans i religiøst liv*, 41–63, Oslo: Cappelen Damm Akademisk.

Wessely, C. (2017), "On the History and Hermeneutics of Comics," *Journal for Religion, Film and Media* 3 (1): 17–43. DOI: 10.25364/05.3:2017.1.2.

Woodhead, Linda og Paul Heelas. (ed.). (2000), *Religion in Modern Times*. Oxford: Blackwell.

Økland, E. (1981), "Den norske barnelitteraturen gjennom 200 år," in T. Ørjasæther (ed.), *Den norske barnelitteraturen gjennom 200 år: lesebøker, barneblad, bøker, tegneserier*, Oslo: Cappelen.

3

Cancelling the *Second Coming*: Manufactured Christian Outrage Online

Evelina Lundmark

Moral Outrage, Religion, and Comics

This chapter explores moral outrage online centered on the publication of a comic—*Second Coming*—and how this event may be understood in relation to Christian nationalism. Comics have a well-established place within American politico-moral discourses, ever since the moral panic centering on comics in the 1950s when they ended up at the center of debates about juvenile delinquency and the American way of life and depicted as a youth-corrupting peril from within (Hajdu 2009). This particular moral outrage began on January 9, 2019, when Fox News reported that DC Comics was set to publish a comic featuring the return of Jesus (Parke 2019), and cited the Christian Broadcasting Network (CBN), who described it as more "blasphemous than biblical" (Jones 2019). The Fox notice accumulated over six hundred comments in the span of a few days, expressing sentiments like how Christians constantly find themselves under attack and taunting DC to do a comic on Muhammad next.

This event is approached as a case study for understanding tensions surrounding depictions of Christian symbolism within the US context, which historically has been characterized by a close relationship between evangelicalism and media, cf. televangelism, and its apparent pragmatic openness in absorbing and employing various audio-visual media in conveying its message (Bowler and Reagan 2014; Hadden 1993). This case exposes how conceptualizations of blasphemy may be embroiled in processes of boundary marking, driven by moral posturing to defend group identity and signal belonging. This chapter contributes to the volume's overall aim of studying linkages between comics and religion by examining a particular "religious" response to a (at the time of the controversy, imagined) portrayal of Jesus. I say "imagined" as no representative from CBN, nor Fox, nor anyone involved in commenting on the blasphemous nature of the *Second Coming*, had read the comic. Moreover, when the comic was later published in July 2019 by Ahoy (AHOY Comics 2019), no similar event reoccurred.

The *Second Coming* itself centers on God asking Sun-Star (a superman pastiche) to teach Jesus how to be more like him: "One omnipotent being to another—will you help me out? You know, take Jesus under your wing … show him how a *real* hero handles his chili?" (Russell 2020, 29, emphasis in original). Throughout the run, God and Sun-Star instead both come to learn from Jesus, and the comic provides commentary on violence and masculinity in comics. This portrayal and the message of *Second Coming* were irrelevant to the event itself, exemplifying how moral outrage can be expressed online in the form of a firestorm (albeit, a minor one), as the sudden explosion of critique was both intensely indignant and lacking in specificity, as is characteristic of a firestorm (Johnen, Jungblut, and Ziegele 2018; Pfeffer, Zorbach, and Carley 2014). Johnen, Jungblut, and Ziegele (2018) have argued that participation is driven both by the desire for social recognition and by a felt moral transgression. Deemphasizing the tendency to view social media phenomena as new or caused by social media, they explore continuity with literature on moral panics and use Goode and Ben-Yehuda's (1994) five characteristics—a concern that something is threatening the group`s moral values, hostility, exaggerated response, consensus, and volatility—to argue that an online firestorm is a form of moral panic, emphasizing that participation is mainly in pursuit of recognition, in the form of likes, or approving comments from strangers (Johnen, Jungblut, and Ziegele 2018).

Moral outrage has further been identified as contributing to political polarization (Carpenter et al. 2021), something that is said to characterize political elites in the United States (Hare and Poole 2014), and it is suggested that this has contributed to a greater degree of polarization in the US population overall following the civil rights movement (Baldassarri and Gelman 2008). Researchers like Whitehead and Perry (2020) instead consider cross-partisan patterns of nationalism, prejudice, and conservatism, and suggest that Christian nationalism is a better framework for understanding the current political landscape in the United States. Following their lead, "I ask how a discourse of moral outrage was articulated in reference to the announcement of the 'Second Coming,' and further if, and how, this discourse reflects Christian nationalism, exploring the circulation of moral outrage." In this chapter, I focus on the comment section of a Fox News notice with the aim of exploring how a discourse of moral outrage was articulated in reference to the announcement of the

Second Coming, and further how this discourse reflected Christian nationalism. I begin with an overview of the US political landscape, focusing on Christian nationalism, then give a brief overview of the incident in question, followed by an analysis of the Fox comment section.

Christian Nationalism

Christian nationalism is an ideology that—building on a mythologized version of US history centering on the idea that the country was founded by white, "traditional," Christian men, based on Christian principles—seeks to enact a racial, patriarchal, and religious hierarchy that they perceive as fundamentally American (Gorski and Perry 2022; Whitehead and Perry 2020). It does not refer to piety, but denotes a cultural framework that some US Americans subscribe to, but that all US Americans relate to, which conflates "religious identity (Christian, preferably Protestant) with race (white), nativity (born in the United States), citizenship (American), and political ideology (social and fiscal conservative)" (Whitehead and Perry 2020, x). Christian nationalism here refers to a distinctly American phenomenon, which should neither be conflated with Evangelicalism (even though there is a lot of overlap) nor with usages of Christian symbolism within other nationalist movements. It builds on the idea that the United States is chosen by God for greatness, and that this status is threatened by "'un-American' influences both inside and outside" (Gorski and Perry 2022, 4); and outsiders within and without are viewed as violent, criminal, and interior (Whitehead and Perry 2020). In line with Mouffe's (2013) conceptualization, I thus argue that Christian nationalism presupposes an antagonistic division of the political field, where everyone who is not part of the ethnonational "us," is conceived as a threat.

Commitment to this hierarchical understanding of US society is decreasing, which Christian nationalists have come to interpret as marginalization and suppression of (their) religious freedom. Indeed, when talking about religious freedom Christian nationalists narrowly refer to a definition of Christian palatable to Christian nationalists, characterized by "a 'premillennial' worldview" connected to the idea that "God requires the faithful to wage wars for good," and thus includes veneration of the military, authoritarianism, and the nation (Whitehead and Perry 2020, 14). Christian nationalism is thus not about adherence to Christian doctrine but is primarily focused on political goals, using "Christian language and symbols to demarcate and defend group boundaries and privileges" (87). Such political goals are not limited to enacting a strict racial hierarchy, but further include gender subordination, as well as a rolling back of rights and protections of LGBTQ+ people. As such, "the 'Christian' label simply signals shared tribal identity or veils political values that would otherwise be socially unacceptable" (Gorski and Perry 2022, 10). Moreover, white Christian nationalist discourse has shifted towards framing, for example, increased LGBTQ rights as an attack on religious freedom, which the authors argue "reflects a paradigmatic response of groups formerly in power (in this case, white conservative Christians) to situations in which they feel that power threatened—namely, to portray oneself as the victim" (Whitehead and Perry 2020, 134). The designated "other" can thus be identified as any number of persons and is referred to in a variety of ways, and includes Muslims, socialists, "leftists," and LGBTQ+ identifying people, conflating everyone on the outside as a threat (Gorski and Perry 2022).

Analyzing the Fox Comment Section: Islamophobia, Polarization, and Martyrdom

While *Second Coming* had been announced six months earlier, the negative reactions did not start until the CBN and Fox notices, after which a petition was started on CitizenGO aimed at canceling the release. This petition described the comic as "outrageous and blasphemous," suggesting that Jesus acts as a "sidekick to an 'all powerful' superhero," and asked readers to "please sign this petition if you agree that DC Comics should pull this blasphemous series" (CitizenGO 2019). The letter petitioners signed mentioned Muhammad—"Would DC Comics publish similar content about other religious leaders, such as Mohammed or Buddha?"—something that was reflected in the comment section of the Fox notice. It also reproduced a description of the *Second Coming*, which identified Jesus as "the roommate of 'an all-powerful superhero, named Sun-Man,'" not the sidekick of Sun-Man. The petition reportedly had over 235,000 signatures, and DC canceled the release on February 13, 2019 (Gustines 2019).

While CBN was the first to report on the comic, Fox News is one of the largest and most trusted news source in the United States (Gramlich 2020). Previous research has focused on Fox' audience as having distinct political attitudes and voting patterns, and "perceptions of political reality that differ from the rest of the television news audience" (Morris 2007, 707). Fox, which is aimed at providing a counterpoint to "liberally biased media," appears to particularly appeal to conservative attitudes, and especially to republicans

(Iyengar and Hahn 2009; Morris 2007). The Fox notice, unlike the CBN one, was accompanied by a comment section, which is the primary material analyzed for this chapter. Comment sections on news media offer ways for people to express their opinions on various political and social issues and can be seen to influence their perceptions of public opinion (Ziegele et al. 2020). While news comment sections thus theoretically function as forums of deliberative public debate, research has at best been inconclusive, at worst showing that such spaces tend towards hate speech (Eberwein 2020; Ziegele et al. 2020), and emotional language in news stories has been shown to contribute to decrease deliberative quality of related comment sections (Ziegele et al. 2020).

The Fox comment section contained 620 comments at the time of data collection (March 3, 2022, not including sixty-three comments that had been removed for violating the commenting policy, and two comments had been removed by users). Fox's comment moderation appears to include filters that pause comment publication until approved by a moderator (Fox News Team 2018). Comments may also be reported by users, they can also edit or delete their own comments, and comment sections may be turned off. According to the FAQ, moderation is used "to maintain a safe and respectful environment" and comments that "include vulgar, racist, threatening, or otherwise offensive language" would be removed (Fox News Team 2018). How moderation is practiced, and what guidelines exist around offensive language are otherwise unknown. Most comments (approximately 550) were left on January 9, 2019, followed by approximately fifty on the 11th, thirty-five on the 14th, thirty on the 12th, twenty on the 15th, twenty on the 10th, and ten on the 13th, with one comment left on the 19th, 20th, and 29th, respectively, and one user coming in and leaving three comments on February 18, 2021. All collected material was inductively coded in NVivo, paying special attention to how *Second Coming* was depicted, and what type of argument was being made against it, or in its favor. In the following section, the results of the coding are presented, focusing on negative framings of the *Second Coming*.

Tendencies Toward Self-Victimization: "They Think They Are Brave for Their Conformist Anti-Christian Nonsense"

Considering the number of signatures the CitizenGo petition got, it might be surprising to learn that the most prominent theme in the Fox comment section appears to be the questioning of Christians, Christianity, and jokes about Christians, followed by Christians arguing with or making disparaging remarks about atheists, and debates among Christians on theological matters. This was, however, followed by complaints about how frequently Christians are mocked in today's society, pronouncements about the blasphemous nature of *Second Coming*, and talk about how atheists, and the creators of the comic, will be punished by God. The prominence of questions directed at Christians, arguments leveled back at atheists, and theological debates mainly refer to discussions between commenters, one example is a user answering a presumably Christian comment with "Rational skepticism for stated and unproven beliefs, is not 'hate.' Drama Queen Alert." Most comments left by Christian antagonists were by the same five users. Their comments range from prodding Christians, dismissing their arguments, to more outright mockery, an example of the latter is "oh they are tender little snowflakes that are melting everywhere over this, they need to lighten up and laugh a little more." This is then contrasted by presumed Christian commenters, where even the most frequent commenters only left a few each. Trying to identify the factors at play with these five commenters is difficult as the only context is that they attack other commenters, but I have written elsewhere about how atheists specifically may participate in similar forms of antagonistic othering (Lundmark 2022).

Critique and mockery of Christians in the Fox comments generally occurred in direct response to comments left by presumed Christians, which were followed by debates amongst Christians. In one comment thread, a user encourages others to share the story about this particular comic on social media, as well as thumbs down any stories from DC to mark displeasure. There are also comments from one of the most frequent Christian commenters questioning if this is really a Christian attitude, and suggesting that "There's nothing they can do to hurt Jesus, especially with a comic book!," Meanwhile, another Christian commenter suggests that the issue is not with attacking Christians, but that this comic questions "the Lord God of all." As another commenter expresses it, the comic is not about religion but "about mocking Christians and Christianity. That's a pretty popular trend that is going to grow." This sentiment appears frequently in the material; that Christianity is constantly being attacked, sometimes specified as happening in mainstream media (unclear if Fox News counts as mainstream in these cases), and sometimes conflated with leftists, atheists, or Democrats that are said to be opposing Christians or Christianity.

Commenter 1

The CW and DC have turned half the superheroes into homosexuals.

Commenter 2

Is that a problem?

Commenter 3

Yes.

Commenter 1

Not unless you think half the human race is homosexual.

Commenter 2

I don't think there are superheroes with super powers.

Did you think the comics are true and the superheroes are real? (the heterosexual ones, obviously)

Transcript "homosexuals" from screenshot Fox news (Parke 2019).

There is a minor tendency in the comment section to associate superhero comics and DC with homosexuality, and that DC is spreading false or evil messages, such as "The comics are there to indoctrinate you to their beliefs. This is an attack on people's beliefs." There appears to be a slippage between accusations of sacrilege or blasphemy, the notion that society is filled with anti-Christian sentiments, and that the "other side" is pushing some form of agenda that includes homosexuality. There are comments that narrow in on the supposed blasphemousness more directly, like "This comic book is a red herring, attempting to offer 'another gospel' other than the authentic one. The entire premise of the comic book is non-scriptural." Several commenters take the opportunity to either talk about the increasing irrelevance of DC or specifically about the irrelevance of the imprint (Vertigo) that was set to publish *Second Coming*; "Their superhero shows on WB kept pushing all sorts of agendas to the point I quit watching them, even though I was a fan of their comics growing up." This agenda is again related to homosexuality; "DC comics is doing a Village people reboot of the Justice League."

> Pretty lame concept. Just a way to take another cheap shot at people with religious and conservative values. I do love how these articles bring out the foaming-at-the-mouth atheists who can't *stand* the thought of someone believing in something that might be greater than ourselves. So much tolerance on the left.

This overlap between Christianity and conservatism is posed in some sense against perceived non-belief or apostasy. On the one hand, this is tied to a perception that anti-Christian messaging is ubiquitous within mainstream media—"There is only one truth . . . . There cannot be multiple truths. Mainstream media attacks Christianity (primarily), God is mocked in most every program on television"—and on the other hand a notion that such sentiments are so common that even non-believers should be bored with them by now.

Commenter 4
Sure, it's blasphemous, but many of you enjoy that. Honestly, it's really unimaginative and uninspired. Shocking and predictably offending people is a calculated, lazy, talentless way to get attention, tapping the guaranteed resonance with the usual sick puerile lot that enjoy the same, as well as the free advertisement that comes with the doctrinally requisite boycotts by the good folk that won't ever, ever, ever forget that DC Comics also markets the formerly lucrative Batman, Superman, and Wonder Woman franchises.
Commenter 5
How can you say it's unimaginative and uninspired if you haven't read it?
Commenter 4
Why do we read things, why do content publishers put out teaser interviews and press releases, how do they calculate the influence of these things? Whatever you posture, don't you feel like we've been here a thousand times before? No thanks, boring.

Transcript "Blasphemy" from Screenshot Fox News (Parke 2019).

As a counterpoint, several of the Christian-antagonist commenters make comments about the appropriateness of mythology being used in comments, such as "Mythology in a comic book is a perfect match." The implication appears to be that Christianity is mythological, and thus fictional; "Not the first time he's [Jesus] been featured in a work of fiction." This centered around a minor argument presumed Christians and Christian-antagonist commenters were having, with Christians irritated with atheists for thinking they understand the Bible and Christianity better than Christians—"A commentary on how Christians misunderstand the Bible and Jesus? Like every other atheist, he thinks possesses great wisdom that we mere mortals cannot comprehend"—and Christian-antagonist commenters are irritated with Christians for assuming they do not understand Christianity: "You are making the ignorant assumption that i havent read the bible, i have many times and see it for the work of fiction it is, I dont fear your myths and superstitions."

Commenter 6
So another leftist strategy to bash religion and religious folk.
Shocking, absolutely shocking, totally shocked I am, color me shocked …

Hey, when do you suppose they'll do a cartoon about Allah and Muhammed? (Edited)

Commenter 7

Why are you assuming they'll use the comic to bash Jesus?

Commenter 6

Only because 99.9% of every lefty enterprise involving religion is used to bash it. But yeah, I can see why you'd go with the .1% possibility.

Commenter 7

The Presence, the Judeo-Christian God, is generally treated well in DC comics. I doubt Vertigo would trash Jesus.

Transcript "bashing left and Muhammed" from screenshot Fox news (Parke 2019).

There are a few threads to untangle when it comes to how Islam is positioned in the comment section. On the one hand, there are questions like the one posed above asking when or if they would make a similar comic about Muhammad, or simply suggesting that they would never be brave enough to do so: "They think they are brave for their conformist anti-Christian nonsense, but would never be brave enuf to mock the child molesting Prophet." On the other hand, we have a conflation of Islam and violence masking implied threats: "I wonder if the artists count themselves lucky that they can create such work without being murdered by Christians. Not every peaceful religious practitioner would suffer these artists to live were they in the same boat." Or suggesting that the lack of violence the comic authors and publishers may expect is proof of the superiority of Christianity: "How many people will die because of this comic? NONE. THIS is how I know Christianity and Islam are not the same."

In the transcript above we also see an association being drawn between "the left" and bashing "religious folk" (here, Christians), something that is suggested would not be done toward Islam: "How many Democrats who constantly slam and ridicule Christians ever do the same to Muslims? I've yet to hear one." These types of comments are entangled in a discussion that appears to collapse conservatism, Christianity, and Republicanism as existing in opposition to an amorphous other sometimes identified as "mainstream media," democrats, or "the left"; "Jesus bashing is of course OK, Would these fools ever dare blaspheme Mohammed or their one true Messiah ... Barak!" In some comments, it appears as if Islam is seen as protected in ways that Christianity is not, such as "I dare them to do a second coming of Muhammod for the sequel (deliberately misspelled to try to get past filters)." In these cases, it is unclear if commenters perceive Fox

News to be part of mainstream media if Fox is also protecting Islam, and who is filtering out mentions of Muhammad. In some cases, it is even suggested that everything outside of Christianity is atheism: "Knowing Jesus is not a religion pal. But … Atheists pretending to be 'religious' to steal a lot of money from people trying to learn. Muslims are one example."

> One more American tradition flushed down the toilet by atheist liberals … the comic book …
>
> lighten up snowflake!

The *Second Coming* was seen as part of a "leftist" agenda or strategy by some commenters, connected both to the positioning of Islam and the perception that religious (Christian) and conservative values go together. In part, the outrage appears to be rooted in an idea that what is Christian, and conservative is what is truly American; "Yet Mohammed cartoons sparked a terror attack in Paris. This is our own PEOPLE doing this! OUTRAGEOUS!!!" Comments on this theme tend to depict a culture war narrative, suggesting that "berating and persecuting white Christians has been popular since oh, about the early part of November in 2008," and that *Second Coming* is "just more Christian bashing by the Left." The culture war framing can also be noted in comments that call for suppression of the comic, while taking part in a discussion emphasizing the supposed suppression of Christians in the United States: "Where do i sign up to join the lawsuit against this?"

Discussion

> Cowards. How about including allah?
>
> What's cowardly—and flatout creepy with all this Islamaphobia - is how many idiots in this comment thread are getting so foamy-mouthed over a) a comic book; b) a comic book they haven't even read yet; c) a comic book which actually shows Jesus to be a loving entity; and d) a comic book which mostly just satires hypocrites and comic book superheroes. Once again, Fox News has misled its gullible audience into grabbing pitchforks and getting incensed over an affront which doesn't even exist. People, please: reconsider your news sources.

The latter comment was left by the sole user, who came in leaving comments in 2021 and appears to have read *Second Coming*. By contrast, the prevailing interpretation on the blogs and Christian news sites that jumped on the story, as well as among the presumed Christian commenters in the Fox comment section outlined above, appeared to be the one originally found in the CBN notice. That "instead of a biblical account of Christ's return, it depicts Jesus as a failure who disappointed God by getting crucified when he first walked the earth. He is sent back to learn how to be a real Messiah by learning from the superhero 'Sun-Man'" (Jones 2019), like the Christian Examiner who referred to it as a "distorted telling of the Savior." Responding as they were to the press release, no one appeared to at that point have read the comic. The lack of specificity characteristic of moral outrage (Pfeffer, Zorbach, and Carley 2014) found in the varied responses, can be exemplified by the CitizenGo campaign mischaracterizing the press release's description while reproducing the press release right next to it. The type of moral outrage expressed thus appear to be an exercise in boundary marking, where *Second Coming* appears as a convenient foe, rather than a focus of genuine moral concern, suggesting that the event might have been driven by moral posturing to defend group identity and signal belonging. This was further emphasized by how the CitizenGo campaign at the time of writing still declared victory in its effort to cancel the comic, despite it having been published. This can be understood in relation to theories on the ways in which political statements are imbued with affect on social media more broadly, where politics becomes a way for people to affectively attune themselves to, rather than engage critically with, political issues (Papacharissi 2015). Assuming that politics become another mode for individuals to attune themselves or signal belonging, necessitates placing emphasis on how public discourse affects democratic space even when social media users may not perceive their actions as that serious, as such actions still have a cumulative effect (Lundmark 2019).

In this chapter, I set out to explore how a discourse of moral outrage was articulated in reference to the announcement of *Second Coming*, and further if, and how, this discourse reflected Christian nationalist narratives. As noted, moral outrage has been identified as contributing to political polarization (Carpenter et al. 2021), and in the case of US political discourse appears to presuppose an antagonistic division of the political field. Christian nationalism here refers to a specific set of assumptions about the history and culture of the United States (Gorski and Perry 2022; Whitehead and Perry 2020). While such views are not transparently expressed in the comments, they are hinted at. The presence of the outrage in itself indicates that some feel threatened, but there are also more specific examples like one commenter who expresses outrage that it is "our own PEOPLE doing this!" or another who refers to comic books as yet another "American tradition flushed down the toilet by atheist liberals." Aside from explicit mentions of Muslims, race is not much discussed in the topic. One reason for this may of course be that the author, Mark Russell, is a white man from Oregon.

The direction of the perceived threat is hard to nail down in the comments but does appear to depict a sort of collapsed other. As Gorski and Perry (2022) note, the other is Christian nationalism, identified as a collection of identities that appear interchangeable, including Muslims, socialists, and LGBTQ+ identifying people, conflating everyone on the outside as a threat. In the comments we see people talk about leftists, liberals, and atheists in unclear ways, and making references to Obama as the second coming of Jesus for liberals, making it appear as if these terms are indeed interchangeable. The corrupting force of this other is apparent in how commenters derisively hint at DC Comics promoting homosexuality, contributing to the slippage between supposed Christian marginalization, and a mainstream media that attacks Christians while promoting a leftist or homosexual agenda, that is simultaneously atheist and pro-Muslim.

> Main stream media attacks Christianity (primarily), God is mocked in most every program on television … . Yes there may be a random joke about another faith. But Christianity is the primary focus. You can "site" a source … but the source I give you is main stream media … it is in our face every day. So any "source" that you sight would just be someone from media saying that "we are fair and impartial" So consider the source.

The tendency within Christian nationalism toward interpreting decline as marginalization and prosecution (Whitehead and Perry 2020) is exemplified in the comment above. This theme weaves through the comment section, and it is suggested that mainstream media controls narratives around Christianity (by attacking and undermining it), and Islam (by protecting it) and that it, as well as *Second Coming* are part of a leftist or liberal agenda. The collapsed other is visible in comments that seemingly suggest that Muslims are just atheists attempting to steal money from people searching for religion. In similar comments depicting Christianity as the one true religion, we also see a conflation of Christianity with conservatism and perceived "traditional" Christian values, which are under attack from *Second Coming*, and from mainstream media, and thus needs to be defended (e.g., "where do I sign up to join the lawsuit against this?").

The antagonistic way in which the other is described in the Fox comments recalls the view of violence as justified when perpetuated by Christian nationalists to defend the purity of the United States as a Christian nation, and disruptive when perpetrated by the collapsed other. This tendency is not very clear, but may be hinted at in how violence was primarily associated with Islam and in comments like "I recommend the author write his next series about Mohammad and have his first signing in Detroit or someplace nice like that," which seemingly conflates Islam with other forms of marginalization and associates both with violence. Violence is thus used to demarcate how much better Christians are. In an interview, the author of *Second Coming* stated that he believed that "once people actually read the book, a lot of them will be embarrassed by how up in arms they were. It's actually a very pro-Christ comic, as he's the character who actually offers a meaningful alternative to violence" (Avila 2019). Russell himself thus maintains that the comic is not a critique of Jesus, but rather of superhero comics and their tendency to valorize violence; "drop-kicking someone into a volcano or throwing them through a plate-glass window only works for solving a very small percentage of human problems. The other 99.9% of problems require empathy and that's the superpower that Christ brings to the table" (Avila 2019). However, given the view of violence within Christian nationalist discourses, this depiction of Jesus may indeed be another point of contention with the comic.

Conclusion

In this chapter, I have looked at how a discourse of moral outrage was articulated in a Fox comment section referencing to the announcement of *Second Coming*, and further if, and how, this discourse reflects Christian nationalism, exploring the circulation of moral outrage. The aim of which was to offer a case study for understanding tensions surrounding depictions of Jesus within the US context, and why—despite historical linkages between Christianity and media broadcasts—some usages of Christian symbolism would inspire the kind of outrage outlined in this chapter. This chapter thus exposed how conceptualizations of blasphemy may be embroiled in processes of boundary marking, driven by moral posturing to defend group identity, and signal belonging. I thus showed how the Fox comments held an undercurrent of comments that assumed a binary between Christianity, religiousness, morality, and conservatism on the one hand, and "leftist" blasphemy on the other. This other side was perceived as pushing an agenda where certain groups are protected (like Muslims) and some interests are "pushed" (like homosexuality), while others are unduly prosecuted, attacked, and ridiculed (like white Christians).

As noted, Christian nationalists are primarily focused on political goals, using references to Christianity to defend and mark belonging to the (white) ethnonational “us.” Outrage centered on perceived threats like the outrage discussed here is not about piety, or even about blasphemy, but rather about protecting against subversion of the “Christian values” preferred by Christian nationalists. The way Christian nationalism fuses national and religious symbolism legitimizes use of violence in defending this by reference to divine will. This legitimation process inhibits dialogue as alternative viewpoints are perceived as threatening. I thus suggest that Christian nationalism presupposes an antagonistic division of the political field, where everyone who is not part of the ethnonational “us,” is conceived as a threat. In this way, the antagonistic construction of an “us” relies on the vilification of everyone who disagrees, as it divides the political field into two opposite antagonistic poles, which further clarifies the tendency in the Fox comments toward collapsing of the other into one amorphous entity which can contain atheism and Islam, liberalism, and socialism, all at once.

References

AHOY Comics. (2019), “Second Coming #1.” July 10, 2019. Available online: https://comicsahoy.com/comics/second-coming-1 (accessed April 12, 2023).

Avila, Mike. (2019), “Exclusive: Mark Russell Responds to DC’s Cancellation of His Jesus-Themed Comic: We Wanted to Be ‘True to Its Vision.’ ” SYFY Official Site. February 15, 2019. Available online: https://www.syfy.com/syfy-wire/mark-russell-dc-cancellation-jesus-themed-comic-second-coming (accessed April 12, 2023).

Baldassarri, Delia, and Gelman, Andrew. (2008), “Partisans Without Constraint: Political Polarization and Trends in American Public Opinion,” *American Journal of Sociology* 114 (2): 408–46. https://doi.org/10.1086/590649.

Bowler, Kate, and Reagan, Wen. (2014), “Bigger, Better, Louder: The Prosperity Gospel’s Impact on Contemporary Christian Worship,” *Religion and American Culture: A Journal of Interpretation* 24 (2): 186–230. https://doi.org/10.1525/rac.2014.24.2.186.

Carpenter, Jordan, William, Brady, Crockett Molly, Weber Rene, and Sinnott-Armstrong Walter. (2021), “Political Polarization and Moral Outrage on Social Media,” *Connecticut Law Review* 52 (3): 1107.

CitizenGO. (2019), “DC Comics to Release Blasphemous Series about Jesus.” Text. CitizenGO. January 11, 2019. Available online: https://citizengo.org/en/md/167848-dc-comics-slated-release-blasphemous-series-about-jesus (accessed 12 April 2023).

Eberwein, Tobias. (2020), “‘Trolls’ or ‘Warriors of Faith’?” *Journal of Information, Communication and Ethics in Society* 18 (4): 575–87. https://doi.org/10.1108/JICES-08-2019-0090.

Fox News Team. (2018), "What Is the Fox News Commenting Policy?" *Fox News*. December 10, 2018. Available online: https://help.foxnews.com/hc/en-us/articles/233195048-What-is-the-Fox-News-Commenting-Policy- (accessed April 12, 2023).

Goode, E., and Ben-Yehuda N. (1994), "Moral Panics: Culture, Politics, and Social Construction," *Annual Review of Sociology* 20 (1): 149–71. https://doi.org/10.1146/annurev.so.20.080194.001053.

Gorski, Philip S., and Perry Samuel L. (2022), *The Flag and the Cross: White Christian Nationalism and the Threat to American Democracy*. Oxford: Oxford University Press.

Gramlich, John. (2020), "5 Facts about Fox News." *Pew Research Center* (blog). 2020. Available online: https://www.pewresearch.org/fact-tank/2020/04/08/five-facts-about-fox-news/ (accessed April 12, 2023).

Gustines, George Gene. (2019), "Comic Book with Jesus as a Character Finds a New Publisher." *New York Times*, March 12, 2019, sec. Arts. Available online: https://www.nytimes.com/2019/03/12/arts/second-coming-jesus-comic-book.html (accessed April 12, 2023).

Hadden, Jeffrey K. (1993), "The Rise and Fall of American Televangelism," *Annals of the American Academy of Political and Social Science* 527: 113–30.

Hajdu, David. (2009), *The Ten-Cent Plague: The Great Comic-Book Scare and How It Changed America*. First edition. New York: Picador.

Hare, Christopher, and Poole Keith T. (2014), "The Polarization of Contemporary American Politics," *Polity* 46 (3): 411–29. https://doi.org/10.1057/pol.2014.10.

Iyengar, Shanto, and Hahn Kyu S. (2009), "Red Media, Blue Media: Evidence of Ideological Selectivity in Media Use," *Journal of Communication* 59 (1): 19–39. https://doi.org/10.1111/j.1460-2466.2008.01402.x.

Johnen, Marius, Jungblut Marc, and Ziegele Marc. (2018), "The Digital Outcry: What Incites Participation Behavior in an Online Firestorm?" *New Media & Society* 20 (9): 3140–60. https://doi.org/10.1177/1461444817741883.

Jones, Emily. (2019), "DC Comics Turns Jesus into a New Superhero—But There's a Big Problem." CBN News. January 8, 2019. Available online: https://www1.cbn.com/cbnnews/entertainment/2019/january/dc-comics-turns-jesus-into-a-new-superhero-ndash-but-theres-a-big-problem (accessed April 12, 2023).

Lundmark, Evelina. (2019), *"This Is the Face of an Atheist": Performing Private Truths in Precarious Publics*, Uppsala: Uppsala Universitet.

Lundmark, Evelina. (2022), "Pumpkins at the Centre of Mars and Circlejerks: Do Atheists Find Community Online?," in Jacob Copeman and Mascha Schulz (eds.), *Global Sceptical Publics—From Nonreligious Print Media to "Digital Atheism,"* London: UCL Press.

Morris, Jonathan S. (2007), "Slanted Objectivity? Perceived Media Bias, Cable News Exposure, and Political Attitudes," *Social Science Quarterly* 88 (3): 707–28.

Mouffe, Chantal. (2013), *Agonistics—Thinking the World Politically*, New York: Verso.

Papacharissi, Zizi. (2015), *Affective Publics: Sentiment, Technology, and Politics.* Oxford: Oxford University Press. https://doi.org/10.1093/acprof:oso/9780199999736.001.0001.

Parke, Celeb. (2019), "DC Comics to Release Controversial 'Second Coming' of Jesus." Fox News. January 9, 2019. Available online: https://www.foxnews.com/entertainment/dc-comics-to-release-controversial-second-coming-of-jesus (accessed April 12, 2023).

Pfeffer, J., Zorbach, T., and Carley, K. M. (2014), "Understanding Online Firestorms: Negative Word-of-Mouth Dynamics in Social Media Networks," *Journal of Marketing Communications* 20 (1–2): 117–28. https://doi.org/10.1080/13527266.2013.797778.

Russell, Mark. (2020), *Second Coming*, Syracuse: AHOY Comics.

Whitehead, Andrew L., and Perry Samuel L. (2020), *Taking America Back for God: Christian Nationalism in the United States.* New York: Oxford University Press. https://doi.org/10.1093/oso/9780190057886.001.0001.

Ziegele, Marc, Quiring Oliver, Esau Katharina, and Friess Dennis. (2020), "Linking News Value Theory with Online Deliberation: How News Factors and Illustration Factors in News Articles Affect the Deliberative Quality of User Discussions in SNS' Comment Sections," *Communication Research* 47 (6): 860–90. https://doi.org/10.1177/0093650218797884.

4

The Reception of Comics on Zoroastrianism

Paulina Niechciał[1]

Introduction

Zoroastrianism is an ancient religion whose origins have been attributed to Zarathushtra, in European languages known as Zoroaster. He was a reformer of ancient Iranian beliefs (see Malandra 2009) and considered a prophet by his followers, who dominated pre-Islamic Iran. However, after the Arab invasion in the seventh century, most Iranians converted to Islam, and some, in the face of discrimination and persecution, settled in India, and became known as Parsis (Boyce 1979). Despite their reduced numbers, Zoroastrianism has survived and, in 2012, the number of people with a Zoroastrian family background was estimated to be 111,201 worldwide, with Parsis greatly exceeding the number of Iranian Zoroastrians (Rivetna 2012). There is also an unknown number of modern converts to Zoroastrianism of different ethnic origins, as well as Iranians, Kurds, and Tajiks, who have not necessarily converted but have returned to pre-Islamic Zoroastrian heritage to distinguish themselves from their dominant Muslim neighbours (see Niechciał 2020a).

Since antiquity, there has been a tradition of Zoroaster's presence beyond Zoroastrianism. Europeans depicted him as a mysterious expert of astrology and esoterism (Panaino 2022). He was imagined to be a descendant of Noah, an enlightened leader, philosopher, wise man, and powerful magician, and has even been credited with inventing magic as a scholarly discipline. His image has been positive, although it has sometimes been influenced by Muslim prejudice. Importantly, how Zoroaster and his religion were portrayed by Europeans has influenced the Zoroastrian discourse and current perceptions of this religion have emerged from an intercultural mixture of interpretations (Stausberg 2005).

An extension of Zoroastrianism outside of the realm of religion may be found in contemporary popular culture. Sociologists of religion explore its presence beyond what has stereotypically been associated with the religious and the sacred, search for religion in the entirety of human experience (Orsi 1997, 7), and analyze how religious heritage appears and is reproduced in secular settings (de Groot 2020, 12). With the diminishing role of institutionalized forms of religion in society, the ground that had traditionally been the field of religious authorities and organizations has been entered into by the media, who now present religious issues and communicate religious images (Hjarvard 2020, 21–3).

Although Zoroastrianism is not a frequent theme in popular culture, it does make its appearance, for example, because of a fascination with Eastern spirituality in new religious movements. The teachings of Guru Ranjeesh, known as Osho (1931–1990), are based on his understanding of Zoroaster. Moreover, readers of literature in many countries may be familiar with the American novel *Creation* by Gore Vidal (1981), who made Cyrus Spitama, the grandson of Zoroaster, the narrator of his book. Contemporary Parsis living in Mumbai are probably best known thanks to the novels of Indian-born Canadian writer Rohinton Mistry, as well as the Netflix release *Maska* (2020)—an Indian drama directed by Neeraj Udhwani, telling the story of a traditional café run by a Zoroastrian family. Additionally, Zoroastrianism-inspired motifs are present in Ubisoft's action-adventure video game series *Prince of Persia*, which have been produced since 1989, in which the starting point is the story of the struggle between the gods Ormazd and Ahriman, based on the Zoroastrian god Ahura Mazda and his adversary.[2]

One of the areas of popular culture that attracts scholarly attention are comics, whose role in maintaining certain imaginaries is particularly interesting, because they are "multimodal": they not only tell the story that people imagine but also show it through pictures (Meskin and Cook 2020, 170; see Orcutt 2010). Among comics are religious comics, which can evoke different reactions from readers, because of the differing attitudes of different religions toward drawing religiously significant objects or figures. While the 2015 attacks on the Paris offices of *Charlie Hebdo* illustrate the controversy surrounding depictions of Muhammad in Islam[3] (see Gruber 2017), in Hindu worship the central act is seeing and being seen by gods, *darśan* (see Eck 1998), and depicting gods or religious acts, helps maintain world and religious order (Koltun-Fromm 2020, 2). Although Zoroastrians surround themselves with portraits of Zoroaster, hanging them in homes or shrines and using them for religious contemplation, this is fairly recent: portraits only became common with the spread of print and lithography and penetrated devotional practice in the mid-nineteenth century (see Sheffield 2012).

Therefore, to study the relationship between religion and illustrated media, sociologists should go beyond the analysis of their artistic forms, production, and distribution, recognizing the role of the audience as its critical commentators (Locke 2012) and emotionally engaged "coproducers of their visual experience" (Koltun-Fromm 2020, 220). Following this path, to shed light on the presence of Zoroastrianism outside the realm traditionally associated with religion, I have focused on the reception of comics with Zoroastrian content, asking whether they reach Zoroastrian audiences and, if so, what this audience thinks of them. I shall discuss the research process, including the choice of sources and methods, introduce the sources, and present the findings.

Research Sources and Methods

Being interested in the reaction to comics, firstly, I assessed their relevance to this study. Publications from Iran did not appear here, because the market for religious comics there—both explicitly promoting religion and less directly referring to religious values (see Esfandi, Ghaderi, and Ghaderi 2015)—is limited to publications exclusively about constitutionally privileged Islam. Although there are graphic publications that refer to pre-Islamic Iranian traditions, the problem arises in the case of publications promoting a religion other than Islam, because they could be considered an attempt at forbidden proselytizing among Muslim citizens.

There are not many publications with Zoroastrian content among the globally available products of popular culture. Fans of Marvel Comics—the company founded in the United States in 1939—may have encountered stereotypical images drawn on an "Orientalized" narrative about the Middle East (Šisler 2008). In 1981, in the Marvel's *Conan the Barbarian* series, an old sorcerer and scholar equipped with a flying carpet named Zoroazztor appeared.[4] Additionally, the Zoroastrian deities Yazatas, depicted as immortal, extradimensional humanoid beings with a tan complexion and black eyes, have appeared in the Marvel Universe.[5] Another American comics series, connected to Zoroastrianism via references to pre-Islamic Iranian mythology, is titled *Rostam: Tales from the Shahnameh* (published since 2003). The eponymous superhero is based on the hero from the eleventh-century Persian epic, *The Book of Kings* (*Shahnameh* in Persian) by Ferdousi.[6] There is also *Zarathustra* (2017; 2019 in English; the first volume of three planned) by Richard Marazano, which grew out of the author's fascination with ancient civilizations and Iranian mythology (2019).

Content analysis showed the inadequacy of the publications cited earlier for this study: although they allude to Iran's pre-Islamic heritage, they do not directly relate to Zoroastrianism. Likewise, I did not include *Persepolis*, the series of graphic novels by Marjane Satrapi, because it only briefly refers to Zoroastrianism (see Satrapi 2004, 7). Therefore, of the items collected, two publications remained, aimed at familiarizing a wide audience with Zoroastrianism, albeit in a different way, as products of different cultural contexts (see Niechciał 2020b):

1. *Zarathushtra*: A repeatedly reissued Indian publication, edited by Anant Pai (2007), presenting the legend of Zoroaster in line with the idea of its publisher to bring local culture and religions to the public via simple, concise comics. (The publisher later released two comics about the Parsi Tata family enterprise, but these do not directly address religion.)
2. *Ainsi se tut Zarathoustra/Silent was Zarathustra*: A French spy thriller in the form of a graphic novel by Nicolas Wild (2016), focusing on the contemporary Iranian Zoroastrian community. (This was not the author's first book set in the Persian-speaking culture but the only one related to Zoroastrianism.)

As Woo indicated, analyses of circulation and surveys that are funded by industry stakeholders do not provide reliable information about readers of the comics (2020, 115). Therefore, I designed a survey to ask about familiarity with two publications and the impressions of their readers. Data was collected in two ways: I distributed a questionnaire to Zoroastrians that I knew from my fieldwork in the United States and Iran and posted it on Facebook and Twitter, targeting groups related to Zoroastrianism. I prepared the questionnaire in English to reach the diaspora and Parsis in Asia, and in Persian to reach Zoroastrians in Iran and those in the diaspora who prefer Persian. I also translated it into my native language, Polish, since in Poland there is a tiny group of converts to Zoroastrianism, and Wild's book has been published here as well.

Ninety-one questionnaires were returned, primarily those in English. The gender distribution was almost equal.[7] Facebook turned out to be the most effective in collecting responses (seventy-one); second best was my direct request (fourteen). I was able to target a diverse age group, but with a predominance of respondents in the 51 to 60 age range. Most of the respondents identified themselves as Parsis and indicated India as their country of residence, followed by the United States and Canada, reflecting the most populous Zoroastrian communities worldwide. I received only one questionnaire from Iran, which I associate with the fear of participating in social surveys, as well as the lower popularity of Facebook and Twitter in Iran than in other countries inhabited by Zoroastrians.

Reception of the Comics

Zarathushtra

The first publication included in the study is *Zarathushtra*, published in 1974 under the Amar Chitra Katha (ACK) brand—one of India's best-selling comics series. This thirty-two-page color publication was written by Bachi Karkaria, an Indian journalist, and illustrated by Ram Waeerkar, an artist who created many iconic characters in Indian comics and worked on many books in the series, including the very first, *Krishna*, in 1969. The editor of *Zarathushtra* was Anant Pai (1929–2011), a pioneer of the Indian comics industry and the creator of the brand in 1967 (Pritchett 1995; see Chapter 12). For Indian culture, this was a breakthrough: previous comics were perceived with skepticism, but ACK's combination of attractive graphics and narrative, educational in nature, shaping moral attitudes, and reaching back to local culture, changed the perspective (Kaur and Eqbal 2019, 40). Although criticized for its narrow perspective and stereotypes, Pai achieved great success, selling tens of millions of copies in English and many Indian languages (Khanduri 2010, 174–5). Moreover, scholars of comics history have noted that the series, through covering religious themes, set a precedent for other comics publishers referring to religion, including Sufi Comics—an Indian publisher of books on the history and teachings of Islam (Stoll 2017, 181).

Zarathushtra tells the mythological tale of Zoroaster, whose birth was surrounded by miracles: the body of his mother glowed, he smiled instead of crying, and miraculously saved himself from the trap set by the enemy (Pai 2007, 9). It was the objective of the ACK to introduce myths to a wider audience within multicultural Indian society, and, as in his other comics, Pai used the name of a renowned expert to ensure the accuracy of the narratives (Khanduri 2010, 174): The back cover of *Zarathushtra* hosts an introduction by the Parsi scholar and high priest Dasturji H. K. Mirza.

Referring to the comic book *Rama*, published by ACK in 1970 and retelling the story from the Sanskrit epic, *Ramayana*, McLain mentions that it manifests the archetypal features of American superhero comics established between the 1930s and 1950s: extraordinary powers, a strong moral code, and specific enemies. However, the comics of ACK, deeply influenced by Western patterns, are grounded in Indian visual traditions and immortalize local heroes, turning them into indigenous superheroes (2009, 1–3). Pai's Zoroaster, who manifested his superpowers and miraculously established a new religion, is also the product of a mixture of different contexts. An important source of this story was the *Zardosht-nama*, a thirteenth-century account of Zoroaster's life written by Zartushi-Behram, a Parsi, who incorporated earlier religious texts, emphasizing the miracles performed by Zoroaster. Just as in the comics, Zoroaster was born smiling and the healing of the legendary King Goshtasp's favorite black horse persuaded the king to accept the new faith. The glowing beams pictured by Waeerkar over the prophet's figure symbolize the *farr*—divine splendor (Rose 2013; see Zartushi-Behram 1843). Furthermore, *Zarathushtra* alludes to Christian themes, echoing theological disputes in nineteenth-century India, where Parsis, challenged by Protestant missionaries and Western scholars, shifted toward interpretations of their faith inspired by Abrahamic religions. These ideas resonate today among scholars and Zoroastrians, who see Zoroastrianism as essentially monotheistic, but contaminated by other ideas over time (Palsetia 2008, 164–7; Ringer 2011, 56–7).

The popularity of *Zarathushtra* is supported by the fact that it is still available for sale or download for free (see Table 4.1). Half of my respondents of different ages have encountered it via different paths: gift, library loan, purchase, and internet search.

Most of the readers were Parsis. Males were slightly outnumbered, which confirms that, although traditionally comics have been identified with male audiences, girls and women also read comics, and not only those directly addressed to female audiences (Gibson 2020, 241). *Zarathushtra* appeared in India before the rise of Hindu-centered nationalism, and the middle-class generation of urban children growing up in the 1960s and 1970s was prepared to be a "new generation" united across linguistic or religious borders. Religious education was not a top priority and was left to popular culture, including movies, comics, and social events (McLain 2009, 9).

Table 4.1 Encountering *Zarathushtra*

Have you ever encountered the comic book titled *Zarathushtra* published in India by Amar Chitra Katha?		
Yes: 39	No: 48	Not sure: 4

Although not everyone remembered *Zarathushtra* well, the respondents had generally positive opinions. For example, they described it as "informative" (Parsi male, India, age 51–60), "good" (Parsi, USA, gender not indicated, over seventy) and valued its illustrations and simplicity in talking about religious values. One person appreciated the form of the story, which, in his eyes, legitimized the religious message received at home: "When you hear the narration by your parents, it seems animated but having an actual comic book that gives you a point of reference made it exhilarating for me as a child" (Parsi male, Canada, 51–60).

Some respondents were familiar with the comics because they had grown up in India: someone mentioned collecting ACK comics as a child, another mentioned reading *Zarathushtra* along with other religious stories in the series. Those who read it as children recalled it especially favorably, for example: "I read it as a child close to 45 years ago so I remember it with child's eyes. I loved it. It felt proud for my identity to be represented in a comic, which I was not used to. I loved the miracles" (Parsi female, Canada, 51–60). Another person admitted: "I had it as a young child and found it to be impressive. Since there is very little representation of us Parsis, this comic / illustration for something that made it a treasure. I felt proud and it became a vehicle for me to share with my non-Parsi friends who wanted to learn more about our religion" (Parsi male, Canada, age 51–60). Building on this positive reception, some respondents recommended *Zarathushtra* to their siblings, cousins, children, and friends, discussed it with family members, and sent it from India to friends or relatives living abroad.

The responses to questions about whether reading *Zarathushtra* brought new knowledge were mixed. One confessed that he "did not know much" about Zoroaster's life before reading the comics (Parsi male, India, age 31–40). Several people admitted that, as they were children at the time, they learned something new, but a third of those who were familiar with the comics explicitly stated that they had not found any new information. Someone who came across this book as an adult admitted to treating it as a "funny thing" and a "curiosity" rather than an informative source (convert, Europe, 61–70).

Zarathushtra was criticized for being very basic, although someone clarified, it was hard to expect anything more from this type of publication. A religious teacher admitted to using it in the classroom. Comics appear in school curricula, but, for the respondent, they turned out to be ineffective: "There was a lot of incorrect info in the book. I was using it in my religion classes to teach kids and had to stop using this book" (Parsi, Canada, gender not indicated, 41–50).

Silent was Zarathustra

The second publication of interest is a French black-and-white graphic novel: the format gained popularity in the 1990s, characterized by literary aspirations and published as a single volume, valued higher than shorter serialized comics (Kukkonen 2013, 84–5; see Cates 2020). Nicolas Wild (b. 1977), both the writer and illustrator of *Silent was Zarathustra*, published it in France in 2013 with the title referring to Friedrich Nietzsche's *Thus Spake Zarathustra* (see Figure 4.1). Despite critical acclaim, according to Wild, there was no interest in publishing the book in the UK and the United States (Fernandes 2014), and the English translation was prepared for the Indian market.

The story is in the form of a humorous first-person narrative. Its protagonist travels to Iran and meets local Zoroastrians, thanks to Sophia, a French-Iranian daughter of Cyrus Yazdani, a Zoroastrian activist assassinated in Geneva in 2006. In part, the book is set in Geneva and covers the testimonies given in court on Yazdani's murder. The narrative is interwoven with flashbacks that reveal Yazdani's life story and includes photographs of ancient Zoroastrian sites and modern Zoroastrians. It presents the life of Zoroaster, but with an emphasis on his message rather than his miracles. On a visual level, he is portrayed, as in the ACK comics, based on his most popular present-day depictions, shaped in the early twentieth century by the Bombay Parsi painter Manchershaw Fakirjee Pithawala (see Sheffield 2012, 97–9). Moreover, readers become acquainted with the nuances of the presence of Zoroastrianism in the Islamic Republic of Iran, where Zoroastrians are a shrinking community[8]. According to the constitution of Iran, like Christians and Jews, they constitute a recognized religious minority and officially enjoy certain rights, but in practice, their rights are restricted, and minorities face discrimination (see Stausberg 2015).

The story of Yazdani was inspired by the true story of an ancient Persian history scholar Kasra Vafadari (1946–2005), whose assassination in Paris is linked by some to his active advocacy for Zoroastrians in Iran ("Obiturary" 2006). Considering the political character of the Islamic Republic of Iran, Wild could not write Vafadari's story openly without exposing the protagonists of his novel and himself to risk. Therefore, he transformed it into a story about Yazdani.

In the survey, Wild's novel did not enjoy popularity (see Table 4.2).

A publication depicting the controversial story of Vafadari as well as the discrimination against the Zoroastrian minority, could not be published in Iran. Although it was published in English in India, which the author had visited

Figure 4.1 Wild, Nicolas. (2016), *Tako milczy Zaratustra*. Warszawa: Timof Comics.

Table 4.2 Encountering *Silent was Zarathustra*

Have you ever encountered the graphic novel titled *Silent Was Zarathustra* (*Ainsi se tut Zarathustra*) by Nicolas Wild, published in France and then translated to English?		
Yes: 1	No: 89	Not sure: 1

several times, only one respondent had encountered the book and another one was not sure, and their responses were not informative.

Conclusions

Zarathushtra and other ACK comics have been the product of tensions between market needs, educational values, scholarly precision, and the need to meet audience expectations; the product of a commitment to Indian history and to national integration (Pritchett 1995, 81). Pai's stress on building a hagiography based on colorful portraits of characters leading exemplary lives (Hawley 1995, 107) is also embodied by Zoroaster, contributing to the consolidation of a certain image of the prophet.

Some respondents valued the simple way in which this comic presents Zoroastrian values. As Koltun-Fromm stresses, comics "encourage us to hear those moral vibrations, and we need not become superheroes to do this ethical work" (2020, 227). As in other ACK comics, the plot is simple, not subtle; the story is short and direct; therefore so even though a good portion of the readers are adults, it is understandable for children (Hawley 1995, 128). I noticed a criticism of some recipients of *Zarathushtra* for it being simple and not informative, but generally, comics are usually full of stereotypes and simplifications, resulting from focusing on details appealing to the common perception of what is presented (Koltun-Fromm 2020, 2–3). The criticism also targeted not meeting the reader's expectations of Zoroaster, as Zoroastrians have different perceptions of their prophet: for some, Zoroaster is a miracle maker, which was central to medieval Zoroastrianism; for others, he is a wise human philosopher, as influenced by Christian missionaries (Sheffield 2012, 89).

It is easy to overlook comics, because the form itself may inspire little respect and be associated with what is opposite to so-called high culture. However, in India, comics have served as channels of contact between English-educated middle-class children and religious traditions of the region (Babb 1995, 8). In the face of modern changes in family structures, they have passed on religious teachings to new generations, replacing the traditional intergenerational transmission of stories by family members (Orcutt 2010, 93). Judging from the survey, *Zarathushtra*, despite the criticism, still fulfils this role. What I believe contributes to it is the fact that whatever concerns Zoroastrianism in popular culture, if it is not found insulting, is appreciated by Zoroastrians despite its shortcomings, because it presents their religion to the outside world. I found two important factors: first, the number of traditional Zoroastrians is dramatically decreasing, so many believe that any way to keep it alive is beneficial; second, after moving from their traditional settlements to new countries, mainly in North America, where their religion is almost unknown in society, Zoroastrians want to introduce it. Thus, comics, as well as any other popular culture products, may be a way to share knowledge of Zoroastrianism with others and legitimize the identity of the followers of this largely unknown religion.

Comics are a global cultural form that not only has international roots, but has also been widely disseminated around the world (McAllister and MacAuley 2020, 107). The choices made by the publisher at a given time have been reproduced by readers in new temporal and spatial contexts, thanks to numerous reissues and the online availability of *Zarathushtra*. Due to transnational Parsi ties, it has appeared in the diaspora, as my survey showed. The face of religion has been transformed: the increasing role of the media in the production and spread of religious images and the process of mediatization of religion imply a multidimensional transformation of religious texts, practices, and beliefs (Hjarvard 2020). Certainly, today's transnational Zoroastrianism is different from what was transmitted through successive generations of priests in the traditional contexts of Iran and India.

Comics may offer the simple pleasure of reading, but they also enrich human experience, including experience of the sacred. The way the sacred reaches people through such a medium undermines the chain of authority: it does not come through priests in designated places, but through ordinary experiences (Gamzou and Koltun-Fromm 2018, 10–14). My respondents admitted to sharing *Zarathushtra* with others: some with those who lived around them, others transnationally. Despite different expectations about how religion should be portrayed, *Zarathushtra* can be a starting point for the discussion that occurs between ordinary members of the religious community away from religious authorities, and its popularity may publicly legitimize the religious message communicated in private.

It seems that *Silent was Zarathustra* by Wild has reached almost no Zoroastrian audience, but I know this might be due to the limitations of the study. Small-scale studies conducted by academic researchers are probably the most insightful regarding understanding the reception of comics, but they do not guarantee that the respondents are typical (Woo 2020, 115).

Despite its limitations, my study of the reception of comics with Zoroastrian content contributes to a picture of how religion functions outside the space stereotypically assigned to it. The study may not only be a voice in academic discussion concerning religion and comics but may also inspire further inquiry. In the survey, I asked whether the respondents had encountered any other comic books or graphic novels; no one mentioned the comics about Rostam or *Zarathustra* by Marazano, but I found repetitive comments about illustrated children's publications. During my fieldwork among Zoroastrians in the United States in 2019, in several homes, I noticed children's cartoons and refrigerator magnets by Delzin Choksey, featuring the figure of a child with large, anime-inspired eyes and in a position that mimics Zoroaster in his popular portraits, intended to present an attention-grabbing version of Zoroaster to children.[9] As with comics, other types of graphic narrative can motivate "new modes of seeing the sacred" (Gamzou and Koltun-Fromm 2018, 16). These are interesting fields of research concerning how Zoroastrian content is perceived by the youngest readers and what artistic means their authors use.

Notes

1 This research was supported by the Strategic Program Excellence Initiative at the Jagiellonian University.

2 See: https://www.ubisoft.com/en-us/game/prince-of-persia/prince-of-persia (accessed February 9, 2023).

3 This does not mean, however, that the key figures of Islam do not appear in comics: For example, in Iranian comics promoting Shi'a values, the face of Muhammad or Hussain is, according to one of the strategies adopted in Islamic art, hidden under a flame of golden light or veiled (see Esfandi, Ghaderi, and Ghaderi 2015, 221–5).

4 See: http://www.marvunapp.com/Appendix7/zoroaster_sorcerer_supreme.html (accessed February 9, 2023).

5 See: https://marvel.fandom.com/wiki/Yazatas (accessed February 9, 2023).

6 See: https://theshahnameh.com/ (accessed February 9, 2023).

7 **Table 4.3** Details of the Respondents

Zoroastrian Identity	A Zoroastrian (one or two Zoroastrian parents) originating from India or other Parsi colonies	78
	A Zoroastrian (one or two Zoroastrian parents) originating from Iran	7
	A convert to Zoroastrianism or a person planning conversion	6
Gender	Male	41
	Female	37
	Not indicated	13
Age	Below 20	1
	21–30	8
	31–40	16
	41–50	20
	51–60	26
	61–70	10
	Over 71	9
	Not indicated	1
Country of Residence	India	39
	United States	22
	Canada	11
	European countries	8
	Pakistan	4
	Australia	3
	Iran	1
	Others or not indicated	3

8 In 2012, there were 15,000 Zoroastrians in Iran (Rivetna 2012), and my observations indicate that this number has decreased significantly.

9 See: https://www.etsy.com/shop/CrispyDoodles?section_id=36746528 (accessed February 9, 2023).

References

Babb, L. A. (1995), "Introduction," in L. A. Babb and S. S. Wadley (eds.), *Media and the Transformation of Religion in South Asia*, 1–18, Philadelphia: University of Pennsylvania Press.

Boyce, M. (1979), *Zoroastrians: Their Religious Beliefs and Practices*, London: Routledge.

Cates, I. (2020), "The Graphic Novel," in C. Hatfield and B. Beaty (eds.), *Comics Studies: A Guidebook*, 82–94, New Brunswick, NJ: Rutgers University Press.

de Groot, K. (2020), *The Liquidation of the Church*, London: Routledge.

Eck, D. L. (1998), *Darśan: Seeing the Divine Image in India*, New York: Columbia University Press.

Esfandi, E., Ghaderi, A., and Ghaderi, A. (2015), "The Notion of Comics in Iran," in J. Ahrens, F. T. Brinkmann, and N. Riemer (eds.), *Comics—Bilder, Stories Und Sequenzen in Religiösen Deutungskulturen*, 201–34. Wiesbaden: Springer VS.

Fernandes, K. (2014), "Writing Comic Books Is a Monk's Work." *ETimes*. Available online: timesofindia.indiatimes.com/life-style/books/features/writing-comic-books-is-a-monks-work/articleshow/45574792.cms (accessed February 9, 2023).

Gamzou, A., and Koltun-Fromm, K. (2018), "Comics and Sacred Texts," in A. Gamzou and K. Koltun-Fromm (eds.), *Comics and Sacred Texts: Reimagining Religion and Graphic Narratives*, 9–17, Jackson: University Press of Mississippi.

Gibson, M. (2020), "Girls, Women, and Comics," in C. Hatfield and B. Beaty (eds.), *Comics Studies: A Guidebook*, 241–52, New Brunswick, NJ: Rutgers University Press.

Gruber, C. (2017), "Images of the Prophet Muhammad: Brief Thoughts on Some European-Islamic Encounters," in S. Fotouhi and E. Zeiny (eds.), *Seen and Unseen: Visual Cultures of Imperialism*, 34–52, Leiden: Brill.

Hawley, J. S. (1995), "The Saints Subdued: Domestic Virtue and National Integration in Amar Chitra Katha," in L. A. Babb and S. S. Wadley (eds.), *Media and the Transformation of Religion in South Asia Religion in South Asia*, 107–34, Philadelphia: University of Pennsylvania Press.

Hjarvard, S. (2020), "Three Forms of Mediatized Religion: Changing the Public Face of Religion," *State Religion and Church in Russia and Worldwide* 38 (2): 41–75.

Kaur, R., and Saif, E. (2019), *Adventure Comics and Youth Cultures in India*, London: Routledge.

Khanduri, R. G. (2010), "Comicology: Comic Books as Culture in India," *Journal of Graphic Novels and Comics* 1 (2): 171–91.

Koltun-Fromm, K. (2020), *Drawing on Religion: Reading and the Moral Imagination in Comics and Graphic Novels*, Pennsylvania: Pennsylvania State University Press.

Kukkonen, K. (2013), *Studying Comics and Graphic Novels*, Chichester: Wiley Blackwell.

Locke, S. (2012), "Constructing a Sociology of Comics by Simon Locke," *Comics Forum*. Available online: comicsforum.org/2012/01/13/constructing-a-sociology-of-comics-by-simon-locke/ (accessed February 9, 2023).

Malandra, William W. (2009), "Zoroaster: Ii. General Survey," *Encyclopaedia Iranica Online*. Available online: www.iranicaonline.org/articles/zoroaster-ii-general-survey (accessed February 9, 2023).

Marazano, R. (2019), *Zarathustra: Volume 1: The Lion That Carried the Flame*, Paris: Europe Comics.

McAllister, M. P., and MacAuley, B. (2020), "Comics Industries," in H. Charles and B. Bart (eds.), *Comics Studies: A Guidebook*, 97–112, New Brunswick, NJ: Rutgers University Press.

McLain, K. (2009), *India's Immortal Comic Books: Gods, Kings, and Other Heroes*, Bloomington: Indiana University Press.

Meskin, A., and Cook, R. T. (2020), "Philosophical Aesthetics: Comics and/as Philosophical Aesthetics," in M. J. Smith, M. Brown, and R. Duncan (eds.), *More Critical Approaches to Comics: Theories and Methods*, 160–74, New York: Routledge.

Niechciał, P. (2020a), "Essentialism in Zoroastrian Boundary Construction," *Anthropology Southern Africa* 43 (2): 119–32.

Niechciał, P. (2020b), "Zoroastrianism in Comics," *Kultura Popularna* 60 (2): 48–56.

"Obiturary: Professor Kasra Vafadari (1946–2005)" (2006), *FEZANA Journal* 19 (1): 104–5.

Orcutt, D. (2010), "Comics and Religion: Theoretical Connections," in A. D. Lewis and C. H. Kraemer (eds.), *Graven Images: Religion in Comic Books and Graphic Novels*, 93–106, New York: Continuum.

Orsi, Robert A. (1997), "Everyday Miracles: The Study of Lived Religion," in D. D. Hall (ed.), *Lived Religion in America: Toward a History of Practice*, 3–21, Princeton, NJ: Princeton University Press.

Pai, A. (2007), *Zarathushtra*, Mumbai: Book House.

Palsetia, J. S. (2008), *The Parsis of India: Preservation of Identity in Bombay City*, New Delhi: Manohar.

Panaino, A. (2022), "Zoroaster 'the Astrologer': Genesis and Development of a Cultural Myth," paper prestented at the Conference *Fascination with Zarathustra: Eastern and Western Perspectives*, UC Irvine.

Pritchett, F. W. (1995), "The World of Amar Chitra Katha," in L. A. Babb and S. S. Wadley (eds.), *Media and the Transformation of Religion in South Asia*, 76–106, Philadelphia: University of Pennsylvania Press.

Ringer, M. M. (2011), *Pious Citizens: Reforming Zoroastrianism in India and Iran*, Syracuse, NY: Syracuse University Press.

Rivetna, R. (2012), "The Zarathushti World—a Demographic Picture." Available online: https://www.fezana.org/files/Demographics/Zworld6Sep12.pdf (accessed February 9, 2023).

Rose, J. (2013), "Zoroaster: Vii. As Perceived by Later Zoroastrians," *Encyclopaedia Iranica Online*. Available online: www.iranicaonline.org/articles/zoroaster-vi-as-perceived-by-later-zoroastrians (accessed February 9, 2023).

Satrapi, M. (2004), *Persepolis: The Story of a Childhood*, trans. M. Ripa and F. Blake, New York: Pantheon.

Sheffield, D. J. (2012), "Picturing Prophethood: KRCOI Zarātushtnāma, Manuscript HP 149 and the Origins of Portraits of the Prophet Zarathushtra," *Journal of the K. R. Cama Oriental Institute* 72: 71–138.

Šisler, V. (2008), "Digital Arabs: Representation in Video Games," *European Journal of Cultural Studies* 11 (2): 203–20.

Stausberg, M. (2005), "Zoroaster: Vi. As Perceived in Western Europe," *Encyclopaedia Iranica Online*. Available online: https://iranicaonline.org/articles/zoroaster-perceived-in-europe (accessed February 9, 2023).

Stausberg, M. (2015), "Zoroastrians in Modern Iran," in M. Stausberg and Y. Sohrab-Dinshaw Vevaina (eds.), *The Wiley Blackwell Companion to Zoroastrianism*, 173–90, Chichester: Wiley Blackwell.

Stoll, J. (2017), "Comics in India," in F. Bramlett, R. T. Cook, and A. Meskin (eds.), *The Routledge Companion to Comics*, 177–95, New York: Routledge.

Vidal, G. (1981), *Creation: A Novel*, New York: Random House.

Wild, N. (2016), *Tako milczy Zaratustra*, trans. W. Birek, Warszawa: Timof Comics.

Woo, B. (2020), "Readers, Audiences, and Fans," in C. Hatfield and B. Beaty (eds), *Comics Studies: A Guidebook*, 113–25, New Brunswick, NJ.: Rutgers University Press.

Zartushi-Behram. (1843), "Zarthusht-Nameh ('Book of Zarathushtra')," trans. E. B. Eastwick. *Avesta.Org*. Available online: avesta.org/other/zartusht-nameh.pdf (accessed February 9, 2023).

Part 2

Religion in Comics

5

Drawn into Krishna: Autobiography and Lived Religion in the Comics of Kaisa and Christoffer Leka

Andreas Häger and Ralf Kauranen[1]

Autobiography in any genre is a form of "presentation of self," a construction of the author's identity. In our study of four comics by Kaisa and Christoffer Leka from Finland, we focus on how religion, in their case the Gaudiya Vashnavism tradition within Hinduism, is integrated in self-representation. As religion is a recurring topic in their comics, which are set in the mundane milieux of the protagonists, we approach these as narratives of lived religion (Ammerman 2014). Our purpose is to analyze the manifold ways in which life and religion are intermingled in the comics. Two of the comics that we focus on follow a conventional pattern of autobiography as they narrate how religion is meaningful and important in the lives of the protagonists. In one case, the autobiographical travel narration not only thematizes the travel as religious practice but the narrative is also structured according to an important religious text. In the final case, a religious text is adapted in the framework of the lives of the two protagonists. Our research question is: What is the role of the autobiographical approach in the depiction and promotion of this minority religion in a secularized Nordic context?

A discussion on religion in autobiographical comics follows next, after which we look at the Finnish religious context. Before moving on to the empirical analyses, the comics production of the Leka couple and self-representation in them are discussed.

Graphic Life Writing and Religion

Graphic life writing, or comics auto/biographies and other personal narratives, has turned out to be a vibrant comics genre in the last half-century (Beaty 2007, 140–1; Kunka 2018, 3). Research has outlined a number of themes central to the genre: childhood, the comics artist's work (Groensteen 1996), the quotidian and the antiheroic (Hatfield 2005), women and trauma (Chute 2010), gender and sexuality, race and ethnicity, and graphic medicine (Kunka 2018). Comics autobiographies and self-representation have become an important means for people, both artists and readers, to negotiate their identities and make themselves visible in culture. Autobiography also offers marginalized groups a means to be acknowledged among social majorities (see Beaty 2007, 143–4; Køhlert 2019, 10).

However, while religion is a crucial theme in a work that often is deemed a starting point for comics autobiographies, that is, Justin Green's *Binky Brown Meets the Holy Virgin Mary* (1972), on the author's struggles with his Catholic upbringing, religion seems marginal to the genre in general. When religion is addressed in comics autobiographies, it often is depicted as a negative force that stymies the protagonist's life. In perhaps the most well-known example, Marjane Satrapi's *Persepolis* (2000–3), religion is predominantly present as the Islamic revolution in Iran, setting off radical changes in the protagonist's and her family's lives. In Green's narrative as well as in Carlos Gimenez's *Paracuellos* (published since 1977) and Craig Thompson's *Blankets* ([2003] 2015), religion as a part of upbringing and the surrounding culture is the basis for traumatic experiences.

Religious Context

As in the other Nordic countries, the religious situation in Finland is characterized by two contrasting facts: the presence of a large national Lutheran church, and a high degree of secularization (Furseth 2018). Finland officially has two national churches, the other being the Orthodox Church with circa 1 percent of the population. There has been a Muslim presence since the nineteenth century. Despite this, it is fair to say that Finland is religiously quite monolithic. Hindus in Finland are a very small minority. There are four registered Hindu communities, with a total membership (in 2018) of just over two hundred and fifty people, but there are around thirty different groups altogether (Uskonnot Suomessa n.d.).

The Lekas belong to a very small group called Sri Caitanya Sangha, with about a dozen members in Finland (Dialogikasvatus 2021). The leader of Sri Caitanya Sangha and the guru of the Lekas is B. V. Swami Tripurari, based in California, to whom some of the Leka publications are dedicated. This group is part of the Gaudiya Vaishnava tradition within Hinduism. This is a strand of Vaishnavism—religious devotion to Vishnu—with its roots in the teachings of the sixteenth century Western Bengali guru and Saint Caitanya, believed to be an avatar of both Krishna and his wife Radha (Klostermeier 1998, 82). The internationally most well-known group within this tradition is ISKCON, or the Hare Krishna Movement. The fact that the Lekas belong to a small minority religion and that this, from a Finnish perspective, "exotic" religion is the subject of their comics is relevant to their impact as comics artists. Thus, they are not considered a threat to the secular order, as artists identifying with and depicting, for example, revivalist Protestantism would be.

We approach religion in the material through the concept of "lived religion." A popular concept in the first decades of this millennium (Ammerman 2016), it sums up a perspective that focuses on practices rather than dogma, on body rather than mind, and on how religion is lived rather than on how it is prescribed. Applying the concept of "lived religion" to media material can seem counterintuitive. However, "lived religion" seems apt in relation to autobiographical narratives. Ammerman (2014) studies lived religion in a life history material and the autobiographical comics studied here are a form of life histories focusing on the personal experience of religion (see Edgell 2012, 253). While the comics can be read as expressions of "lived religion," they may also provide their readers with scripts for lived religion.

Kaisa and Christoffer Leka and Self-Representation

Kaisa (b. 1978) and Christoffer Leka (b. 1972) have, starting in 2010 with *Tour d'Europe*, coauthored six books published through their own Absolute Truth Press. Both have authored comics on their own before. Kaisa Leka is still probably best known for her autobiography, *I Am Not These Feet* (2003), which focuses on the amputation of her legs and her receiving prostheses. In Finland, the Lekas have received several accolades. Their potential readership, however, is transnational as most of their works are published in English.

In our analysis we focus on the following four works: *Your Name is Krishangi* (Leka 2004), *On the Outside Looking In* (Leka 2006), *Tour d'Europe* (Leka and

Leka 2010), and *Time after Time* (Leka and Leka 2014; hereafter we refer to the comics as *Krishangi, Outside, Tour*, and *Time*). In addition to a few non-autobiographical comics (Leka, C. 1997, 2003; Leka 2007, 2009), these are the ones in which religion is the most articulated. The four books present the lives of the protagonists—"Kaisa" and "Leka" (Christoffer is referred to by the couple's surname)—in different genre traditions, and with religion intermingled in their lives in varying ways.

The two oldest books—*Krishangi* and *Outside*—represent autobiography in a conventional sense. In line with "the autobiographical contract" (Lejeune 1989), the narrator and protagonist are equaled with the single author–artist Kaisa Leka, and the narratives convey stories of the personal development of the protagonist. They also present religion as a crucial aspect of personal life and change. *Tour* is a travel narrative, where the story suggests a comparison between road cycling and spiritual life and practices. The comic also integrates religious teachings with the structure of the travelogue. Finally, *Time* can be described as an adaptation of Hindu mythology in comics form. The mediation of mythology, however, is interwoven with the lives of the two protagonists, and therefore this comic is also representative of autobiographical narration.

Comics scholars have raised the question about autobiographies having multiple creators (El Refaie 2012, 52). The autobiographical self of the four books changes, from first being Kaisa's self and religious development (*Krishangi*), to one where Leka's developing self becomes a part of Kaisa's developmental story (*Outside*), to a collective of the two selves in many ways equally present in the stories (*Tour* and *Time*). In all four books, however, Kaisa and Leka are the ever-present protagonists, in dialogue with each other, providing a constant exchange and change of perspectives between the two.

El Refaie (2012, 19) notes that contemporary autobiographies often are dialogic. According to her, "This dialogism, in which each voice and each perspective exists in relation to others equally valid, creates a sense of ironic ambivalence, where 'truth' can never be established once and for all, since it is always being simultaneously avowed and dismantled." In line with this, the works of the Lekas can be described as dialogic autobiography. Crucially, dialogism is also significant for understanding the position of religion in the narratives. Religious beliefs, dogmas, and practices are continually reviewed and positioned in the lives of the protagonists in their dialogues. Religion constitutes a third voice in the comics, sometimes in a very concrete fashion as, for example, in the words of a guru or in the retelling of myths, but it is also integrated in the protagonists' verbal exchanges.

Self-representation in autobiographical comics has a very concrete dimension: in them, artists repeatedly depict themselves in series of visual self-portraits. This forces the artist to engage with the embodiment of identity and conventions of body image (El Refaie 2012). In the Lekas's comics, drawn in a simplified style of line drawings with scant background detail, the author-protagonists' selves and most other characters take animal form. Kaisa and most other characters are mice, and Leka along with his family are ducks (Figure 5.1). As the different characters of the slightly Disney-esque species look alike, their individuality is marked by an initial on the shirt: Kaisa with "K," Leka with "L," and so on.

The depiction of characters in a non-elaborate visual form can be interpreted in different ways. In an analysis of *I Am Not These Feet*, Romu (2016, 206) suggests that the simple figure and its lack of cultural, gendered, and other attributes, foregrounds "the shared human experience," which grants the reader interpretative freedom to project their own visions of embodiment onto the character. Equally viably, Quesenberry (2017, 418, 423) claims that

Figure 5.1 Kaisa Leka, *On the Outside Looking In*, Absolute Truth Press, 2006, n.p.

the non-human self-representation allows for the accentuation of a specific characteristic in a figure, for example, disability in Kaisa's mouse character. Furthermore, the non-human characterization reduces the "inference or 'noise' in the representation of a specific experience" (418), by downplaying visible differences of, for example, gender or ethnicity. In relation to the representation of religion, the simplified characters, with their association to well-known popular cultural icons, may be read as offering an object of readerly identification that is not limited by specific characteristics. The simplified characters may also be seen as a means to reduce distractions and direct attention to what is important, for example, the representation and discussion of religious ideas.

We now turn to the analysis of the different comics. Our methodological approach can be described as inductive, giving precedence to the material. When analyzing how religion is treated in these comics, we pay heed to the comics' narration as both verbal and visual as well as sequential. The four comics in our material represent different takes on autobiographical representation and on the depiction of religion in the authors' and protagonists' lives.

Life, Religion, and Personal Development

While the earlier *Your Name Is Krishangi* focuses on one particular and especially significant religious event in the lives of the Lekas, *On the Outside Looking In* is a more encompassing coming-of-age story, where religious matters play a crucial role. The latter depicts how Kaisa and Leka find Hinduism and Krishna, and learn about, discuss, and criticize the teachings and practices, while the former focuses on their initiation by Swami Tripurari. In this section, we show how religion is interwoven in the life narratives and the development of the protagonists. The narratives provide a particular, personal, and lived take on Hinduism, which is both serious and humoristic and both embraces the religion and maintains a critical distance to certain aspects of it. This double approach suggests an invitation to the reader to identify with and embrace the religious message, while providing the space for dissociation as well.

Taking a broad retrospective look at the two protagonists' lives, *Outside* is divided into three parts. In the first two, Kaisa and Leka, respectively, reminisce about growing up. In the third part, they jointly remember their life together.

The first two parts present coming-of-age stories that accommodate the meaning of religious development in the lives of the two protagonists. Kaisa's story focuses on childhood insecurities concerning being oneself, suffering from disability, being bullied, and making friends. In terms of religion, Kaisa develops from a person angry with an unfair god responsible for her disability and an inclination toward atheism to someone who shows an interest in the Hare Krishna movement. The high-school-aged Kaisa wonders,

> If there is a God and he's good, then why does he let me suffer like this? / Isn't it kind of unfair of him to make some people disabled while others are healthy? / And if God loves people, how can he send them to hell for eternity without giving them a second chance? / You know what, God? If you're out there, I'd just like to say this: I hate you! (Leka 2006, n.p.)

In this context, Hinduism starts to make sense to her. Kaisa's road to Hare Krishna goes through food and her vegetarianism. Her first encounters with the movement are depicted in a humorous way. At first, Kaisa is not that interested in or convinced by the religious tradition, but "the food's great," she notes when she comes in contact with it (Leka 2006, n.p.). The interest in the tradition is not described as a sublime epiphany; quite the contrary, it is rather mundane and even based on materialistic indulgence.

While Kaisa's interest in religion is approached with humoristic distance, it is connected to the personal problem of disability and to the ethical choice of vegetarianism. Leka's introduction to the Hindu tradition, again, is part of a slaphappy childhood and development into adulthood. His interest is presented as a continuation of his involvement in punk and straight edge cultures, and the coincidental reading of a religious book found on his parents' bookshelf. This leads to further study and Leka finding "Krishna consciousness" (Leka 2006, n.p.). This takes him to the Krishna temple in Helsinki, and the narrative depicts him as an active participant in the movement. However, critique of the Hare Krishna temple and movement is central to the narrative. The local temple's "atmosphere became authoritarian and anti-intellectual" (n.p.), Leka tells Kaisa in the frame narrative.

The first part of *Outside* ends with Kaisa taking her matriculation exam and deciding that she needs to move forward in life. The second part ends with Leka voicing his dissatisfaction with the Krishna temple. Both endings show the respective protagonist thinking, "I really need to get out of here!" The third part shows how the two—together—"get out" or at least onward from their previous life phases. It is also a romance story, as it recounts Kaisa and Leka's life together from the moment that they first met. Their studies and work, as well as Kaisa's disability and operation, are constituents of the story, but the final part is heavily dedicated to the couple's ongoing reflection on religion.

When the two protagonists' dialogue on religion starts, Kaisa states that "I personally don't believe in anything" (Leka 2006, n.p). Consequently, in the beginning, the conversation has the pattern of teacher and student, with Kaisa raising questions and Leka replying, evoking the *satsang* institution within Hinduism. Later, Kaisa recognizes herself as "a Hare Krishna," an epiphany approached with humor in the comic (Figure 5.1). As a sign of belonging, this is the first retrospective scene in which both Leka and Kaisa have necklaces of beads, a simple but clear marker for Krishna devotion in the comics. As a sign of distance, however, the protagonists' dialogue starts to scrutinize the Hare Krishna Movement's and specifically the Helsinki temple's ideas on gender. In this question, the roles of teacher and student are downplayed, as Kaisa's views on the issue are forcefully voiced. The issue of gender equality is also crucial with regard to the protagonists' enthusiasm over Swami Tripurari's teachings.

At the end of the third part of the memoir is a dialogue that echoes the ends of the first two. Here, Kaisa reflects on her practice of having her prosthetic feet visible instead of hiding them with prosthetic covers. She notes that "there's a huge difference between being pushed outside and choosing to stay outside social norms." The ending suggests that the protagonists have managed to "get out" of their former surroundings and lives. While the dialogue focuses on disability, the ample reflection on religion in the comic as well as the story ending with Swami Tripurari's visit suggest that the discussion also refers to the choice of a life in a religious minority position outside the normative standards of society.

The more limited autobiography *Krishangi* tells the story of how Kaisa and Leka receive initiation by Swami Tripurari during their honeymoon trip to California. Here, the autobiographical perspective coincides with the travelogue and with the diary format as the narrative segments are dated (cf. El Refaie 2012, 44). Although the story includes some typical depictions of air travel and tourist activities, it centers on religious life. Interspersed with common tourist experiences, the narrative focuses on experiences that are less ordinary, both from the perspective of the general tourist and the protagonists. Early in the narrative, they attend a Ratha Yatra, a religious procession. It is Kaisa's first experience of this ritual, and she greets it with great eagerness: "This is the coolest thing I've ever seen!" (Leka 2004, 13). One third of the story takes place at Swami Tripurari's Audarya monastery, described as "a spiritual community in the redwood forest" (23). Here, the story's climactic moment occurs: the initiation of Kaisa and Leka.

The guru's suggestion of Kaisa and Leka's initiation comes as a surprise to them. It is both pleasant and a reason for unease. A key discussion in the comic

Figure 5.2 Kaisa Leka, *Your Name Is Krishangi*, Absolute Truth Press, 2004, p. 37.

concerns the readiness of the protagonists to be initiated (see Figure 5.2). In a self-ironic way, they discuss their unpreparedness for the much valued step in their spiritual development. As Kaisa dramatically states, "We're completely unqualified! And most certainly unable to meditate for two hours a day!"

The ambivalence between the joy of being initiated and the responsibility that it implies is discussed repeatedly. While the protagonists are affected by the words of the guru and see the seriousness of initiation, their attitude is a source of humor. For example, in one installment in the comic, after having been initiated, Kaisa and Leka are watching TV, and Kaisa points out that they "should go out and meditate now!" They agree to stay in after Leka's retort, "Yeah, but the Simpsons are on next" (Leka 2004, 57). This discussion not only plays on the protagonists' ambivalence in regard to religious commitment, but also shows how religion is incorporated in their lives, as one part that shares space with other cultural interests like the Simpsons. Religion, although the comic's central theme, is intermingled with other aspects of the protagonists' lives and identities.

The self-ironic, humorous stance toward the protagonists' relationship to religion does not imply ridicule of religious teachings or practices. Quite the contrary, it can, as the following example illustrates, be read as humility, and thus reverence, of the tradition. This reverence is also visible in how the guru's words are presented. Speaking of initiation, his word-filled speech balloons occupy three full pages with only his character in the corner of the page indicating the source. Only the titles of the pages frame the guru's words from the narrator-Kaisa's perspective, "Swami speaks about initiation / I'm a bad listener … / … but the words touch me" (Leka 2004, 26–8), again suggesting the valuation of the religious message and the simultaneous unassuming perspective of the narrator–protagonist, opening up a space for the reader where both the reception of the religious message and a distance to it are possible.

The Travelogue as Religious Text

Tour d'Europe (2010) is one of several travelogues in the Leka oeuvre. It depicts a bicycle trip from Finland to France. The comic is in black and white. To add to the austere look, the drawings are almost exclusively line drawings, with no nuances or shades. As the main theme is a bicycle trip, a large proportion of the pages are dominated by a road consisting of a few lines, with the two main characters on bicycles.

The subtitle of the album reads: "The Yoga of Road Cycling." The strenuous trips depicted in several Leka comics are often connected to yoga, exemplifying how lived religion comes across in these comics, but never more so than in *Tour*. In this section, we look at how the parallels between cycling and yoga play out in this comic. We point out four ways in which yoga and cycling are paralleled in *Tour*: the formal connection between the comic and Bhagavad Gita; explicit mentions of cycling as yoga; renunciation and asceticism as part of a long cycling trip; and the road as a metaphor for Krishna.

The connection between yoga and cycling in *Tour* is taken to the extent of shaping the narrative after the Bhagavad Gita (hereafter *BhG*), one of the central texts in Gaudiya Vaishnavism. The comic has eighteen chapters, just as *BhG*, and each chapter borrows its title from the corresponding chapter in the original, from chapter 1, "The Yoga of Despair," to chapter 18, "The Yoga of Freedom."

There are also many themes borrowed from *BhG*, often recurring in the exact corresponding chapter, including direct quoting.

The comics of the Lekas are often dialogue-driven, and a recurring theme of discussion concerns their reflections and "philosophizing" over life, faith, and the efforts of bicycling. These reflections are sometimes more, sometimes less explicitly tied to their religion. Yoga is referred to repeatedly in the short prose introductions to each chapter of *Tour* but also occasionally in the dialogue of the comic. One example is from a discussion in chapter 5 on the constant companion of the road cyclist, the wind. Leka says, "Everything seems to change when you have a tail wind," to which Kaisa adds: "Well, you'd have to be quite the yogi to see both head wind and tail wind as equal" (Leka and Leka 2010, 122–3; Figure 5.3). The wind turbine dominating the image illustrates the idea that all wind directions are equal. The discussion is a reference to a passage in the corresponding chapter in *BhG* (5.18): "The truly learned, with the eyes of divine knowledge, see with equal vision a Brahmin, a cow, an elephant, a dog, and a dog-eater."

The physical demands of the journey, being at the mercy of the weather, and the sometimes ascetic conditions of living can be summed up under the concept of renunciation, which is a central theme in *BhG*. These renunciations, being part of the journey and of the life of a yogi, exemplify how the protagonists' lived religion is depicted in the comic. On one occasion (Leka and Leka 2010, 64–5), Leka ascertains that "whenever we do something of consequence, there's an element of sacrifice involved." Kaisa agrees, saying "It's a mistake to think that we could avoid discomfort in this world"—and adds a comic twist to the serious discussion, questioning her husband's sanity, as he had conceived of this trip.

Their reaction to these sacrifices during the journey varies. Kaisa complains about the hardships of the journey: "So this is it then … headwind, rain, second-rate accommodation, no rest, no proper meals … and my butt is killing me" (Leka and Leka 2010, 56). This quote describes the difficulties of traveling by bike and on a budget. But it is also an example of a less "yogi-like" attitude toward the inevitable difficulties of such a journey. Thus, the sentiments expressed are examples of how the narrators present themselves as inferior yogis, as in the discussion of whether they are worthy of initiation, the central theme in *Krishangi*. One concrete example of the cycling couple being quite content with the less than luxurious circumstances is when old bread and olive oil become a "delicious sandwich" (235).

Food, both in terms of renunciation and indulgence, is a common theme in this comic, as in other Leka comics, and a central aspect of how lived, embodied,

Figure 5.3 Kaisa and Christoffer Leka, *Tour d'Europe,* Absolute Truth Press, 2010, p. 123.

religion is present throughout this and other Leka albums. They are vegetarians, following *ahimsa*, and are often looking for vegetarian shops or restaurants (Leka and Leka 2010, 424–5). The tension between asceticism and pleasure is always present in their relation to food, as when they enjoy their french fries, first making sure they are fried in vegetable oil: "Munch munch" (85).

One feature that is repeated on several occasions in the album is the special way of talking about the road. "Our fate really lies in the hands of the road, whether we choose to accept it or not," Leka says (Leka and Leka 2010, 209). In the final chapter, after arriving, Leka muses about the journey being the destination, adding that "we should forget everything else and just give up our separate interest and try to understand the way of the road" (464). This suggests to us that the road here is a metaphor for Krishna, in line with the parallel between cycling and yoga central to the album. In the final example, Kaisa again brings comic relief in cheering as she crosses the finish line first.

The connection between yoga and cycling is, to sum up, twofold. On one hand, the road cycling in the story becomes a metaphor for yoga, a way to explain yoga to the uninitiated. This aspect is explicit in the supporting prose passages. On the other hand, cycling is also a form of yoga, and especially this type of long and very strenuous cycling, as it entails renunciation from their normal level of comfort as well as brings the cyclist into a different, meditative state of mind (Leka and Leka 2010, 374–7). Seeing cycling as yoga or a form of meditation strongly evokes the embodied aspect of lived religion: the central religious practice of the tradition is carried out through a bodily practice.

Lived Mythology

Time after Time (Leka and Leka 2014) stands out in the work of the Lekas due to its theme and particular structure. There is a frame narrative with the main characters working, arguing, and eating, but above all, reading and discussing *Dasavatara*, the tales of ten avatars of Vishnu/Krishna, and the myths act as the main narrative of the album. The different parts of the long, colorful album are represented in distinct styles.

In the frame narrative, set in the Leka home in Finland, the couple is again portrayed as a mouse and a duck, although in more colors and inhabiting a much more colorful milieux than in the other comics. The Hindu myths are represented in a more elaborate and even more richly colored style, where line drawings are not as imperative, and colors are less clearly separated; the style evokes associations of traditional Hindu iconography. The mythological parts are framed to look like an old book with yellowing paper and the edges of an open book.

In this section, we look at how the ancient myths turn into an aspect of the lived religion of the protagonists, and at how the depiction of the myths in the comic, through narrative and image, become both a part of and a contrast to their daily lives.

The tales of the avatars are told in different Hindu texts, but most prominently in the *Bhagavata Purana*, also known as the *Srimad Bhagavatam*, the main holy text of Gaudiya Vaishnavism (Broo 2006, 185). They are retold in many different popular versions, previously also in comic form (e.g., Pai 1978); as a full-length animated film (*Dashavatar* 2008); and in contemporary prose (Vaswani 2018).

The narrative solution of frame and adaptation in *Time* is illustrated by the book's cover (Figure 5.4). The lavishly framed image shows a view from the Leka home with Kaisa, Leka, and four different avatars of Krishna sharing the space. As Leka is reading aloud (his mouth is open) a book called *Time after Time*, the cover metatextually depicts the commixture of the frame narrative and the adaptation narratives. The image suggests that the reading brings alive the stories about Krishna, but it also implies the importance or reality of the religious tradition in the lives of the protagonists. Reading and discussing the texts is a part of lived religion in this case.

As indicated earlier, the source of the avatars is somewhat ambiguous: are they incarnations of Vishnu or, as is the tradition within Gaudiya Vaishnavism, of Krishna? And if the latter, how can Krishna be one of the incarnations? This conundrum is also discussed in a dialogue between Leka and Kaisa in *Time*; they conclude that:

L: "There's no need to fight over this. Both are right in a sense"
K: "Ah? Kind of like water and ice?"
L: "Vishnu's like the majestic face of God and Krishna is the friendly, more easily approachable face"
K: "Ok, I get it … Do go on!" (Leka and Leka 2014, n.p.)

This dialogue is a typical example of how the protagonists discuss theological issues arising from the reading, and how they attempt to provide accessible answers.

The fantastic tale of the second avatar, the tortoise Kurma, can serve as an example of the narrative dynamic of the comic. It tells of the churning of the milk ocean, which produces a number of substances, objects, and

Figure 5.4 Kaisa and Christoffer Leka, *Time after Time*, Absolute Truth Press, 2014, front cover.

beings—including a cow—and finally the nectar of immortality. Kaisa comments by exclaiming: "Stop right there! That's just too crazy!," and continues, "The previous one made at least a bit of sense, but this is just too much! I mean, flying cows? For real?" (Leka and Leka 2014, n.p.). The same humorous distance as in the other comics, serious discussion followed with a sarcastic comment, is central to *Time*. It is combined with the sometimes-sharp questioning of myths, which also takes ambiguous form: "For real?," the question suggesting the potential reality of myth.

In addition to the protagonists' discussions about the myths, the myth retellings themselves suggest a distanced and humoristic narrative perspective on the mythological stories. The dialogue and visual representations are at times incongruous with the stories told. For example, when one of the Asuras is decapitated, he exclaims, as his immortal head flies off, "So long, suckers!" (Leka and Leka 2014, n.p.). Such an exclamation, or the drowning child Prahlada depicted as being pulled down by a concrete block with the text "1 ton," provide for humor based on the incongruence between the sacral text and the prosaic formulations. However, this stylistic technique can also be read as a means to make sense of stories assumedly obsolete and unbelievable in a contemporary context.

The tale of the final avatar, to appear in end times, is represented in a more realistic style, placing the myth in our time. The apocalypse is illustrated by skyscrapers advertising "Steakhouse" and "Girls," and by an abandoned oil field. These images propose that contemporary, modern life represents "end times," and that selling sex, eating meat, and exploiting natural resources are signs of this. This is coupled with the traditional depiction of the Kalki avatar on his winged horse with his attributes (Leka and Leka 2014, n.p.). Other visual accounts of Dasavatara, like those mentioned earlier, also represent the end times with contemporary images of industry and violence, sharing the same view of the imminent apocalypse with the Lekas. The similarity indicates how *Time* may be inspired by other popular, visual accounts of the myths.

The main inspiration for *Time* is, however, the mythological tales; this is evident both in text and image. The original narratives are complex, and many aspects have been left out (cf. Vaswani 2018). On the other hand, lines in *Time* can be quite faithful quotes from Bhagavata Purana, as in the tale of the boar avatar Varaha, when Brahma says, "Who is this extraordinary creature that emerged from my nose?" (Leka and Leka 2014: n.p.; cf. *Bhagavata Purana* 3.13.21). The imagery also closely follows tradition, for example, in the depiction of the gods. Vishnu, Krishna, and Rama have blue skin; Vishnu has four arms and sits on his snake throne holding his traditional attributes; three-headed Brahma is riding his white swan; and so on. The depiction not only helps identify the characters but also shows adherence to the tradition.

Earlier, Vishnu and Brahma are referred to as "characters" in the comic, but they are obviously more than that; they are gods. This difference can be further elaborated by reference to a distinction between two types of religious images within Hinduism: mythological, as in retelling myths, and devotional (Cooksey 2016, 8). This distinction is evident in *Time*. The images serve the narration of the stories of the avatars, but some images also serve another purpose. There are a few full-page frontal images of the principal deities, such as Vishnu on his throne and similar images of Brahma and Krishna. One central feature of these splash pages is that the gaze of the deity is directed at the reader. This relates to a particular form of devotion within Hinduism, *darśan* (Elgood 1998; Klostermeier 2008), to see the god and to be seen. The image—a statue in a temple or a page in a comic book (McLain 2011)—is both a depiction of the god and the god themselves (Klostermeier 2008, 79). The visually elaborate and colorful full-frontal images in *Time* can be read as invitations to darśan. It is essential that such devotional pictures are well crafted and beautiful for the god to enter (Elgood 1998, 14, 30–1). Furthermore, the often very ambitious crafting, in binding and graphics, of *Time* and other Leka publications, can be viewed in light of this: their beauty is a devotion on the part of the craftsmen and invites the reader to join in this devotion.

The Dasavatara tales become part of the lived religion of the protagonists through reading, discussing, and even ridiculing them. Furthermore, the retelling of these myths in the form of this beautiful comic can be considered part of the lived religion of the Lekas. The reverent, even devotional, artwork becomes a way to make the sacred myths come alive. The contrast between the mythological elements and the scenes from the couple's home accentuates the importance of religion, its otherness, while the reading and related practices make this otherness a part of their—and our—lives.

Conclusion

The perspective encapsulated by the concept of lived religion focuses on everyday religiosity. The autobiographical comics of Kaisa and Christoffer Leka offer the reader life writing that is based in the everyday but also directs attention to that which is exceptional. The narratives filter the everyday and emphasize certain aspects of life. The works we have studied crucially place religion as a part of the lives of the two narrator-protagonists. The comics achieve this in different ways: while *On the Outside Looking In* and *Your Name Is Krishangi* situate religion and religious practices in the developmental narratives of the protagonists, *Tour d'Europe* foremost establishes a structural resemblance between, on the one hand, travel and cycling and, on the other hand, religion and yoga. Finally, *Time after Time* primarily adapts a religious text or myth but frames it within the everyday of the two artists. The comics provide insight into lived religion, in the ways in which religion is interwoven in the lives of the protagonists and, by extension, the artists. As narratives, the comics, of course, do not provide a direct view into everyday religiosity; as textual practice they represent different aspects of lived religion, such as the personal, embodied, and lay practices of religion.

The embodiment of religion is a theme of *Tour*, in which the bodily practice of road cycling is compared to yoga. The comic manifests how religion is central to a practice that usually has worldly connotations. Food and diet are another occurring theme in the Lekas' comics, from Kaisa's first meetings with the Hare Krishna movement to the discussions about restraint and indulgence, and to the religiously motivated vegetarianism. Religion is thus presented as an aspect of the mundane practices of eating and grocery shopping.

The Lekas' comics, although anchored in the everyday, also are representations of the textual traditions, commentary, and learned discourse on religion. The comics assert that the disparity between doctrine and life, between the prescribed and lived, or between religious elite and lay practitioner, is blurred.

Humor plays an important role in the representation of religion in the comics. Firstly, the ironic self-representation implies reverence for the religious tradition, by contrasting religion with the unworthy or unknowing protagonist. Secondly, the juxtaposition of serious discussion and recitation of religious wisdom with humorous commentary and skeptical wisecracks suggests a narrative distanciation from the religious tradition. It is a sign of a skeptical position with regard to uncompelling, for example, too fantastic, elements of religion, which, however, may make these elements more palatable to the protagonists and to the reader. The humorous distance and skepticism is also a narrative force that drives the discussion further, toward more satisfying explanations.

The dialogic dynamic of serious discussion and a humorous point of view is quintessential for how the Lekas' comics invite readers to approach religious themes. The dual address opens up for different approaches, both a contemplation of the religious message and a critical position of disbelief, and even a reading that completely ignores religion. The dialogues between Kaisa and Leka offer moments of education both for themselves and for the reader. In *Outside*, for example, Kaisa asks questions and Leka gives replies about religious matters, and in *Time*, Leka reads the religious text, Kaisa expresses her wonder about it, and the continuing discussions try to find solutions to the pending issues. In addition to the protagonists' own discussions, educational authority also belongs to the third voice of religion, as personified by their guru (present both as a speaking character in the comics and through a letter in *Time*) or represented through the religious texts. Regardless, the narrative educational setup invites the reader to join the protagonists in their learning process. In a secular context like Finland, the personal perspective of autobiography is perhaps more palatable to the reader than a more institutionally based representation of a minority religion.

The aesthetic, pedagogical, and theological mediation of religion in the autobiographical comics of Kaisa and Christoffer Leka integrates religion in the lives of the protagonists, narrators, and authors. The comics describe a lived minority religion in a personalized, learned, and informative manner, intermingling religion with the lives and identities of the protagonists.

Note

1 The authors would like to thank the anonymous reviewer for helpful comments and Sofia Blomqvist for her thorough language revision (Go Minutemen!).

References

Ammerman, Nancy T. (2014) *Sacred Stories, Spiritual Tribes: Finding Religion in Everyday Life*, Oxford: Oxford University Press.

Ammerman, Nancy T. (2016), "Lived Religion as an Emerging Field: An Assessment of Its Contours and Frontiers," *Nordic Journal of Religion and Society* 29 (2): 83–99.

Beaty, Bart. (2007), *Unpopular Culture: Transforming the European Comic Book Culture in the 1990s*, Toronto: University of Toronto Press.

Bhagavad Gita. Available online: https://www.holy-bhagavad-gita.org.

Bhagavata Purana. Available online: https://prabhupadabooks.com/sb.

Broo, Måns. (2006), *The Little Book of Bhakti-Yoga*, Porvoo: Absolute Truth Press.

Chute, Hillary L. 2010, *Graphic Women: Life Narrative and Contemporary Comics*, New York: Columbia University Press.

Cooksey, Rachel. (2016), "The Influence of Raja Ravi Varma's Mythological Subjects in Popular Art," *Independent Study Project Collection* 2511. Available online: https://digitalcollections.sit.edu/isp_collection/2511/ (accessed April 12, 2023).

Dashavatar. (2008), [Film] Dir. Bhavik Thakore, India: Anushvi Productions, Available online: https://www.youtube.com/watch?v=b5HmmrdrWAY=.

Dialogikasvatus. (2021), Hindulaisuus: Sri Caitanya Sangha. Video. Available online: https://www.youtube.com/watch?v=4pSSWqRjvEs (accessed April 12, 2023).

Edgell, Penny. (2012), "A Cultural Sociology of Religion: New Directions," *Annual Review of Sociology* 38 (1): 247–65.

El Refaie, Elisabeth. (2012), *Autobiographical Comics: Life Writing in Pictures*, Jackson: University Press of Mississippi.

Elgood, Heather. (1998), *Hinduism and the Religious Arts*, London: Bloomsbury.

Furseth, Inger. (2018), *Religious Complexity in the Public Sphere: Comparing Nordic Countries*, London: Palgrave Macmillan.

Groensteen, T. (1996), *Système de la bande dessinée*, Doctoral Thesis Toulouse: Toulouse 2.

Green, Justin. (1972/2009), *Binky Brown Meets the Holy Virgin Mary*, San Francisco: McSweeney's Books.

Hatfield, Charles. (2005), *Alternative Comics: An Emerging Literature*, Jackson: University Press of Mississippi.

Klostermeier, Klaus K. (2008), *Hinduism: A Beginners Guide*, Oxford: OneWorld.

Kunka, Andrew J. (2018), *Autobiographical Comics*, London: Bloomsbury.

Køhlert, Frederik Byrn (2019), *Serial Selves: Identity and Representation in Autobiographical Comics*, New Brunswick: Rutgers University Press.

Lejeune, Philippe. (1989), *On Autobiography*. Translated by Katherine Leary, Minneapolis: University of Minnesota Press.

Leka, Kaisa. (2004), *Your Name Is Krishangi*, Helsinki: Absolute Truth Press.

Leka, Kaisa. (2006), *On the Outside Looking In*, Helsinki: Absolute Truth Press.

Leka, Kaisa, and Christoffer Leka. (2008), *Audarya-Lila: The Death of Tuomas Mäkinen*, Helsinki: Absolute Truth Press.

Leka, Kaisa, and Christoffer Leka. (2010), *Tour d'Europe: The Yoga of Road Cycling*, Porvoo: Absolute Truth Press.

Leka, Kaisa, and Christoffer Leka. (2014), *Time after Time*, Porvoo: Absolute Truth Press.

Leka, Kaisa, and Christoffer Leka. (2017), *Imperfect*, Porvoo: Absolute Truth Press.

Leka, Kaisa, and Christoffer Leka. (2020), *Russian Diaries*, Porvoo: Absolute Truth Press.

McLain, Karline. (2011), "The Place of Comics in the Modern Hindu Imagination," *Religion Compass* 5 (10): 598–608.

Pai, Anant. (1978), *Dasha Avatar: The Ten Incarnations of Lord Vishnu*, Mumbai: Amar Chitra Katha.

Quesenberry, Krista. (2017), "Intersectional and Non-Human Self-Representation in Women's Autobiographical Comics," *Journal of Graphic Novels and Comics* 8 (5): 417–32. https://doi.org/10.1080/21504857.2017.1355831.

Romu, Leena. (2016), "Graphic Life Writing in Kaisa Leka's *I Am Not These Feet*," in Mikhail Peppas and Sanabelle Ebrahim (eds.), *Framescapes. Graphic Narrative Intertexts*, 203–12, Oxford: Inter-Disciplinary Press.

Satrapi, Marjane. (2000–2003/2007), *The Complete Persepolis*, New York: Pantheon Books.

Thompson, Craig. ([2003] 2015), *Blankets*, Montreal: Drawn & Quarterly.
Uskonnot Suomessa (n.d.). Available online: https://uskonnot.fi/in-english/ (accessed April 12, 2023).
Vaswani, J. P. (2018), *Dasavatara: The Ten Incarnations of Lord Vishnu*, Ahmedabad: Jaico Publishing House.

6

What Would Preacher Do? Tactics of Blasphemy in the Strategies of Satire and Parody

Michael J. Prince

Introduction

Garth Ennis and Steve Dillon's sixty-six-issue graphic novel series *Preacher* is blasphemous. Scream it from the rooftops, post it behind a sputtering red Cessna on an aerial advertising banner, and be sure to mention it in your Amazon customer review, as hundreds have (Maxfield 2012). Of course, some of the reviewers hem and haw, admitting a guilty pleasure that, in spite of being Evangelical Christians, devout Methodists, or Roman Catholics, they actually *enjoyed* reading *Preacher*, could not put it down. Others cannot resist making a teaching moment of their two-star review, pointing out that, all in all, *Preacher* is lousy theology. "Ennis and Dillon hold religion in undisguised contempt. Therefore, they don't realize the questions they raise are centuries old, or that their characters are little more complex than paper dolls. They just hold the characters, and their faith, up to mockery and derision, and think they've created a story" (Nenstiel 2021). Even serious scholarship is not immune to righteous indignation: "Here, Ennis' Northern Irish Protestantism (even if latent) comes to the fore. Ennis expresses himself as an outraged Puritan, implying that it is better to destroy than to allow contamination (whether societal or religious) to continue" (Grimshaw 2010, 153). Now, given that the *Entertainment Weekly* review blurb on the Amazon page *endorses* it with "features more blood and blasphemy than any mainstream comic in memory. Cool," one is hard pressed to avoid the suspicion that a good-sized chunk of the comics reading public just cannot take a joke.

This is undoubtedly a condition of the times, especially within the perceived conflicts between the waning authority of religion's institutions, and an almost limitless horizon of "things which are no longer sacred." As Kees de Groot points out, 'the market has become more powerful than the state, the church, or the family once were. We are tempted to buy the products that provide elements of an 'authentic' identity" (De Groot 2006, 96). Mike Grimshaw makes strong claims for the *Preacher* series' "[representing] Gen X in search of itself, a generation reading of a loss (the death of God) heard of in their parents' generation, but now experienced in *graphic* detail" (Grimshaw 2010, 161). And fan pages, letters to comics' publishers, cosplay, and Comic-Cons are evidence that readers of graphic novels do encourage in-group identification. Within that, or overlapping it, is another group that is open for the blasphemy excesses this series tactically employs, in this case hinging discursively on a shared notion of irony and ironic expression. Linda Hutcheon notes insightfully that "discursive communities" are a precondition for meaningful communication:

> [The] whole communicative process is … *made possible* by those different worlds to which each of us differently belongs and which form the basis of the expectations, assumptions, and preconceptions that we bring to the complex processing of discourse, of language *in use*. … [It] is this community that comes first and that, in fact, enables irony to happen. (Hutcheon 1994, 89, emphasis in original)

After Thomas Kuhn, Hutcheon defines these discursive communities "by the complex figuration of shared knowledge, beliefs, values, and communicative strategies" (Hutcheon 1994, 91). Among these communication strategies are those that, on occasion, participate in what Stig Hjarvard refers to as a "mediatization of religion" (Hjarvard 2016, 8). Does a dispersed group of comics "fans," individually or at a gathering, constitute De Groot's third type of "liquid religion?" (De Groot 2008, 288). I would venture to say, for some, yes; but even at its weakest, the mediatization of fundamental religious questions, narrative tropes, and symbols can be read (as Grimshaw does) as symptomatic of prevalent social attitudes, if for no other reason than Vertigo, the publisher of the *Preacher* series, wants to make money from their product. And to achieve this, they must find their appropriate discursive community.

Preacher was published serially from 1995 to 2000 and was reissued in a six-volume collection about a decade later. It is an eschatological satire, a parody of the *Second Coming*, only with an extremely warped figure representing the Jesus of the Parousia. As such, blasphemy is tactically deployed for most intents and purposes as part of the rhetoric of satire. To be sure, the series certainly merits its "Suggested for Mature Readers" label, but each excessive visual or textual flourish fits comfortably under the aegis of what a work participating in the satiric mode does: cajole, shock, mock, and condemn, all the while exerting control of the medium and genre and involving the reader in a sense of inclusiveness marked by familiarity with extratextual references, and the appropriate mode of humor.

Ennis and Dillon's comic epic utilizes literary and visual techniques to make a commanding work of Menippean satire, which employs a variety of genre, visual, and literary cues. Chief among these are the two dominant genres exploited in this work, Christian-inspired fiction and the Western. Further, within these genre articulations and expectations, there are some elements of parody, a frequent fellow traveler of satire. With regard to "religious"discourses, *Preacher* contains a complex angelology and eschatology, with the protagonist "Jesse Custer" as a complex placeholder for Jesus Christ. However, in spite of a rich assortment of blasphemies, these will be shown to be fairly pedestrian compared to the religion-based ontology that this series *naturalizes*, a feature of "banal religion." *Preacher* uses blasphemy as a tactic in the broader strategy of an epic Menippean satire. In short, I will show that *Preacher* may give a bit more than it takes at the table of religious exchange.

Religion and Blasphemy in a Comics Series

Blasphemy is different things for different people. *The Catholic Encyclopedia* lists three kinds: "It is heretical when the insult to God involves a declaration that is against faith"; "It is imprecatory when it could cry a malediction upon the Supreme Being"; and "It is simply contumacious when it is wholly made up of contempt of, or indignation towards, God" (Melody 1907). While at the federal level, the United States has no laws against it, some states did, trying an individual in the nineteenth century for unflattering statements about Jesus's mother; and a publisher for denying the existence of God. The Supreme Court ruled to stop all prosecutions in 1952. England and Wales abolished their statutes against blasphemy in 2008 (Vile 2009).

The comics serial *Preacher* is difficult to summarize. Like a television series, a strong draw for the readers is the interest in the characters, and to find out what happens to them in the following episode. This opens up for frequent and complex digressions. A single sentence summary, however, will verify the charges of blasphemy: a small-town preacher, Reverend Jesse Custer, is possessed by an unholy miscegenation of an angel and a demon, embarks upon a quest for God, and ultimately convinces a hitman to "rub out" the Heavenly Father for being a deadbeat dad and abandoning Earth. Throughout the sixty-six episodes, heresy, imprecation, and contumacy are committed numerous times.

The increasing stream of religious liquidity in the Western society, however, changes a discussion of blasphemy in a humorous work. Just twenty years ago, one could inquire of the television series *South Park*, as does Kevin J. Murtagh, whether Parker and Stone "are doing something morally wrong by using blasphemy for comic effect?" (Murtagh 2007, 29). Still, Murtagh's definition of *blasphemous humor* is helpful: "some sort of presentation that is intended to be amusing or funny, in which something deemed sacred is portrayed in a disrespectful or irreverent manner" (31). The first sticking point here is with "sacred": sacred for *whom*? The series *Preacher* calls to it an audience who may not have a strong notion of the sacred on any level, religious, nationalist, or consumerist. Rather, religion for this audience can be seen as a marker for those outside of their ingroup-affinity.

As Jesse Custer's backstory is that of an abused child of a conservative Pentecostal Christian family of a certain southern backwater ilk; this childhood narrative bears a strong critique (*Preacher, Book One*: 249–335, *passim*). But the denigrating depiction of a religious group has less to do with the religion than the "ethnic" group, for lack of a better term, "white trash." For example, when Jesse and his sweetheart Tulip are brought to Jesse's childhood home, the driveway is bordered by burning crosses, invoking an iconic connection to the Ku Klux Klan (*Book One*, 225). In some respects, however, the stern religious aspect of his childhood gives Jesse a messianic sheen, which the passage of time will bring to full light. Murtagh justifies the blasphemous humor in *South Park* as providing pleasure of the audience (even at the cost of others) and by encouraging discussion (Murtagh 2006, 35–7). That show frequently ends with a learned lesson. No such didactic reflection is available in *Preacher*. Contrary to what one would expect in strongly blasphemous characterizations of angels, churchmen, institutions, and God, the critique is frequently aimed at the *secular habits and human sensibilities* of these allegedly holy agents, oddly folding back on a transgressed morality on the part of those characters. The blasphemy of Ennis and Dillon is therefore not solely in the humor, but rather as a tactic to censure characters representing religion.

Preacher is a comics series, and as such brings with it some of the narrative constraints of other series, such as radio and movie serials and television series. However, copious digressions notwithstanding, the installments of *Preacher* were part of the same overarching story arc, unlike an interminable American sitcom, which runs until it "jumps the shark" or otherwise depletes the interest of its audience. *Preacher* was composed with a dramatic climax and conclusion in mind (Hibbs 2020). In this respect, it is similar to a Dickens serial novel. Each issue centers on a part of the overall narrative, generally concerning a particular coterie of characters. But, whereas the characters in a TV show are chiefly determined by the actors, in *Preacher*, and all other comics, the visual portrayals contribute to their characterization, both as individuals and in the narrative. It is then a serial graphic novel, as full of variety and digressions as *The Pickwick Papers*, yet as an illustrated epos of Ennis and Dillon's commentary on American society and the integrity of the Abrahamic godhead. Their critique of the Abrahamic God, and Christian religion in general has been recognized as "the plot's driving force, the author's most prominent intellectual examination of US culture and myth" (Salisbury 2013, 133). Yet, frame for frame, America, its people, its self-image in the media, its sustaining cultural mythology is satirized more than religion.

Nevertheless, religion is central to *Preacher*. Hjarvard writes that in fictional media "religion has become one among many other cultural resources for storytelling, yet since mass media generally … are in the business of getting the audiences' attention, religious messages are subordinated … and have to comply with generic conventions" (Hjarvard 2016, 10). Blasphemy in and of itself is not a genre convention. However, characters in doubt about their religious faith, in conflict with agents of religion (earthly as well as angelic), and in search of the *meaning* of it all are the new generic conventions of the adult serial comic and graphic novel. In the modalities that thrive in a state of religious liquidity, blasphemy can be employed in the repertoire of sustained irony at the core of satire.

Genres, Satire, and Parody

The impulses behind Ennis and Dillon's *Preacher* series were iconoclastic against organized religion but also against two crucial supporting cultural myths of Western and, especially, American society: the Christian founding myths and those associated with the Western frontier. This would not be done directly, but implicitly with the arsenal provided by satire and parody. Inspired by the cinema, Ennis constructed the series with an eye to combine uneven parts of David Lynch's *Wild at Heart* (1990), with a romance to set the world on fire;

Kathryn Bigelow's *Near Dark* (1987) with its more demotic vampires; and Clint Eastwood's *Unforgiven* (1992), a Western with a critical view on the gunfighter mystique. Also, during this time Ennis was living in the United States, so the work was inspired by American cinema, and portrayals of American culture. The mélange of these plot and character elements was in the end packaged in a contemporary *Western* (Hibbs 2020). However, unlike the films that inspired it, *Preacher* is an interwoven series of narrative vignettes. As such, the structure lends itself to promiscuous visits to diverse genre topographies, for two reasons. First, as Kathryn Hume has observed, "satire is better seen as a mode adaptable to various genres" (Hume 2007, 303); and second, one signal characteristic of Menippean satire is its use of different genres to achieve its attack (Griffin 1994, 31–3). *Preacher* is a Western, to be sure, but it also participates strongly in the generic expectations of the Christian novel, the horror genre, including (and especially), the vampire narrative. There is a bit of the action-film, the thriller, the detective story, a conspiracy narrative, with visits to old Europe, and the uninformed backwards American South. This great variety is what one would expect of the *lanx satura*, the "full plate" of Menippean satire. And the plate is nothing if not full in Ennis and Dillon's series.

To help the reader navigate the complex plot, the character gallery, and the way these are related to the genre, a slightly expanded, *selective*, plot synopsis is in order. Jesse Custer, a small-town minister, is imbued with a child spirit who is the issue of a love affair between an angel and a demon. This being is called *Genesis*, and it has come to earth in search of a *soul* it can inhabit, in this case, Custer's. Genesis gives its host a superpower, the "word of God," which compels anyone who hears his order to perform it, and it also imparts to Jesse inside knowledge on the true nature of Lord God. He created the world in order to have beings who would love Him. The mixture of angel and demon was an effort to expand His power and province even further. Instead, this creature represents an existential threat, so the Yahweh figure "gets out of Dodge," so to speak, leaving heaven, abandoning earth and His creations. Custer's quest is to use his superpower to compel the Lord to appear to the world and confess that he has been remiss in His duties. So, in the cosmological frame of the series, an absent God is the answer for evil in this world. At the end, when Custer realizes that this plan will not work, he enlists a gunslinging zombie, the Saint of Killers, to kill God (*Book Six*, 352–3).

Before discussing how *Preacher* participates in the satiric mode, these genres should be explored to examine the ideas, values, and expectations they may carry, as well as the icons, myth narratives, and tropes they make available. The

Gothic horror elements are present in the protagonist's sidekick, Cassidy, as a vampire; the Saint of Killers, as an "undead"; and a visual palette that features a fair share of gore. Grimshaw makes an interesting point about Gen X's reliance on Gothic horror as a multiple-meaning-bearing generic discourse (Grimshaw 2010, 149). Yet, not only does *Preacher* not deliberately try to evoke the scariness of a genuine work of horror, it only tangentially parodies it or uses it for satirical embellishment. In spite of some instances of the demonic supernatural, a subplot based on vampires, and plenty of abject splatter, horror is merely present as other genres unfold. The real genres that are "played with" are the Christian novel and the Western.

In *West of Everything*, Jane Tompkins describes how the Western novel genre displaced Christian-inspired literature popular in late nineteenth century America. The template for the Christian novel is Charles M. Sheldon's 1896 book, *In His Steps*, about a preacher who vows for a whole year "to ask before he does anything, 'What would Jesus do?'" It was "far and away the most popular book of its time … Sheldon reports in a 1936 forward to the novel that according to *Publishers Weekly* it had sold more copies than any other book except the Bible." Tompkins mentions four other novels from the same period that make "Christian heroism their explicit theme." Less than ten years after Sheldon's novel came out, Owen Wister's *The Virginian* initiated a genre that would come to rival and ultimately dominate Christian literature (Tompkins 1992, 29–32).

The social gospel religion that Sheldon's work popularized was the descendant and last gasp of the evangelical reform Christianity embodied in the popular fiction of the mid-nineteenth century. The female, domestic, "sentimental" religion of the best-selling women writers—Harriet Beecher Stowe, Susan Warner, Maria Cummins, and dozens of others—whose novels spoke to the deepest beliefs and highest ideals of middle-class America is the real antagonist of the Western (Tompkins 1992, 37–8).

Whereas these domestic novels were indoors, the new genre was outdoors; the Western is male-orientated, the domestic novel was largely focused on women and the family with female heroines; and finally, whereas the religious underpinnings of society were present and reinforced in the domestic novel, the Western was at best agnostic, and where there was a sense of the divine, it was in the scope of natural beauty. Secular, worldly, and violent, the Western genre broke the Puritan grasp on American identity and replaced it with the concerns of surviving a world of Hobbesian violence. While Tomkins positions these thematic genres in opposition, *Preacher* deftly conflates them in several ways.

To begin at the beginning, the first titled subsection of the series is called "Gone to Texas." The protagonist, Jesse Custer, is a minister to the rough and tumble hayseed town of Annville. So, at the outset, the terrain of the Western frontier overlaps that of saving souls. But in determining the intertwining of the two genres, the character gallery sets up the structural overlap. Let us start with the protagonist, Jesse Custer, a name that deserves closer attention, for Jesse Custer, is the big J. C. of this narrative. There is a long tradition for this, such as the tall soldier Jim Conklin in Stephen Crane's *The Red Badge of Courage*. Given the series' entire plotline, Ennis's hero's name is about as ham-fisted as an author can get. I would suggest this lack of subtlety is deliberate, for as a "Christ figure," a one-time staple of literary discussion and analysis (Detweiler 1964, 111), Custer is a perverted one. His name invokes a conflation of social bandit Jesse James, who fought the corporations exploiting the frontier settlers (morphing into a dime-novel hero in the process), and the US Army General George Armstrong Custer, arguably the most famous Indian fighter, if one of the less successful (Slotkin 1994, 8–9; Slotkin 1998, 133–9).

A second cue to Jesse Custer's double role as Western hero and Christ figure is in the nickname given him by a hallucinated manifestation of John Wayne: "Pilgrim." The appearance of the iconic Western actor is a childhood association with Jesse's dead father. Wayne's advice, "Yah gotta be one of the good guys" (*Book One*, 292–304), comes late in the first collected volume. But he uses this term in his first utterance in the comic: "Well, Pilgrim … Couldn't help but notice ya ain't mentioned *me* yet' (*Book One*, 39). John Wayne's calling Jesse "Pilgrim" is an intertextual cue to the 1962 film *The Man Who Shot Liberty Valance*; it was the nickname used by Wayne character Tom Doniphon for James Stewart's character Ransom Stoddard, an idealistic and impractical East coast lawyer who moved west. It was intended pejoratively, generally reserved for one from the eastern states who finds himself out of his depth in the challenging environment of the frontier west (*Legends of America*). Ennis achieves an intriguing palimpsest on two levels. The obvious is the intertextual reference to John Wayne as a Western hero in films. The other is more subtle, but something which is often at work in this series. The "Pilgrim" invokes an important work of literature for the foundation colonial societies of North America, Paul Bunyan's *Pilgrim's Progress*. The tribulations of the protagonist in that book suggest that Jesse Custer is in for a rough time. The instance of the protagonist hallucinating a "guardian angel" of sorts out of an amalgam of John Wayne Western characters iterates a satiric attack on an aspect of American identity, updating "What would Jesus do?" with "What would John Wayne do?" If it is, as Jane Tomkins says, that the "Western *answers* the domestic novel … [by rejecting] evangelical Protestantism …; it seeks to marginalize and suppress the figure who stood for those ideals" (Tompkins 1992, 39), then Jesse's twinned thematic charge, as Western and Christian hero, ironically seems to be answering back to the Western.

One way is to have the acme of the Western hero as a protective familiar spirit, a guardian angel, who warns Jesse of the true nature of his greatest nemesis, the "Saint of Killers," and urges Jesse to "watch him" (*Book One*, 68–9). As an indication of genre conflation and contrast, the zombie assassin combines Christian religious tradition and hierarchy (even the angels in heaven refer to him as a "saint") with the bleak life-and-death struggles of the Western genre. He is a hired gunman of supernatural abilities, incidentally one who regards killing angels a valid act. Visually, he is first revealed in a Western genre topos: the abandoned mine. Further, he is portrayed as the quintessence of the "black hat" gunman—think Jack Palance as Jack Wilson in *Shane*. The moral valence of the angels and religion in general is shifted with their employing of this wraith to hunt Custer. Ironically, though, it is the Saint of Killers who ultimately will assassinate the principal Yahweh figure in a parody of the Western showdown. In terms of genres, there is a certain logic at work here: if God is dead, the Western has helped kill Him. Yet, this character possesses some complexity borne from the Western. Though Custer has convinced him to challenge God, the murder is also a gesture of Frontier revenge: the Saint of Killers punishes God for not being present to protect his family against a pack of murderous outlaws.

The genre marker is clearly articulated right before the final issue in a Bill Hick's quotation about his childhood wish to be "an avenging cowboy hero" (*Book Six*, 351). By the concluding pages, the obvious cowboy hero is Jesse Custer, since he is riding off into the sunset on a horse with his good lady behind him. But at the same time, it is not Custer who performs an act of vengeance, but the Saint of Killers. The how and why of this is tidily sown together in issue #66 with three-long letters, Jesse's to his beloved Tulip, Cassidy's to Jesse, and Cassidy's to Tulip. The fact that Ennis and Dillon had to resort to epistolary exposition to conclude the series in a meaningful way is testament to just how varied (to put it mildly) the plot gyrations have been.

To participate in the satiric mode, Kathryn Hume tells us, certain markers have to be present in sufficient "intensity." A target must be attacked; this target may be historical or more universal. Humor and wit distinguish the satiric from merely the invective. There ought to be textual evidence of "the author's glorying in his or her literary performance"; since we are dealing with a comic,

I would include here visual flourishes as well. An element of exaggeration or extreme extrapolation from the present historical-material circumstances may also be present. At the same time, the reader may recognize a "moral or existential truth," "some version of authorial malice," and an aspect of "inquiry" when sheer indignation is not so present (Hume 2007, 305). Grimshaw, among others, identifies the attack on Christianity, and yet at the same time iterates the *presence* of a strong base of residual religiousness (Grimshaw 2010, 162). As I will highlight below, a major factor justifying the critique of God is not just apocryphal, it is wholly invented: God's desire to gain even more power via an angelic miscegenation.

Up to now, I have emphasized the impressive control of rival genres, the Western and the Christian narrative, as indicative to a commanding "literary performance." At the same time, there is a double-coding in *Preacher* in the parody exercised within the respective genres. Parody lampoons the text it inhabits, playing off of genre expectations. It works with excesses and permutations to make its point, similarly to satire, with a metafictional and a comedic aspect (Rose 1993, 254). As a book of Christian faith, *Preacher* reads as somehow too literal; as a Western, too esoteric.

Preacher's Angelology and Eschatology: Banal Religion *in Extremis*

This equivocal genre quality becomes apparent in the ontology of Ennis and Dillon's world, in a depiction of the powers of religion, earthly and heavenly, as incompetent, corrupt, and unpalatably corporate. In short, the problems with the Abrahamic faith portrayed in *Preacher* come down to divine beings' succumbing to *human* weaknesses, from a Yahweh figure, who fears being alone, to peevish low-level angelic bureaucrats. The mortal agents fare even worse. Ennis and Dillon rely on traditions already in place, and embellish when they must, to recreate heaven, and the role of angels on earth. English literature has done this before with John Milton's *Paradise Lost*, and while there is no evidence of direct textual references, Milton's Pandemonium and the early twenty-first-century earth do share some characteristics. However, rather than expulsion, Jesse and Tulip as the new Adam and Eve seem to be riding back toward a landscape of freedom by the end of the series.

The primus motor for the entire *Preacher* narrative is the conception of the child, which is to be called "Genesis," the child of a male angel and a female demon. Late in the series, the reader learns that this union was, if not encouraged, at least sanctioned by the Lord God as a way of increasing the province and variety of beings who could love Him. This child, however, was too powerful and had to be imprisoned in *heaven*. This was the state of affairs at the start of the story. In order for there to even be such a creature, a complex intertextual referencing system had to be brought into the narrative to justify the existence and practice of angels' interbreeding, and the existence of demons on earth.

Since they mated, it is logical to assume that the angel mated with a *fallen angel*, and here popular literature has a rich tradition to draw upon, chiefly the book of *Genesis* and John Milton's *Paradise Lost*. Genesis 6:2 says that "the sons of God came in to the daughters of men, and they bore children to them"by way of introducing the situation that justifies the great flood. So, having Elohim come down and take wives on earth was a thing. *Paradise Lost* essentially describes earth as under control of fallen angels, one of which, Satan, is nominally in charge. While Milton himself was only indirectly informed of an apocryphal book, *1Enoch,* which elaborates on the angel-human interbreeding (Williams 1940, 298–9), it may be that Ennis and Dillon have further buttressed their view of the fallen angels from this text. In some traditions, Nephilim are said to have mated and produced children, and it is likely one of these whom a "Seraphi" mates with in *Preacher*. This is established in the first episodes of the series.

It begins in Texas, and at the outset it is clear that Jesse is not atheistic, he is anti-church. The reader is presented with a preacher on the cusp of losing his faith, and his visit to the bar in Annville positions Jesse as the suffering leader of a wayward flock. The action then moves to heaven, which contains the prison "Genesis" has escaped from. This is unequivocally rendered as *a space-station*. Fifty years ago, this stopped being science fiction, but the portrayals of the Seraphi and the Adephi also teeter on this science fiction edge: the Seraphi do have wings, but the Adephi would not look out of place in Stanley Kubrick's *2001: A Space Odyssey*. In addition, heaven is portrayed as bureaucratically hierarchical, but based on a class of nobility. The "working class" Adephi are *in fear* of the "Seraphi," the highest rank of Christian angelology. They are described in Isa. 6:1-8, and are mentioned in the *Book of Enoch* and *Revelations*. The Adephi are not part of the Christian Angelic Hierarchy, though one does claim to be "one of the host ... of angels" as he is dying. But since the term itself is one letter away from *adelphi*, which means "brothers," they do fulfill the role of some monk-like order. The hair fashion and uniform dress in plain blue tunics would imply the same. And when one of them is killed by the Saint of Killers, it is clear, they are mortal. When they are confronted by an angry grieving Seraph carrying his dead brother, the Adephi fear them as masters (*Book One*, 21). In addition, the spatialization of heaven and earth is intriguing: the Seraphi had been in the "stratosphere," indicating earth orbit; and Genesis "came charging out of the rising sun" (21), which, while not clarifying where exactly heaven is, places it at a distance determined by interplanetary space. And finally, with the Seraphi "left in charge," the implication is that earth has been abandoned by God. In the logic of the narrative, God is not imaginary, God is not dead, God *has run off.*

Literalization is a rhetorical device in satire to poke fun by presenting something so that the reader perceives the metaphorical meaning, but a character in the narrative takes the same statement literally (Quinlan 1967, 517). However, Ennis and Dillon are doing this on a much broader level: they are literalizing a Biblical cosmology, and it is portrayed as *corrupt.* Heaven is an interplanetary outpost, inhabited by peevish bureaucrats and snooty supervisors. It is a *workplace*; and the angels are doing a *job*: running a maximum-security *prison* for a demon bastard child. Given that Milton's tale is culturally available for the author and artist, if not necessarily for the reader, it is a further jibe to invert the demon prison in *Paradise Lost*, earth, with heaven.

Another presupposition of Christianity is not literalized, but rather *naturalized* by the fact that Genesis has gone to earth to obtain a *soul.* When the Adephi first decides that they must retrieve this being, one of them suggests that "it will attempt to bond with a fully developed consciousness. With a soul" (*Book One*, 21). And further on, an Adephi explains his target to the Saint of Killers. "It holds a power like unto that of God Almighty. It seeks to join with the spirit of mortal man: if it succeeds, the two together will know the secret ways of Paradise as no other mortal has done. Together they could end us all" (*Book One*, 30).

Genesis' merging with Jesse Custer, as a divine being combined with mortal, is mimetically similar to Jesus's coming to earth. Yet, instead of Satan plotting against Him, it is the *angels* of the Abrahamic religious tradition. To be sure, this inversion may well be the single strongest blasphemy in the *Preacher* series, implying that the forces of Satan have been replaced by God's ordained stewards of earth. The church, under this guise, is itself an agent of Satan. The depiction of Jesse possessed by Genesis on page 35 sustains the satirical inversion: Jesse is suspended in the air, black and white in his clericals, and yet he is part of a larger being, with cloven hooves and red skin below and the lighter hair and outspread angel wings. Later, when Jesse is trying to make sense of the information Genesis has imbued him with, the reader is shown a Seraphi with a female demon mounted on him in a variety of intercourse referred to as "Cowgirl."

The reference to a couple who have done something of which God disapproves, invokes the First Couple driven from the Garden of Eden. Genesis' merging with a mortal will result in a parody of Adam and Eve as depicted in *Paradise Lost*. Forbidden knowledge is still something the Elohim emphatically guard, but unlike the first couple, a more powerful knowledge is on hand, one that can "end" the Heavenly Host. This is the knowledge that Jesse Custer wrestles with and tries to make sense of.

Now, I do not want to suggest that the readers of this comic are therefore believing Christians. After all, the conclusion to this epic is the murder of an unarmed God, albeit by one of His more questionable creations. Rather, it would be more accurate to say that this improvised angelic hierarchy extends into a world that would resonate with the readers of fantasy and horror. Still, the vocabulary is charged with an acknowledgment of "a soul" and "a spirit of mortal man"; and it is to imbue a mortal with "a power like until that of God Almighty." In the sheer enjoyment of the visual presentation and action-packed plot, the reader may overlook connecting this with Jesse Custer. Yet, again, a mortal man imbued with the powers and understanding of God? Hmm. Where have we heard that before? I would suggest that whatever else *Preacher* may be, when it comes to identifying the protagonist as a Christ figure, it is none too subtle. Jesse Custer *could* be the Anti-Christ. But he does attempt to fix the corrupt Texas hamlet of Annville; he attacks the corrupted earthly representatives of Christ, the Grail; and he tries to relieve humanity of the quandary of the presence of evil by getting the Lord God to come clean, as it were. In these particulars, the overall drift of Jesse Custer's actions suggests that he is here to combat the Anti-Christ, clearing the Temple of earthly vanity and corruption, right and proper. God is not dead, in this instance; He is in each and every one of us, and at the end of this narrative, He is riding the horse away from the metropolis and into the desert.

It seems, then, that in the cosmology the narrative plays out, Ennis and Dillon take away with one hand—heaven is a space station, humankind is the product of a vain and lonely supreme being—and serve with the other: the human soul is real; morally correct behavior counts for more than elevated social status. It is this latter theme, the importance of correct behavior in relation to one's fellow man or woman, which is the clear normative ethos in this satire; and, within the parameters of the satire, the blasphemy is essential to this message as a carrier wave on which righteous behavior can be inscribed. It is difficult to dispute Grimshaw's conclusion that *Preacher* is Puritanical in its absolute stance on disputing existing (if waning) authorities (Grimshaw 2010, 153), but I am inclined to view this more as a feature than a bug. The excesses of the series suggest some genuine value in wiping the slate clean.

The strongest invective is reserved for the human members of a religious order called "the Grail," a group who has the task of keeping intact the bloodline of Christ. These earthly powers, trading in the coin of religion, are also combatted by Jesse Custer. While something akin to an ordinary religious service is not depicted after the catastrophe at Annville, something analogous to "church fathers" are present in this institution. Other Christian elements are mentioned. The Grail is introduced as another part of the Godhead hierarchy in charge of earth (*Book One*, 72), and they fear the spiritually imbued Jesse Custer. The Allfather, who is consulted by this organization, appears dressed as a Pope, only comically obese.

While much more could be discussed on this, three points speak to the element of the satiric. First, the idea that there is an "essence of Christ" in the blood is lampooned by depicting the current heir of this heritage as a blithering idiot. As the executive agent Starr puts it: "Son of God or son of man, … you can't fuck your sister and expect much good to come of it" (*Book Two*, 225). So, the current heir to "the blood of the lamb" has maintained that purity by ironically exercising the Pharaonic taboo. Second, the profound conflicts within the series participates in what Michael Barkun has identified as a characteristic of millennialism, "stigmatized knowledge," information of the ilk of UFOs aliens and Atlantis (Barkun 2013, 36–8). In this case it covers the angelology and the blood line of Christ. Stigmatized knowledge is a feature of some types of satire, usually involving secret societies, of which Ishmael Reed's *Mumbo Jumbo* stands out as an example. Finally, in the fullness of time, Starr, who is in charge of the Grail, wishes Jesse Custer to be the new vessel of the blood of the lamb, again, iterating and strengthening Custer's position as a Christ-figure in the narrative.

Blasphemy in *Preacher* is not the *intent*, but in our times of liquified religion, is available as a marker for in-group/out-group boundaries. Irony (and by extension, satire) finds its own audience. In *Preacher*, the blasphemy portrays those associated with the Christian religion as pederasts, sadists, and backbiting bureaucrats. In this case, they become just another set of one-time sacrosanct entities at the ready for defamation in the name of artistic, in this case, satiric intertextual aesthetics. As blasphemy is employed, the objects of religious worship are made literally ridiculous. It is in this conjoined ridicule that the readers revel, not endorsing an insult to a "real" God, but going along with the intriguing premise that the Elohim are just as petty and egotistical as some functionaries within their own perishes and dioceses. Whatever else may be going on here, it is *not* an appeal to cognitively nested ostensive physical reality, the atheism of Richard Dawkins. Non-cognitive supernatural events are the norm in this series, with Jesse's being possessed by a spiritual entity being the most fantastic element of them all. Obviously, there are others, for instance, the vampire trope. However, the overarching generic attitudes of the Western provide a materialist alibi for the supernatural goings-on.

Preacher, blasphemy and all, does qualify as what Hjarvard terms a "banal religion." "[The] various logics of the media influence the ways in which religion is represented and condition the ways in which authority to speak about these issues is constructed" (Hjarvard 2016, 14). In this case, the work is the product of a comics production label deliberately cultivating an adult audience, not with eroticism, but iconoclastic ridicule. It plays fast and free with the very pillars of the "religious" symbol set of Western society, as well as some esoteric, arcane, and outlying aspects parodying stigmatized knowledge. The allegory the author and artist construct blatantly positions Jesse Custer as Jesus Christ; the ossified bureaucracy of heaven and their accomplices on earth, as Pharisees. On the cosmic level, the battle of good versus evil plays itself out as Jesse's having been imbued to fight the Anti-Christ on Earth. Its contribution, in spite of its iconoclastic climax, is to bring into circulation some "religious imaginations and practices … fundamental for any kind of religion" (13). Its subject matter is loss of faith, and the regaining of—if not faith—at least a personal and connubial equilibrium: in the end, *Preacher* is a comedy. Comedies generically serve to endorse a social order, perhaps the weakly moralistic, secular society of the readers. In this way, John Milton's *Paradise Lost* could be charged with blasphemy when Satan collects twelve disciples, in imitation of the Apostles; but in terms of the late Renaissance English-speaking world, it, too, was participating in social discourse as a banal religion (Milton 1971, 392–490). And what of Charles M. Sheldon, reading aloud in his drafty church at the end of the nineteenth century? The allegory may be tighter, but the *media* and popularity, as well as the way these works have mixed themselves up in discussions of religion, qualify them, too, as banal religion. But these works, and *Preacher* too, serve to bring important issues and questions to light, as a nutrient in the noological sphere on which religious authority can take root.

According to material provided by the Jehovah's Witnesses, blasphemy also "includes the act of claiming the attributes or prerogatives of God, or of ascribing these to another person or thing" (Watch Tower 1988). Again, Jesse Custer, the complex Christ-figure in a Christian Western satire, is certainly guilty of blasphemy. In a world where God appears to be absent, is it wrong, is it *blasphemous,* for someone, *anyone,* to try to sort it out? What would Preacher do?

References

Barkun, Michael. (2013), *A Culture of Conspiracy: Apocalyptic Visions in Contemporary America*, Berkeley: University of California Press.

de Groot, Kees. (2006), "The Church in Liquid Modernity: A Sociological and Theological Exploration of a Liquid Church." *International Journal for the Study of the Christian Church* 6 (1): 91–103. doi: 10.1080/14742250500484469.

de Groot, Kees. (2008), "Three types of liquid religion." *Implicit Religion* 11 (3):277–296. doi: 10.1558/imre.v11i3.277.

Detweiler, Robert. (1964), "Christ and the Christ Figure in American Fiction," *Christian Scholar* 47 (2): 111–24.

Ennis, Garth, and Steve Dillon. (2009), *Preacher, Book One*, originally published in single magazine form, *Preacher 1–12*, New York: DC Comics.

Ennis, Garth, and Steve Dillon. (2010), *Preacher, Book Two,* originally published in single magazine form, *Preacher 13–26*, New York: DC Comics.

Ennis, Garth, and Steve Dillon. (2014), *Preacher, Book Six,* originally published in single magazine form, *Preacher 55–66*, New York: DC Comics.

Griffin, Dustin. (1994), *Satire: A Critical Reintroduction*, Lexington: University of Kentucky Press.

Grimshaw, Mike. (2010), "On *Preacher* (Or, the Death of God in Pictures)," in A. David Lewis and Christine Hoff Kraemer (eds.), *Graven Images: Religion in Comic Books and Graphic Novels*, 149–65, New York: Continuum.

Hibbs, Brian. (2020), "Interview with Garth Ennis 'GARTH ENNIS for PREACHER!,' " *Comix Experience* YouTube channel. Available online: https://www.youtube.com/watch?v=JbjEIFvUT00&t=0s (accessed February 25, 2022).

Hjarvard, Stig. (2016), "Mediatization and the Changing Authority of Religion," *Media, Culture, and Society* 38 (1): 8–17.

The Holy Bible: Old and New Testaments in the King James Version, Nashville: Thomas Nelson, 1970.

Hume, Kathryn. (2007), "Diffused Satire in Contemporary American Fiction," *Modern Philology* 105 (2): 300–25.

Hutcheon, Linda. (1994), *Irony's Edge: The Theory and Politics of Irony*, London: Routledge.

Legends of America, "Western Slang, Lingo and Phrases—A Writer's Guide to the Old West," Available online: https://www.legendsofamerica.com/we-slang/11/ (accessed February 27, 2022).

Maxfield, Clive. (2012), "Book Review: Preacher by Garth Ennis and Steve Dillon." EDN.com January 19, 2012. Available online: https://www.edn.com/book-review-preacher-by-garth-ennis-and-steve-dillon/ (accessed February 23, 2022).

Melody, John. (1907), "Blasphemy," in *The Catholic Encyclopedia* Vol. 2, New York: Robert Appleton Company, 1907, via *New Advent.org*. "Blasphemy." Available online: https://www.newadvent.org/cathen/02595a.htm (accessed February 24, 2022).

Milton, John. (1971), *Paradise Lost*, Alistair Fowler (ed.), London: Longman.

Murtagh, Kevin J. (2007), "Blasphemous Humor in *South Park*," in Robert Arp, (ed.), *South Park and Philosophy: You Know, I Learned Something Today*, 29–39, Oxford: Blackwell.

Nenstiel, Kevin L. (2021), "Hellfire and Damnation (the Lite Version)," Amazon.com customer review August 17, 2021. Available online: https://www.amazon.com/Preacher-Book-One-Garth-Ennis/dp/1401240453/ (accessed February 23, 2022).

Quinlan, Maurice J. (1967), "Swift's Use of Literalization as a Rhetorical Device," *PMLA* 82 (7): 516–21. Available online: https://www.jstor.org/stable/461160 (accessed February 24, 2022).

Rose, Margaret A. (1993), *Parody: Ancient, Modern, and Post-Modern*, Cambridge: Cambridge University Press.

Salisbury, Derek. (2013), *Growing Up with Vertigo: British Writers, DC, and the Maturation of American Comic Books*, MA Diss., University of Vermont. Available online: https://scholarworks.uvm.edu/graddis/209 (accessed February 24, 2022).

Slotkin, Richard. (1994), *The Fatal Environment: The Myth of the Frontier in the Age of Industrialization 1800–1890*, New York: HarperCollins.

Slotkin, Richard. (1998), *Gunfighter Nation: The Myth of the Frontier in Twentieth-Century America*, Norman: University of Oklahoma Press.

Tompkins, Jane. (1992), *West of Everything: The Inner Life of Westerns*, Oxford: Oxford University Press.

Vile, John. (2009), "Blasphemy," *The First Amendment Encyclopedia*. Available online: https://www.mtsu.edu/first-amendment/article/894/blasphemy (accessed February 24, 2022).

Watch Tower. (1988), "Blasphemy," in *Insight on the Scriptures*, 337–9. Brooklyn, NY: Watch Tower Bible and Tract Society of New York.

Williams, Arnold. (1940), "Milton and the Book of Enoch: An Alternative Hypothesis," *Harvard Theological Review* 33 (4): 291–9.

7

Islam and Anxieties of Liberalism in Craig Thompson's *Habibi*

Kambiz GhaneaBassiri[1]

Craig Thompson's *Habibi* (2011) is a beautifully illustrated love story that tackles contemporary struggles for justice through visuals of Islam. When Pantheon Books released it, with some fanfare, on the decennial anniversary of 9/11, it made as notable an artistic intervention in post-9/11 popular US conceptualization of Islam as any. Its significance as a work of social critique that reflects the society in which it was produced, however, has been overshadowed by the controversy the book has garnered since its publication. Some have praised it as "a remarkable feat of research, care, and black ink" (Smith 2011, 76) and as "a masterpiece that surely is one of a kind" (Shea 2011, 352). Thompson has been described as "the Charles Dickens of the genre" (ibid.), and, in 2012, *Habibi* earned him the coveted Will Eisner Award for Best Writer/Artist. Others have critiqued *Habibi* for its "jumbled storytelling" and for unironically "indulging" in Orientalist fantasies (Cresswell 2011, 26). They have faulted Thompson for his nauseating "appropriation" of Islamic culture and for promoting stereotypes of Islam "by overly sexualizing women [and] littering the text with an abundance of savage Arabs" (Damluji 2011).

This chapter aims to move discussions of *Habibi* beyond its monumental artistry and questions about the judiciousness of Thompson's portrayal of Islam. It examines what this epic narrative, by one of the most prominent graphic novelists today, reveals about the US society as it has sought to come to terms with the place of American Muslims in its religiopolitical landscape after 9/11. Thompson has explained that *Habibi* "was born in the wake of 9/11" as he sought to redress the Islamophobia, xenophobia, and racism that had become "rampant everywhere" in the United States (Thompson 2020). "In the wake of the tragedy," he told *Guernica* magazine, "I felt a stronger sense of American guilt and awareness of our tacit participation in exploiting cultures elsewhere in the world" (Armstrong 2011). Thompson reports it was "embarrassing to be American and see people behaving the way they were towards Muslims or people that they thought were of Arabic (*sic*) descent" (Thompson 2020).

To address this sense of national guilt and personal shame, Thompson worked to learn more about Islam and perceptions of Muslims in US popular culture. It took him seven years to complete *Habibi*. During that time, he read the Qur'an in translation and learned Arabic calligraphy. He read books on Islamic art as well as Richard Burton's popular rendering of *One Thousand and One Nights* and immersed himself in Western portrayals of "the Orient" in nineteenth-century French paintings (Armstrong 2011). He familiarized himself with the principal religious teachings of Islam and conceptions of divine love in Sufism. He also befriended Muslims. His efforts resulted in a highly stylized, multilayered, contentious text that brings Islamic teachings, negative stereotypes of Muslims, American liberal Protestant conceptions of mysticism, and means of dealing with religious diversity into conversation with one another. This conversation is not always coherent, but its theme is clear: the traumatic legacy of racism, sexism, colonialism, industrial capitalism, and environmental exploitation. The figurative table around which *Habibi*'s meandering conversation takes place, and the structuring principle of its graphic narrative, is an erotic theology of selfless love that Thompson regards as redemptive. Its portrayal reveals a sense of fragility and anxiety in post-9/11 United States about the viability of liberal values rooted in mysticism and love for creating a just society that can be inclusive of Muslims.

An Overview of *Habibi*

Habibi is a fable set in the fictitious land of Wanatolia[2] that most Americans would associate with Islam because of its deserts, harams, sartorial styles, Arabic writings, and arabesque ornamentations. Muslim-majority countries manifest as places of fantasy in *Habibi*. Here, "the old and the new brush against each other," Thompson explains; "my experience being in the Global South, as they call it, you can see people living in a very medieval way—alongside Western development and globalization" (Armstrong 2011). This perceived incongruity between time and space in the Global South makes the lived history of Muslims in the region irrelevant for Thompson, allowing him to use visuals of Islam "to wind [his] way between fantasy and reality—bending time and space to create a transcendent sacred order" along the lines of his own mystical visions (Koltun-Fromm 2020, 45).

At the core of this mystical vision is a love story between Dodola and Zam, who meet as children in a slave camp and manage to escape into the desert, where they live in an abandoned ship. Dodola, who is nine years older than Zam, exchanges sex for food with men from passing caravans. As Zam grows older, he becomes sexually attracted to Dodola. One time when Dodola approaches a caravan for food, Zam witnesses her being raped. He decides to go out into the city, unbeknownst to Dodola, to look for provisions so that Dodola would not have to prostitute herself. Dodola ends up being abducted and sold to the cruel and lascivious sultan of Wanatolia as a sex slave. She bears the sultan a child, who is later murdered as he would be a potential threat to the throne. She becomes an addict and is haunted by her love for Zam. Zam's desire for Dodola continues to rage within him. He joins a South Asian community of eunuchs (*hijras*) and castrates himself to purify himself from sexual urges. He is captured and enslaved as a servant in one of the harems of Wanatolia's sultan who is also holding Dodola captive. The sultan tires of his sexual relations with Dodola and arbitrarily condemns her to drowning. Zam manages to save her and, with the help of a crazed man and a marabout, to bring her back to health amid the social, economic, and environmental devastation caused largely by Wanatolia's dam and water bottling industry. Later, Zam finds work in this industry, and the two become increasingly intimate. They unite sexually and spiritually in a moment of mystical enlightenment before deciding to use the little money they had managed to save up to rescue a little girl from slavery rather than buy a boat to sail away into their mystical bliss (652).

Liberal Anxieties

Through Zam's desire for Dodola, who is sexually objectified and abused throughout much of *Habibi*, Thompson expresses, in personal terms, a broader anxiety associated with liberalism. He expresses this anxiety at three levels: at the level of personal relations, at the level of intercultural and interreligious relations within American society, and at the level of international relations within the context of global capitalism. If a key feature of a liberal society is for its members to have the freedom to pursue their individual desires and happiness, what happens when the personal desires of some sexualize and objectify others to enable their abuse? This personal anxiety is reiterated at a societal level in

Habibi through Thompson's use of Orientalist imagery: What if what American society finds beautiful and commercially viable about representations of Islam are its Orientalized and exoticized visuals that have been complicit in colonizing and otherizing Muslims? Thompson reframes this question globally through the portrayal of industrial capitalism, which, in Wanatolia, has resulted in the commodification of natural resources (specifically water) and the exploitation of the environment for the benefit of some nations at the devastating expense of others (see, in particular, 573–6). What if the modern amenities liberal democratic economies produce and depend on for the happiness of their citizens are also the source of environmental degradation and the exploitation and oppression of others?

Thompson's Proposed Solution to Liberal Anxieties

It can be inferred from the words Thompson chose to explain his response to the rise of Islamophobia—"guilt" and "shame"—that his thinking about the anxieties he perceives in liberalism has been shaped at least in part by his religious formation. In his 2003 semi-autobiographical graphic novel, *Blankets*, he explores the significance of his religious formation for his professional life by depicting his upbringing in a fundamentalist Protestant family before he decides to go to art school. He narrates his eventual break from organized religion through a love affair that led him to the personal realization that, through selfless love of another person one can commune with the divine spirit within (Thompson 2003, 561–71).[3] *Habibi* revisits and furthers this erotic theology in an Islamic veneer. In the final chapter of *Habibi* Dodola teaches Zam how to experience sexual union spiritually (see Figure 7.1); "pleasure … isn't the center of sex. It's breath," she tells him. "During sex," she explains, "my spirit always disconnected from my body … When Zam anchored me, the dark clouds dissolved. I grasped hold of my vapor [i.e., spirit]—and drew it back into my body" (635–9). Through this spiritualization of sex, Zam and Dodola, depicted against a backdrop of paradisical Arabesque designs come to the enlightened realization that "There are no separations" (640–2). Their united spirits or breaths during sex are depicted through the Arabic letter ح, which makes an aspirated "h" sound and is the last letter in the Arabic word for spirit/soul (*rūḥ*), which, according to the Qur'an, God blow into humanity at the time of their creation (Q 15:29; 32:9; 38:72).

During the climax of mutually gratifying sexual union, there is no distinction between the object desired and the subject desiring. This makes the erotic love of

Figure 7.1 Dodola and Zam's experience of mystical enlightenment during the climax of their sexual-spiritual union. Craig Thompson, *Habibi*, p. 642. By courtesy of PenguinRandomHouse.

another for their own sake redemptive. If, by fulfilling the desire of one's beloved, one also fulfills one's own desires, then one no longer has to feel ashamed as Zam did, for wanting the other. Nor does one have to resort to power and violence that objectifies or exoticizes the other to fulfill one's desires.

After coming to this realization, Zam and Dodola look in the market for a vehicle with which they can leave Wanatolia. They settle on a boat. While Zam tries to negotiate down its price. A slaver approaches Dodola with a slave girl who can help her "handle all the dirty work and back-breaking tasks" as well as "take care of [her] hubby's special needs" (655). Recalling their own lives before their mystical realization, when they lived in a world in which the fulfillment of one's own desires was the source of others' oppression, Dodola and Zam immediately and in unison decide to purchase the girl and adopt her as their own child—a redemptive act of selfless love rooted in the liberal values of human equality and the inalienable right to the pursuit of happiness.

Habibi, Mysticism, and American Religious Liberalism

The idea that a mystical union can result in selfless acts of love is by no means unique to the Christian tradition in which Thompson was enmeshed (see Thompson 2003), but this idea has had a distinct legacy in the United States. *Habibi* is a post-9/11 expression of this legacy. The term "mysticism" has historically referred to movements within Christianity that sought to awaken the divine within the soul to evoke an immediate and individualistic experience of the divine. These took on a variety of forms, but despite their differences, premodern mystical approaches to Christianity held in common, in the words of the influential liberal Protestant theologian Ernst Troeltsch (1865–1923), a "hostile attitude toward the world, because the divine Spirit rises far above the sensual, the worldly, and the finite." Through "mortification of the natural impulses of the flesh," the mystic achieves "liberation that consists in the suprasensual surrender of spirt to [the Holy] Spirit" (Troeltsch [1911] 1991, 327). According to this understanding of mysticism, Dodola and Zam's story, after they had their sexual-spiritual union, should have ended with their release from the turmoil of Wanatolia, but in the wake of the European Enlightenment, the belief that humans have within them a means to unite with the Holy Spirit came to also have social and political implications. If Christianity, from an Enlightened historical perspective, is the divine Spirit working through humanity, then the same divine principle must be at work in all humans regardless of their religious beliefs. During the eighteenth and nineteenth centuries, such an understanding of Christianity promoted religious tolerance and provided a means of redressing the sectarian wars that ravaged Europe. It also promoted civic tolerance. Insofar as the working of the Spirit in individuals is the same everywhere, then individual consciences need to be kept free of state interference for the Spirit to do its work, and individuals need to be guaranteed freedom of religious belief and expression by the state.

The perceived affinity between Christian mysticism and the political ideals underpinning America's liberal democracy was such that, in 1911, Troeltsch wrote: "Freedom of conscience … has its origin in the circles of mysticism." "Under the influence of the Enlightenment theory of natural law or of the rights of humanity," he noted, "this freedom of conscience was included juridically among the natural rights of all people … [And it was] first presented in rationalistic and juridical form by the American constitutions" (Troeltsch [1911] 1991, 339). While Troeltsch makes a historical argument, for our purposes, the historicity of his argument is not as relevant as what his observation reveals about liberal Protestant attempts to define a central role for Christianity in the development of American liberal democracy by universalizing the belief that the surrendering of an individual's spirit to the Holy Spirit is the latent purpose of all religions. It is how God works in the world. By guaranteeing freedom of conscience, the state not only promotes religious tolerance and social harmony but also facilitates the mystical fulfillment of God's work through the lives of its individual citizens, thus assuring its own prosperity and moral superiority.

Such "claims to universal truth," as historians of liberal Protestantism have observed, "masked structures of domination rooted in race, gender, and nation" (Hedstrom 2013, 16). In the United States, the notion that the state's guarantee of religious freedom facilitates the work of God on Earth allowed liberal Protestants to espouse equality and social justice as ideals underpinning the establishment in American society even while they faced the realities of Jim Crow, colonial violence, and economic inequality. As the historian Leigh Schmidt observed in his study of the uses of mysticism among American liberal Protestants at the turn of the twentieth century,

> this modern construction of mysticism was part an Orientalist strategy of appropriation and part a vision of union solely on liberal Protestant terms, but it also served as a category to open up dialogic possibilities across cultures and traditions. The social, political, and theological conviction embedded in it was that the bridges of sympathy marked an improvement on the bombardments of colonialism and the boasting of Christian missiology. Clearly, mysticism, when imagined this way, erased differences, but it also dreamed of a common ground in a cultural domain filled with conflict and violence. (Schmidt 2003, 290)

The mystical idea underpinning *Habibi* that—at a time of conflict and violence, like post-9/11—union with the divine through the love and recognition of the divine in others is a source of not only personal but also social redemption is thus nothing new, but rather a reiteration of a decades-old solution to civic and religious intolerance in American history rooted in liberal articulation of Protestantism.

Analytical Framing of *Habibi*

While Thompson's solution may not be new, what is striking, but to-date little discussed in analyses of *Habibi* is the way Thompson appropriates Islam in a medium of popular culture culture not only to address issues of social and environmental justice but also to explore whether spiritual union through love of the other is a possibility in the Islamic tradition and, conversely, whether American society can make possibly room for Islam and Muslims through liberal values rooted in mystical love of the other.

Habibi explores these possibilities by depicting Dodola and Zam as figures who are from the stereotypical Muslim Orient, but simultaneously represent oppressed and impoverished social groups to the contemporary readers in the United States. At the very beginning of the book, we are informed that Dodola comes from a poor Muslim family. Her illiterate father marries her at the age of nine to a much older man who is an Arabic and qur'anic scribe (10–11). Her marriage to her husband is depicted negatively as evidenced by the visual prominence Thompson gives to the coins exchanged between the bridegroom and her father and by Dodola's assertion that her parents "sold" her into marriage (10). Yet, despite this reference to a popular Islamophobic trope, Thompson's aim is not to critique Islam through child marriage.

While he begins *Habibi* with a scribe contracting a marriage with nine-year-old Dodola, just as Muhammad is said to have married "A"isha at this age, he also associates himself with the scribe. Thompson puts pen to paper for a living, just as Dodola's husband "copie[s] manuscripts for a living. The Sacred QUR'AN and the hadiths, One Thousand and One Nights, and the works of the great poets" (15). These texts that the scribe copies are all sources that Thompson uses to produce *Habibi*. It thus seems that Thompson draws an analogy at the outset of *Habibi* between himself and the scribe and between the scribe and Muhammad, to place himself in the Prophet's debt rather than to stand in judgment over him.

Thompson pushes these analogies further into a realm of Islamic cosmology and erotic theology. The very first frame of *Habibi* depicts a drop of ink on a white backdrop with this sentence above it: "From the Divine Pen fell the first drop of ink" (9). This frame echoes the first verses of the Qur'an revealed to Muhammad:

> Read [aloud] in the name of your Lord who created, created humanity from a blood clot. Read! Your Lord is most gracious, who taught by the Pen. He taught humanity what it did not know. (Q 96:1–5)

In *Habibi*, these qur'anic references to creation of humans through reproduction and the creation of knowledge through the Pen are collapsed through an analogy Thompson draws between the pen and the penis as instruments of creation. After the scribe takes Dodola to his house, he bathes her and comments on her purity. Then he consummates their marriage. Thompson depicts this scene in three frames that take up half of a page (Figure 7.2). In the first, Dodola is crying while her husband exposes himself to her.

Figure 7.2 The scribe's consummation of his marriage to Dodola. Craig Thompson, *Habibi*, p. 13. By courtesy of PenguinRandomHouse.

The scribe reminds her that he was married to her according to Islamic norms and performed an ablution on her: "I am your husband. There is no shame." His reed pens are clearly foregrounded in this frame, making the analogy between the pen and his penis as instruments of creation overt. In the second frame, Dodola is looking at him with tears in her eyes, while he says, "Look at this. It is beautiful." In the third frame, the scribe holds up the bedsheet that has a drop of Dodola's blood on it, signaling simultaneously her purity, virginity, and role in creation as well as the successful consummation of their marriage. The spot on the sheet echoes the drop of ink that falls from the "divine pen" in the very first frame of the book. While the scribe's statement, "Look at this. It is beautiful," seems to refer to the bloodspot on the sheet, the sequencing of the dialogue in relation to the images in the frames insinuate that it should also be read as a description of the scribe's penis with which he makes a mark on the sheet using Dodola, just as the divine pen makes a mark on the world using ink.

Thompson goes on to intertwine Dodola's marriage to a scribe with the story of God's revelation to humanity as well as the biblical and qur'anic stories of Adam's creation. Unlike the contemporary American reader who may be repulsed either by the idea of child marriage or by *Habibi*'s commencement with an inflammatory Islamophobic trope, Dodola's experience of her marriage is not trailed with tears. She states that her much older husband "taught me to read and to write, just as ALLAH taught Adam the NAMES" (16–17, emphasis in the original). Throughout the book, Dodola recalls for the reader stories from the lives of the prophets that her husband taught her, just as the Qur'an recalls the stories of prophets through whom God revealed God's will to humanity. The scribe's desire for sex and his subsequent marriage to Dodola are thus an attempt to allegorically place *eros*, symbolized through the pen both as a phallic symbol and an instrument of God's creative power and knowledge, at the beginning of *Habibi* as well as at the origin of human existence and Muhammad's revelations.

Given this multivalent depiction of Dodola at the beginning of *Habibi*, the Orientalized and sexualized depictions of her in much of the rest of the book should not be seen as mere Islamophobic representation of the oppression of women in Islam. In fact, Thompson attributes Dodola's oppression as a poor woman to the violent severing of her relationship with the qur'anic scribe (and by extension the foundational sources of Islam through which Thompson articulates the mystical union of the divine with humans in an Islamic veneer). Thompson deploys nineteenth-century Orientalist depictions of "the Islamic world" to critique the objectification of women and the racialization of Africans by men whose appetites for sex and money went unchecked because of patriarchy and a freemarket economy (see Figure 7.3).

Thompson further explores whether spiritual union through selfless love can be expressed in an Islamic idiom when Dodola meets Zam, the child of a Black, female slave. The two meet in a slave camp. Dodola sees that the slavers are about to kill Zam. She instinctively rises and claims him as a brother to save him. Only a couple of enslaved girls question how Dodola and Zam can be siblings given the difference in their skin color (59); this suggests that Thompson wants readers to view them as sharing the same lot in society despite their differences. *Habibi*, however, does not equate the plight of Black Americans with that of Muslim women. Just as Dodola's character paradoxically encompasses both the stereotype of the oppressed Muslim woman and the beauty that attracts God's attention at the beginning of creation (allegorized through the scribe and his pen), Zam's character also encompasses both the oppressive legacy of slavery in the Americas and God's favoring of the downtrodden evinced in the story of Hagar/Hajar and Ishmael/Isma'il. For Zam's character to encompass this paradox, Thompson goes out of his way to make sure that his readers do not associate slavery and anti-Black racism solely with Europeans and the Transatlantic Slave Trade nor solely with Islam. He thus depicts Dodola and Zam's enslavers as Arabs, but his physical depiction of Zam as an adult is reminiscent of stereotypical images of the Black help in Hollywood films (387–8).[4] The scene in which he introduces the reader to Zam's mother also visually recalls the crammed spaces and cages associated with the Middle Passage of the Transatlantic Slave Trade between West Africa and the Americas (226). He also tells readers that Zam's birthname was Cham thus associating him with the Curse of Ham (495), which was deployed by some followers of Abrahamic religions to justify the enslavement of Blacks as an inferior people (Goldenberg 2003; Johnson 2004). Dodola, however, renames Cham as Zam, after the well of Zam Zam, which according to the Islamic tradition erupted by God's command in Mecca to sooth the thirst of Ishmael/Isma'il, the biblical ancestor of Arabs who was the son Abraham/Ibrahim fathered with his "bond servant" Hagar/Hajar (43). Cham thus represents the bleak legacy of slavery in the Americas. As Zam, however, he stands to receive God's favor, just as Hagar/Hajar and Ishmael/Isma'il did when God produced the well of Zam Zam for them. Thompson thus associates Zam with two narratives of blackness and slavery, one rooted in God's curse of Ham in the biblical religions and the other in God's favoring of Ishmael/Isma'il in the Qur'an.

Figure 7.3 Thompson's Orientalist depictions of "the Islamic world," in this case Jean-Leon Gerome's *Slave Market* (*c.* 1866), alongside images of slavery and attitudes toward race based in the Transatlantic Slave Trade. Craig Thompson, *Habibi*, p. 63. By courtesy of PenguinRandomHouse.

On the Possibility of Spiritual Union through Love in Islam

When Dodola and Zam, two personifications of poverty and racial and sexual oppression, find one another, they immediately share an inexplicable bond of affection, but they are separated from each other. While living in separate oppressive conditions, their longing and search for one another becomes their *raison d'être*, raising the question of whether their love can help them survive their cruel circumstances. Scenes in which qur'anic calligraphy guides Zam's search for Dodola (397) recall for the reader the mystical origins of their love. And the social and moral value of their love is acknowledged throughout the book by the favors and generosity it elicits from other oppressed individuals as well as through the supernatural assistance they receive in the form of prophetic stories (308), healing practices (473–5), magic (40), and other divine interventions (136–40).

Despite these supernatural indications that their love would assist them in overcoming their circumstances, Dodola and Zam do not turn to a benevolent deity or acts of devotion to escape their lot in life. Rather, they seek their escape from the world by disconnecting from their bodies. In their social and economic circumstances, their bodies are objectified, commodified, and abused as vessels of sexual gratification and forced labor. They are not just commodified, objectified, and enslaved by others; they also commodify, objectify, and mutilate themselves to survive physically and psychologically. Dodola, for example, speaks of "learn[ing] the laws of commerce" when she begins to prostitute herself to desert caravans to feed Zam and herself (117): "I'd once used my body to my advantage, but even then, it didn't belong to me, possessed, instead, by the LUSTS of men" (107). Zam's self-castration as a means of dealing with his sexual urges (335–6), which from the behavior of others in society he learned to associate with the abuse of women (149–57), is another example of how the mortification of the body becomes a means of survival. In both cases, their participation in the economic and patriarchal social structures in which they find themselves results in their alienation from their bodies. They thus cannot overcome their circumstances physically. Their salvation, as we shall see, in Thompson's view, must be spiritual.

The psychological burden and existential crisis induced by self-alienating economic and social structures throughout *Habibi* culminate in a scene in which Zam stands above the dam that has wreaked havoc in the region; he contemplates destroying the dam by throwing himself into its machinery. He is simultaneously depressed for having to work for the capitalist industry that had built the dam and for his inability as a eunuch to give Dodola a child:

> If only my heart would explode and crumble this dam. Tear down this wall, release this River, drain this empire, and nourish the slums below. If I could tear it down with me, I might have value. Let me atone for all the sins of men. Let me release the DELUGE pent up in me. Let me die. (604, emphasis in original)

He decides not to jump off the bridge. Recognizing the futility of trying to physically overcome systems of oppression, he turns inward toward self-reformation, by recalling a *hadith* about how, "after battle, the prophet said, 'We have returned from the LESSER JIHAD to the GREATER JIHAD.' When asked, 'What is the GREATER JIHAD?' he replied; 'It is the struggle against oneself' " (605, emphasis in original). Thompson thus identifies within normative Islamic sources a possibility for spiritual reformation akin to liberal Christianity, but as the reference to the "lesser jihad" (i.e., military struggle) in the above *hadith* suggests, this possibility in Islam is contingent upon how Muslims interpret their religion. It is, therefore, anxiety inducing for liberal Americans who wish to know whether an ethic of self-reformation through love in Islam can foreclose the possibility of militant interpretations of Islam.

The next and final chapter of *Habibi* begins with a flashback to Dodola's marriage to the Qur'anic scribe. This time, the scribe's pen, which was foregrounded in Thompson's depictions of the consummation of their marriage (Figure 7.2) is nowhere to be seen. In its place, the scribe holds his penis over a water basin to perform the ablution after coitus (Figure 7.4). Here, Thompson centers Dodola's sobbing on the page rather than the pens used to inscribe God's will with ink. The scribe attempts to calm her with a story about Jesus's birth through "divine conception" (Figure 7.5). Thompson juxtaposes the story of the procreation of Jesus without intercourse in the final chapter of the book with the lascivious allusion to Muhammad's marriage to Aisha at the outset of his narrative. The entwinement of divine and human love familiar to Sufi literature with which the book—and Dodola's troubles—began are rendered in a Christian framing at the end of the book through Mary's spiritual conception of Jesus, ironically recalled through its Qur'anic telling. (Figure 7.5). The story of Jesus' divine conception calms Dodola, and while she is in the scribe's adoring arms, he says to her, "By Allah … You're just a child." "After that," Dodola informs the reader, "he left me to behave as such" (611). By framing the scribe's realization of the problematic nature of his sexual relationship with Dodola within the story of Jesus' birth in the Qur'an, Thompson suggests that for Islamic teachings and

Figure 7.4 Dodola and her husband after the consummation of their marriage. Craig Thompson, *Habibi,* p. 609. By courtesy of PenguinRandomHouse.

Figure 7.5 Dodola's husband narrates the story of Jesus's divine conception and miracle to calm Dodola after sex, Craig Thompson, *Habibi*, pp. 610–11. By courtesy of PenguinRandomHouse.

traditions to accord with modern sensibilities, they may need to be spiritualized along Christian lines. As such, he seems not only to validate but also to share liberal anxieties about Muslim participation in America's liberal democratic society. Despite the aesthetics of the Islamic tradition, which *Habibi* seeks to painstakingly reproduce through its calligraphy and Arabesque designs, for Muslims to participate in America's liberal democracy, Thompson seems to suggest that they, like the scribe, need to learn to distinguish between physical and spiritual dimensions of religion. They need to reconceptualize how the life of Muhammad can be both exemplary for them *and* in accord with liberal sensibilities.

Thompson's reframing of the scribe's marriage to Dodola toward the end of *Habibi* depicts how Thompson imagines this reconceptualization. When the scribe acknowledges Dodola as a child (within the framing of the birth of Christ) rather than an instrument of divine creation (framed within the context of Muhammad's marriage to "A"isha), she begins to play prophet by herself rather than rely on the scribe to teach her: "I'm Jesus walking on the water. I'm Solomon talking to the animals. I'm the Prophet flying on the magical buraq (*sic*)!" (612). While playfully imitating various prophets, she spills ink on the Qur'an. Blaspheming! The ink dropped from the divine pen with which *Habibi* began and its analogue, the blood spot on the marital sheet that was deemed beautiful because of her beauty and purity, in the final chapter, becomes a stain on the Holy Book. The scribe, who relates to God by reproducing the literal word of the Qur'an, calls her a "little bitch." "YOU'VE DESTROYED MY WORK!" He slaps her "across the face" (613, emphasis in the original).

Thompson uses this incident to critique Muslim scripturalism as fundamentalism laden with violence. He humanizes the divine *eros* with which he began *Habibi*. He takes the scribe and Dodola's relationship out of the sacred landscape in which sexuality, creation, and God's revelation were enchantingly intertwined and places it within the profane context of patriarchy: "And don't get started on that crying again!" the scribe tells Dodola after slapping her. "A man demands his silence!" (613).

This disenchantment of Dodola's relationship with the scribe as patriarchal empowers Dodola not to see herself solely as the object of desire but also as the subject of *eros*. This time she is the one to initiate sex with the scribe. The scribe's pen is notably absent in this scene. In its place is the mundane erection of a shy man anxious about his sexual urges.[5] Thompson depicts Dodola's hand over the scribe's erection at the very center of the page. Here, Dodola wields the phallic symbol of *eros* and creation, which she says, "when dealt with gently, made him fragile, vulnerable, and scared" (614). The penis can thus be both symbol of creation and patriarchy depending on how religion (in this case, Islam) is interpreted. Consequently, Dodola at the end of *Habibi* gains control over her sexuality by herself becoming erotic, allowing for her spiritual-sexual union with Zam (discussed earlier).

Dodola and Zam's survival and union at the end of *Habibi* represent the redemptive love that Thompson believes humanity needs to inwardly overcome lust and greed, symbolized through prostitution and slavery, and to outwardly overcome the degradation that industrial capitalism has wrought upon the environment and the more impoverished nations. Thompson ends *Habibi* by identifying this love literally with the selfless love for God that the Sufi saint, Rabi'a al-Adawiyya (d. 810), sought when she metaphorically called for setting heaven on fire and dousing the flames of hell so that "God's followers worship … not out of hope for reward … nor fear of punishment … but out of love" (662–4). Rabi'a, here, as the patron saint of a spiritualized love in Islam, stands in contrast to Dodola's husband whose life's literally is dedicated to reproducing the word of the Qur'an. This allows Thompson to express his erotic theology of selfless love through both Islam and Christianity to argue that love is a vital source for liberal interpretations of both these religions on which Muslims and non-Muslims can draw to coexist and to survive the challenges of racism, sexism, poverty, environmental degradation, and sexual trauma, just as Dodola and Zam have. Thompson, however, is neither a utopian nor a romantic. He has a penchant for discerning social and phycological anxiety. He ends the book by depicting Dodola, Zam, and Rabi'a walking as a family against the flow of a nonchalant diverse crowd, one that one would expect to find in a liberal society with clear expressions of anxiety on their faces (662). The very last page spread of the book also highlights the fragility of love and its unique potential for the salvation of humanity by depicting the Arabic word for love as a life raft hovering over a turbulent ocean (664–5).

The Role and Significance of Esotericism in *Habibi*

In an interview in October 2011, Thompson indicates that *Habibi* is "not really about religion." He explains, "I was inspired maybe more by all of the esoteric takes on those faiths; in Christianity, the Gnostics; Kabbalah, in Judaism; and the Sufis, in Islam; *the sense of the ecstatic perception of the divine*; *the sort of bringing down of barriers between cultures*" (Thompson 2011, author's emphasis). Indeed, *Habibi* is a product of long-standing esoteric traditions in the United States that "redirected and rechanneled [the imagined otherness of the Orient] into culturally available templates for making sense of difference … on the fringes of liberal Protestantism" (Albanese 2007, 331; see also, GhaneaBassiri 2010, 114–15). By way of example, Thompson immediately follows Dodola and Zam's spiritual-sexual union with an esoteric explanation of what they experienced: "In the magic squares, the letters are not arranged in numerical order yet each square encompasses a point, and when they are connected in increasing value, a design of perfect rotational symmetry emerges" (643). Tellingly, Thompson follows this esoteric explanation with a shared story in the Qur'an (37,102–11) and the Bible (Gen 22:1-19). He depicts the angel Gabriel bringing Abraham/Ibrahim a ram to sacrifice to God in place of his son who is regarded as Isma'il in the Qur'an and Isaac in the Bible. In the pages of *Habibi*, however, in light of Dodola and Zam's erotic enlightenment, the fact that the Qur'an and the Bible disagree about who exactly was the descendent of Abraham/Ibrahim whom God saved is alchemically made irrelevant. In Thompson's imagined retelling of this famed story, Isaac and Isma'il come together as brothers happy to see a ram's neck on the sacrificial alter rather than their own. Indeed, Thompson seems to expect the reader's witnessing of Zam and Dodola's "ecstatic perception of the divine" to effect a spiritual realization that would "bring down barriers between cultures" for them. Later, when the couple decide to purchase a slave girl and adopt her as their daughter, Thompson uses magic squares again to reveal to the reader the hidden role of love ciphered in the title of the book, *habibi*, "my beloved" in Arabic (658–9).

Ultimately, Thompson resorts to esotericism to eschew dealing with Islamic teachings about love on their own terms. By way of illustration, Dodola and Zam's relationship draws on the story of Layli and Qays, an ancient love story set in Arabia that is most widely known today through Nizami Ganjavi's (1141–1209) masterful epic *Layli and Majnun*. Dodola and Zam, just as Layli and Qays (who comes to be known as Majnun, "the crazed one") fall in love as children, and are separated from one another when they reach puberty. In Nizami's story, however, it is the society around the lovers that is responsible for disrupting the purity of their love. In Thompson's tale, Dodola and Zam's loving companionship as children is disrupted by Zam becoming sexually aware of Dodola and wanting to protect her from sex work (132f). While in Nizami's story, the sources of Layli and Majnun's suffering are the social expectations and cultural norms of their communities, for Dodola and Zam, their inborn instincts are as much a cause of their suffering as are their social and economic circumstances. Dodola's maternal instincts[6] lead her to prostitute herself to be able to feed Zam, and his inborn sexual desires compel him to castrate himself. The Christian theological notion that suffering bodies are redemptive overlays, if not overpowers, the lover-beloved motif in Sufi literature that Thompson appropriates for his graphic narrative.

Another example of Thompson resorting to esotericism to avoid dealing with Islamic teachings and aesthetics on their own terms is seen in the fact that he often leaves Arabic calligraphy untranslated and his allusions to Sufi literature unexplained (see, for example, 404–5). These references to and symbols of Islam are expected to be sufficiently universal to be able to mysteriously communicate their significance to their audiences. They are denuded in *Habibi* from the Islamic tradition that give them meaning in Muslims' lives and instead are reimagined and reconstructed through Thompson's Arabic Calligraphy and Arabesque designs (Backus and Koltun-Fromm 2018).

Ironically, while *Habibi* seeks to address American anxieties about the presence of Muslims in America, it comes to sensualize those anxieties through its own illustrations. The book's depiction of sexual violence with stereotypically hairy and horny Muslim men instills in the reader an anxious sense that a societal embrace of Muslims or Islamic traditions, which do not diminish bodily desires,[7] risks undermining the notion of selfless love through which the liberal religious establishment has sought to accommodate differences and to push the possibility of redemption into the realm of spiritual self-reformation rather than physical or political acts of defiance. The social and political consequences of this spiritualization have gone beyond portraying Islam esoterically to make it palatable for the American public. They have also meant that non-whites and non-males, whose experiences of oppression have been intimately tied up with their bodies (like Dodola and Zam) have been marginalized in America's national self-understanding and body politic because their experiences of oppression belie the limits of liberal values in American history and point to the potential for redemption through violence. By centering Black, female, and Muslim bodies in a story about personal, spiritual triumph over adverse circumstances, *Habibi* counters this marginalization while still reflecting the anxiety surrounding the potential of liberalism to be inclusive and to bring about a just society without violence.

Conclusion

Habibi posits that the selfless love of the other can provide a mutually recognizable theology that liberal Muslims and Christians can use to engage one another as co-citizens outside of the constraints of racism, sexism, unjust economic structures, and the degradation of the environment. While such theological self-reflections on difference and justice have a long history among liberal Protestantism in the United States, their expression through Sufi motifs of love in an award-winning medium of popular culture is striking and deserves sociological analysis. It demonstrates that a decade after 9/11, following US military ventures in Muslim-majority countries and increased instances of Islamophobia in American society and politics, American anxieties about whether Muslims can be part of America's liberal, democratic society shifted to become anxieties about the capacity of liberalism to assimilate Muslims. The anxiety induces by this question in American public life, given the history of racism and sexism in this country, is what *Habibi* sought to both articulate and alleviate through its application of an erotic theology of redemptive love to Islam.

Notes

1 I wish to thank Kees de Groot, Kaveh Bassiri, Alma Flores, Lori Pearson, Kamala GhaneaBassiri, Max Wink, and an anonymous reviewer of the book for their assistance and valuable feedback on various iterations and parts of this chapter.

2 Wanatolia seems to allude to "Western Anatolia," a meeting point between Europe and Asia, as well as the so-called Western and Islamic worlds.

3 For a discussion of Thompson's erotic theology in *Blankets*, see Jungkeit 2010, 323–34.

4 His portrayal bears striking similarities with the iconic character Mammy played by the Academy Award winning actress Hattie McDaniel in *Gone with the Wind*. This makes sense because by this time in the story, he has been castrated and emasculated.

5 Just as Thompson self-identified with the scribe as a writer and an artist, here too, he may be self-identifying with the scribe's sexual anxieties.

6 That Dodola's initial feelings for Zam were instinctual and maternal are demonstrated by the fact that Dodola instinctually jumps to his rescue in the slave camp. Dodola also wakes from her state of depression and lethargy to mother the child she herself bears with the sultan when that child is three years old (274), three being Zam's age when she first met him. Furthermore, she later explicitly states, "I wasn't ready to mother anyone other than you. Since then I've realized I'm not your parent, but your PARTNER" (581).

7 For a discussion of eroticism in Islam, see Tourage 2007.

References

Albanese, Catherine. (2007), *A Republic of Mind and Spirit: A Cultural History of American Metaphysical Religion*, New Haven: Yale University Press.

Armstrong, Meakin. (2011), "Craig Thompson: Fundamentals," *Guernica*, September 15. Available online: https://www.guernicamag.com/thompson_interview_9_15_11 (accessed June 20, 2022).

Backus, Madeline, and Ken Koltun-Fromm. (2018), "Writing the Sacred in Craig Thompson's *Habibi*," in Assaf Gamzou and Ken Koltun-Fromm (eds.), *Comics and Sacred Texts: Reimagining Religion and Graphic Narrative*, 5–24, Jackson: University Press of Mississippi.

Creswell, Robyn. (2011), "The Graphic Novel as Orientalist Mash-Up," *Sunday Book Review of the New York Times*, October 16: 26. Available online: https://www.nytimes.com/2011/10/16/books/review/habibi-written-and-illustrated-by-craig-thompson-book-review.html (accessed April 12, 2023).

Damluji, Nadim. (2011), "Can the Subaltern Draw? The Spectre of Orientalism in Craig Thompson's Habibi." Available online: https://www.hoodedutilitarian.com/2011/10/can-the-subaltern-draw-the-spectre-of-orientalism-in-craig-thompsons-habibi/ (accessed May 13, 2022).

Ganjavi, Nizami. (2021), *Layli and Majnun*, trans. Dick Davis, New York: Penguin Books.

GhaneaBassiri, Kambiz. (2010), *A History of Islam in America: From the New World to the New World Order*, Cambridge: Cambridge University Press.

Goldenberg, David M. (2003), *The Curse of Ham: Race and Slavery in Early Judaism, Christianity, and Islam*, Princeton: Princeton University Press.

Hedstrom, Matthew S. (2013), *The Rise of Liberal Religion: Book Culture and American Spirituality in the Twentieth Century*, Oxford: Oxford University Press.

Johnson, Sylvester. (2004), *The Myth of Ham in Nineteenth-Century American Christianity: Race, Heathens, and the People of God*, New York: Palgrave Macmillan.

Jungkeit, Steve. (2010), "Tell Tale Visions: The Erotic Theology of Craig Thompson's *Blankets*," in A. David Lewis and Christine Hoff Kraemer (eds.), *Graven Images: Religion in Comic Books and Graphic Novels*, 323–34, London: Continuum.

Koltun-Fromm, Ken. (2020), *Drawing on Religion: Reading and the Moral Imagination in Comics & Graphic Novels*, University Park: Pennsylvania State University Press.

Schmidt, Leigh Eric. (2003), "The Making of Modern 'Mysticism,'" *Journal of the American Academy of Religion* 71 (2): 273–302.

Shea, Lisa. (2011), "A Magic Carpet Ride," *Elle*, September: 352. Available online: https://www.elle.com/culture/books/reviews/a11768/habibi-review (accessed September 17, 2022).

Smith, Zadie. (2011), "Reviews: New Books," *Harper's Magazine*, September: 73–6.

Thompson, Craig. (2003), *Blankets*, Marietta: Top Shelf Productions.

Thompson, Craig. (2011), *Habibi*, New York: Pantheon Books.

Thompson, Craig. (2011), "Craig Thompson 'Habibi' with Bill Kartalopoulos," *Strand Book Store*. Available online: https://www.youtube.com/watch?v=8r0mg6H_YNg (accessed September 17, 2022).

Thompson, Craig. (2020), "Craig Thompson on Ginseng Roots, Blankets, and More: Interview," *The Comics Cube*. Available online: https://www.youtube.com/watch?v=OFAPc8JdWds (accessed May 13, 2022).

Tourage, Mahdi. (2007), *Rumi and the Hermeneutics of Eroticism*, Leiden: Brill.

Troeltsch, Ernst. ([1911] 1991), "Stoic-Christian Natural Law and Modern Secular Natural Law (1911)," in *Religion in History*, 332–53, trans. James Luther Adams and Walter F. Bense, Minneapolis: Fortress Press.

Part 3

Comics as Religion?

8

Implicit Religion and Trauma Narratives in *Maus* and *Watchmen*

Ilaria Biano

Introduction

While *Maus* and *Watchmen* were published between the late 1980s and early 1990s, they still manage to be alive and well on the cultural scene—and in the news—in ways that clearly testify to their solid place in a nevertheless still developing canon of comics and graphic novels. Searching through the pages of these two books for what has rendered them so powerful and meaningful we can find, as this chapter aims at showing, an intertwinement of trauma narratives and religious concerns within the fundamental sociohistorical and cultural contexts of their production. As "complex narrative structures" dealing with "weighty issues" (Van Ness 2010, 5) such as the Holocaust, Cold War, morality and justice, memory, and identity, *Watchmen* and *Maus* emerge in fact as relevant as cultural manifestations of some critical aspects of their pertinent contexts. Besides being both examples of trauma graphic novels, *Maus* and *Watchmen* present, in very different ways, narratives strongly imbued with religious themes, allegories, and symbolism, mainly attached to a "traditional" view of the religious realm, as bearing identity and meaning, but placing them in unconventional contexts.

Building on a cultural-critical and contextual approach to the representation of religion in media and popular culture, the article will specifically highlight a nexus between the cultural transmission and reproduction of the collective trauma on which these narratives rely and an implicit religious dimension of these traumas, also suggesting how these elements play a crucial and not yet considered a role in the processes of canonization, in the construction of the symbolic capital, in the building and persistence of their legitimacy by intercepting, and conveying an implicit religious trait of the structure of significance of contemporary culture.

Implicit Religion and/as Commitment to Trauma

As a framework trying to make sense of the increasingly evident shortcomings and heuristic limitations of secularization theory, particularly in Western societies, Implicit Religion was first elaborated by Edward Bailey and spread between the 1980s and 1990s, focusing on those cultural manifestations of central elements of the religious experience outside conventional and institutional religions. By searching for the "sacred" within what conventionally may be considered as "secular," Bailey's Implicit Religion builds on concepts such as commitment and integrating foci (focal points in society "that integrate wider areas in life" and where implicit religion will reveal itself; 1998, 23) that, when applied to the realm of popular culture, may help grasp "collective and individual experiences that engage beliefs and values within a particular cultural context" highlighting also relevant power dynamics (Spoliar 2022, 69). Implicit Religion suggests that we "think about the extent to which categories such as sacrality, ritual, and faith can be applied to traditionally 'non-religious' behaviours," but most of all recognizes that "implicit religion can be combined with explicit faith in greater or lesser degrees" (Crome 2015, 454). In the context of popculture and especially fiction, the Implicit Religion frame has been applied in most cases to the study of fandoms and fan cultures. The focus here will be slightly different, but will rely on Bailey's conceptual tools.

By applying the Implicit Religion framework to *Maus* and *Watchmen* it is possible to better understand their cultural relevance and their place in the canon beyond what the existing literature has since pointed out. In the way in which the texts combine explicit and implicit forms of religion, oftentimes overlapping them, and building the religious/secular "divide" more as a continuum, it emerges that feature of Implicit Religion highlighted by Karen Pärna (building on Meerten ter Borg): a tool "to explore how modern societies deal with questions relating to human existence" and meaning making experiences, as well as overwhelming emotions, fears, and uncertainties (Pärna 2010, 6). In this sense, the implicit religious dimension can be found in anything that is based on "collective beliefs and references to objects or ideas that are placed above ordinary human experience" (170).[1] Both *Maus* and *Watchmen* in fact engage with this blending of explicit and implicit religious registers in their narratives relating it to their being trauma narratives.[2] This is a crucial move, especially for contextualizing them both in the cultural and political landscape of the late 1980s and early 1990s and in the contexts of their later ongoing centrality in the cultural field and public debates and thus for highlighting a crucial aspect of their canonicity. As we will see, the trauma is expressed through, and as a form of, implicit religion as related to issues of meaning and commitment.[3] The kind of messages they vehiculate are at the same time extremely context-related and an expression of trauma as a site for forms of "implicit religion of contemporary society" such as the "encounter with the holy" in history that Bailey has indicated as "a commitment to the human" (1997, 273). This kind of "structural" trauma can be seen as the deepest layer of "the fabric" of contemporary societies (Taylor 2020, 383). Some scholars go so far as to suggest that "from the monotheistic-Western perspective ... the holy and the traumatic are two sides of the same coin" (Ataria 2017, xviii). In this sense, *Maus* and *Watchmen* represent in different ways, but with a sort of cultural consonance, examples of (pop)cultural products that are paradigmatic of the traumatic zeitgeist of the *fin the siècle*, with all the sacrality culturally attached to it. And this aspect is a constitutive part of their symbolic capital.

Maus and the Cultural Transmission of "The Central Trauma" of the Century

Serialized between 1980 and 1991 and published in two volumes in 1986 and 1991, *Maus* is first of all a memoir. Art Spiegelman, the author, is a cartoonist and, at the time, editor of a few magazines; these included *Raw*, one of the main alternative comics magazines explicitly devoted to bringing together graphic and literary cultures—in which *Maus* was serialized after a previous appearance in 1972 on the first issue of the magazine *Funny Animals*. *Maus* is both an account of the relationship between Spiegelman—or Spiegelman's alter-ego—and his father Vladek, an Auschwitz survivor, while he interviews him for the book, and the story of Vladek and his wife before, inside, and after the camp. One of the main features of the comic is the fact that the characters are represented as animals: Jewish people are depicted as mice, Germans as cats, and Poles as pigs. The main themes of the narrative are memory, trauma, violence, and persecution as related to history and identity. *Maus*'s place in the canon is linked to the relevance of such themes in the moment in which it was published.

At an explicit level, religious themes emerge especially in the everyday life and beliefs of Vladek during his imprisonment, as well as in the story of him as a survivor infused with a sense of divine intervention. For example, for Tabachnick, the "deep religious significance" of *Maus* resides precisely in Vladek's experience of the camp and emerges in episodes such as when he dreams that he will be released on the day in which the passage of the Bible known as Parshas Truma would be read at the synagogue—which, in fact, is what then happens (Tabachnick 2004, 3). On the other hand, Spiegelman represents himself more as a secular character or, as he later defined himself, "a rootless cosmopolitan, alienated in most environments" (Spiegelman 2011, 133). As Spiegelman said, "I didn't know that I did want to do a book about the Holocaust. If anything, I was in allergic reaction to my own Jewishness" (39). However, Spiegelman has also said that working on *Maus* "somehow involved coming out of the closet as a Jew" (39). In fact, the narrative is structured as a dialogical encounter between father and son and between the "emotional" and the "rational." A dialogue that has the outcome of making Art—and the audience with him—aware of and empathetic with Vladek's point of view and, through it, with his trauma. It is in the process of framing his father's life story and experience against the backdrop of the Holocaust that Art himself, both as a character and as the author, comes to explore "his own victimization and survivorhood" and the effects "of having grown up with European Jewish parents irreparably damaged" (Demsky 2020, 530).

This is a crucial point that links *Maus* to its cultural milieu, that is, the development of the fields of trauma and memory studies—in the late 1980s and early 1990s especially in the US context—as initially related to the growing relevance of literature about the Holocaust, in which the "Maus event" (Spanjers 2019) played a crucial role. This role unfolds on at least two levels. On the one hand, the culturalization of the Holocaust in the United States, not only as a Jewish-American cultural heritage restructuring the cultural, historical, and religious identity of a community but more broadly as a part of American cultural memory. On the other hand, the study and the definition itself of the field of trauma and memory studies, to which *Maus* became an almost inevitable point of reference, establishing a "critical vocabulary" for talking about the dynamics of the transmission and reproduction of transgenerational trauma—as in the case of Marianne Hirsch's (1992) "generation of postmemory," indicating dynamics of interiorization of parents' memories on the part of their children. These aspects represent a constitutive part of *Maus*'s cultural field: they both contributed to the positive environment toward it and at the same time were, with time, fueled by *Maus* itself to become an integral part of that culture and research fields.

Spiegelman himself has defined the context of his work as a real cultural zeitgeist—one that he didn't really necessarily endorse (2011, 46–8). But its relevance goes beyond this. *Maus* also contributed to creating the condition of possibility for a valuable social and cultural transmission of the traumatic collective memory of the Holocaust and of its victims and survivors in a broad cultural field as a form of commitment to the responsibility intrinsic in bearing that memory as a collectivity of both survivors and witnesses. If Spiegelman has in fact defined *Maus* as "a diasporist's account of the Holocaust" (153), he also stated that "in terms of the way the Holocaust has entered into Jewish American consciousness, there's something sad and dangerous ... It becomes this closed-off martyrology" (Jacobowitz 1994, 54–5). In this sense, Spiegelman acknowledges the criticalities intrinsic in the religious associations of the word Holocaust itself and what it came to signify with its reference to the ideas of sacrifice and offering. Nevertheless, throughout *Maus*'s storyline, the traumatic, violent but also quasi-religious experience involved in the story of the father is actually "transfigured" into a founding trauma—to use the words of historian Dominick LaCapra—"holding the elusive (perhaps illusory) promise of meaning and identity for the son in the present" (LaCapra 1998, 155). If the religious dimension unfolds in the text as a cultural and identitarian mark transmitted intergenerationally through a traumatic tale, it is in the intergenerational transmission of the cultural trauma—both from father to son and from Spiegelman to his audience—that the implicit religious dimension of the traumatic experience, of this founding trauma, is articulated, oftentimes through the postmodern and metanarrative register of the work (cf. https://archive.org/details/mausiisurvivorst0000spie/page/40/mode/2up). This fidelity to trauma emerges as an identity builder and as one in which "the bond with the dead may invest trauma with value" as a form of "painful but necessary commemoration ... an endlessly melancholic, impossible mourning" (LaCapra 2001, 22).

A trauma that is complex by definition: personal for Vladek and for all of those who directly experienced it, cultural and collective for the Jewish community, but that also constitutes, as Spiegelman himself phrased it, "the central trauma of the Twentieth Century" (Dreifuss 1989, 34). If comprehension and closure are not attainable, it is in the fidelity and transmission of the trauma, in the non-forgetting, that it is possible to show respect and recognition for the experience and suffering of Vladek and all the others. When it is the trauma—direct and vicarious—that becomes a source of identity and recognition, the commitment to, and meaningfulness of the traumatic experience may represent a form of implicit religion. LaCapra warns against the "sublime" dimension of limited events and indicates as the most problematic aspect of *Maus* precisely the risk of converting the Holocaust into a founding trauma and thus "a paradoxical, perhaps impossible source of meaning and identity" (177). And yet, cultural collective traumas, especially when they become objects of cultural analysis and transmission in cultural products and texts such as *Maus*, do become founding traumas and the social and cultural transmission of those traumas involves an implicit religious dimension as a form of commitment and responsibility. As emphasized by the aforementioned initial reluctance of Spiegelman in dealing with his family and personal history, *Maus* thus emerges as a tentative exercise of "working through." A trauma narrative that, in the impossibility of reaching any closure, reinvents itself as an instrument not only of memory but of identity. In so doing it contributes to implementing the fidelity to cultural trauma as an integrating focus. Linda Hutcheon had already noted back in 1999 how the postmodern challenge to the status of historical "fact" enacted by *Maus* managed to bring the past and its witnessing to life in "ways that have won it a worldwide" attention and success alongside the possibility of relating to those facts and witnessing (4). The ability of *Maus* in making something as untranslatable as trauma comprehensible and a source of identification and commitment, is thus not only intertwined with the processes of reception of *Maus* in different contexts—and also with the criticalities it faced over the years[4]—but also an integral element of its relevance, success, and on-going centrality in public debates, too—in other words, of its symbolic capital.

Watchmen and the Quest for Humanity

Created by writer Alan Moore and comic artist Dave Gibbons, *Watchmen* was published between 1986 and 1987 by DC Comics. As a work of fiction, it is set in an alternative 1980s world, in which superheroes are actually masked vigilantes with no superpowers, who had great relevance in twentieth-century American history. In 1985, Nixon is in his fifth term after winning the Vietnam War. The *Watchmen*, however, have been outlawed since 1977 following a drop in their popularity. Only Dr Manhattan, a scientist who was exposed to extreme radiation, acquiring great powers and the ability to see the past, present, and future all at once, works for the government amid escalating cold war tension. Central themes are the fight between good and evil, human suffering, and the impending apocalypse. Its place in the canon is mostly related to the unsettling of the superhero genre and to the peculiar sociopolitical critique, typical of its author: it questions the very notion of goodness and exposes the dangers of all-encompassing power. Through these powerless, beaten, and struggling Minutemen, "readers were forced to confront the legitimacy of heroism" (Phillips and Strobl 2013, 38) and the role of supposedly redeeming figures—real or fictive, with or without superpowers—bringing salvation.

At the heart of *Watchmen* lies a denouncement of political and social injustices through the metaphor of the superhero in the context of a traumatic era. *Watchmen* depicts a world in crisis and a group of vigilantes supposed—more or less—to watch over it, while struggling themselves with their own personal issues. These "mostly impotent superheroes" (Blake 2010) are affected and traumatized by the same real-world problems they are supposed to face. The trauma of the Cold War and in particular the threat of nuclear destruction, as well as the political trauma of those let down by the very institutions they were devoted to, emerge in *Watchmen* as affecting the collectivity both at a personal and national—possibly global—level. The "traumatic collapse of the socio-political structures in the psyche of the individual" (Romero-Jodar 2017, 156) provoked by the destruction of political, social, and cultural assumptions constitutes the background against which—criticizing Thatcherism, Reaganism, and capitalist politics—*Watchmen* articulates its allegorical use of religious themes through which it expresses its sociopolitical commentary.

The role of—explicit and implicit—religious elements in *Watchmen* is linked to its being a text in the science fiction genre. As McGrath notes, science fiction texts often represent a middle ground in which questions about meaning and human existence are articulated by mixing and matching "mythmaking process(es)" with "the powerful gaze of science" realizing "new and sometimes surprising forms" between religious and secular, sacred and profane, beliefs and rationality, explicit and implicit forms of religion (McGrath 2015, 483). In this sense, it is relevant how *Watchmen* coincides in Moore's career and personal life with a shift from an atheist and rationalist view toward a magical philosophical worldview. Moore sees in *Watchmen* "the symbolic end" of his "writing rationally" and at the same time a first "step beyond the rational" toward an incorporation of magic and paganism both in his fiction and his life, which he interprets as a creative and artistic form (Babcock 2007). *Watchmen* embodies this ambiguity and blurred boundaries. Both the powerless Minutemen and Dr Manhattan embody a religious allegory, albeit in quite different ways, and represent these two facets rooted in Moore's more general worldviews. Through their peculiar condition of flawed superheroes, they embody different forms of morality in relation to the choices they make and their actions in the face of life-shattering events and possibly global threats

(Hughes 2006; Kreider 2013; Prince 2011). In particular, Dr Manhattan explicitly assumes a religious dimension. He is a god-like figure more than a conventional superhero. A rationalist and positivistic scientist in his human shape who gains an omnipotent and messianic status and a huge ultimate power over humanity. Nevertheless, he struggles between the attachment to his lost humanity and the pessimistic clarity resulting from his subatomic philosophy.

Through its allegories, *Watchmen* projects the implicit religious dimension on the political traumas of the 1980s. While what we saw in *Maus* is a dynamic related to a fidelity and commitment to trauma as a form of impossible closure that transmutes into a source of memory and identity, in *Watchmen* that same impossibility of closure for a collective political trauma identified by the author with the condition in which humanity finds itself—in British society, but not only—in the late 1980s is transmuted in the text and through the text as a political stance. In this sense, the fidelity to trauma emerges as an active form of transmutation of trauma into political and social "action" based on the strong commitment derived from the bonds and sense of belonging created by the political-cultural trauma. As Romero-Jodar noted, *Watchmen* "rewrites history so as to take a political stance on a social situation that is leading to a general traumatization of society" (2017, 147).

Watchmen highlights how the relationship between humanity with a self-proclaimed superior authority—be it a politician, superhero, or god—always ends up with the entity becoming uncaring and indifferent and with humanity being let down (cf. https://archive.org/details/watchmen0000moor_e6p3/page/402/mode/2up). Thus, the only realistic and desirable form of commitment is to humanity itself, to its imperfection, and to the chaos and unpredictability of life that "is part of the normal, natural order of things" (Cooke 2000). The traumatized Minutemen ultimately try to "find *themselves* in seeking," acknowledging the imperfection that makes them human just like all the other humans: looking for meaning (Dietrich 2009, 149). And Moore and Gibbson are able to convey this message through a traumatic narrative, but also by infusing this depiction with a clear, implicitly religious message devoted to personal responsibility and political engagement.

This core message is the strength of *Watchmen*'s narrative, and it emerges in the processes of reception of the book; it relies on a narrative that "transcends the context" while narrating a story that is so clearly context-related (Luoma-aho 2014, 246). This aspect emerges clearly by considering *Watchmen's* transmedial diachronic reception. Leaving aside the movie adaptation of 2009 by Zack Snyder that presented some criticalities in the context of a rather didactic adaptation, more interesting is the 2018 HBO's miniseries created by the author of *Lost* and *The Leftovers*, Damon Lindelof. The show, which enacts a reformulation in which the deep significance, the semantic of the text remains the same while being told through other words, was in fact intended not as an adaptation or reboot, as much as a "remix," capable of maintaining Moore's central concerns and, at the same time, of conveying an up-to-date version of the message through a completely new, contemporary story. While presenting some of the original characters, the story revolves around the historical-structural violence and injustices against the African American community, and it does this not only by creating a new human-super hero, Angela Abar, a Black woman, but also by rooting her origin story back in the history of the 1921 Tulsa massacre—in which white residents attacked and killed several members of the Black community as well as destroyed their properties and houses—and by revealing that one of the original Watchmen, Hooded Justice, was in fact a survivor of the massacre and the grandfather of Angela. Lindelof stated that he envisioned *Watchmen* as a story "about self-proclaimed 'heroes' fighting an intangible enemy almost impossible to defeat. In the 1980s, that enemy was the threat of nuclear Armageddon. In 2019, is the long overdue reckoning with America's camouflaged history of white supremacy" (Evans 2019). A powerful resignification in this sense is that of Dr Manhattan, who once again plays a symbolic role: he had renounced his powers and incarnated himself in the body of a Black man for the love of the protagonist and through her of the idea itself of humanity. It is through his story, and that of Angela, that the original secular, individual spirituality discernible in Dr Manhattan's story, is linked here with the cultural trauma of the African American community and the battle for rights and justice. It transposes the deconstruction and reconstruction of the superhero in its metaphorical dimension from the Cold War of the 1980s, to the United States of the Black Lives Matter movement and its spiritual connotations. *Watchmen* the miniseries thus testifies, with its existence and its structure, to the specific symbolic capital of *Watchmen* the graphic novel.

The Implicit Religion of Trauma Culture in the *fin de siecle* "New" Comics

In the November 2021 issue of *Harper's Magazine*, author Will Self published an essay titled *A Posthumous Shock*; the subheading of the article was *How Everything Became Trauma*, but on the cover the essay was referred to with the sentence *Against Trauma. How an Obscure Psychological Theory Took Over Our Lives*. Self was not the only one turning against trauma theory and its legacy; similar essays were published between 2021 and 2022 in the pages of *The New Yorker* and *The New York Times*. Self's main thesis is that trauma is primarily a "function of modernity in all its shocking suddenness" and what we've come to call trauma is in fact merely "an extreme version of a distinctly modern consciousness." For Self, trauma theory succeeded principally because it provided "a grand narrative of human moral progress" centered on suffering. While Self's intuition is challenging and, in a way, parallels some aspects of what this article aims at exploring, that is, the implicit religion of trauma culture in its pop-cultural manifestations, Self's aversion for the concept seems limiting. In the literary and cultural field, trauma theory emerged at the end of the 1980s and the beginning of the 1990s, and while strictly linked with the growing knowledge and scholarly interest in the horrors of the Holocaust, it spread rapidly—and particularly in American culture—as a lens through which to interpret a variety of individual experiences and historical events. As Anne Rothe has highlighted: trauma has become a "discursive knot" in Western and especially American popular culture transforming the Holocaust from an event in European history into a metaphor for evil and generating "the narrative paradigm—the basic plot structure and core set of characters—for representing such vastly diverse experiences" (Rothe 2016, 52). And yet the idea that trauma is nothing more than a modern consciousness and a metaphor for any modern human struggle does not elide the core of trauma theory. For Ataria, "trauma stands at the very core of Western culture" (2017, xvii) and is understandable only in the context and as a function of (modern) culture. At the same time, contemporary culture "cannot be understood without understanding the trauma that shaped it" (xvi). It is "by understanding the traumatic structure of contemporary culture [that] we can understand how this culture generates new traumas by means of repetition compulsion" (xvi).

Turning then to the relevance of the Implicit Religion framework for interpreting (pop)cultural manifestations of the late twentieth century, could we talk of a commitment of Western culture to its structural trauma and its meaning-making dimension? And if the answer is positive, where else to search for its manifestations if not in popular culture? Cultural and pop-cultural products in particular are powerful instruments in the processes of intergenerational transmission and reproduction of cultural collective traumas but also of beliefs and meaning making. Thus, these texts bear with them (while narrating specific historical and/or cultural traumas) that wide, generational, structural trauma of modern culture. *Maus* and *Watchmen*—with their differences in terms of genres and background—still represent a case study of these dynamics and, vice versa, these dynamics give us a better understanding of their symbolic capital and their canonicity. By reading them in fact in the double, connected frame of Implicit Religion and trauma culture, these texts emerge as exemplary not only of the rising graphic novels but also of the cultural zeitgeist at the end of the short century—or at the beginning of the long nineties. Both texts are epochal meditations at the end of the century on the sense of history and evil. Their traumatic nature, although relating to specific historical and collective traumas (the Holocaust and the Cold War), nevertheless also expresses through them a "generational"—and even structural—trauma of Western society and its "humanity." This aspect cannot be underestimated when considering their symbolic capital.

As noted by Gauthier, one of the strengths—and also of the weaknesses in a way—of the concept of Implicit Religion is the fact that it grasps how "individuals and communities are dynamically structured by 'religiologics' which precede, exceed, determine and allow for them" outside of dogmas, institutions, and liturgies (2007, 265). As Bailey put it, implicit religion is about "what people are determined *about*, as well as determined *by* … the causes *for* which they live, and the causes for which they might, if necessary, die, as well as the causes *of* their life, and their death … their profoundest and most all-embracing assumptions, concerns and identities … what distinguishes human beings, both collectively and individually" (Bailey 1998, 14, emphasis in original). Texts such as *Maus* and *Watchmen* explore the nature of the structural trauma of contemporary culture through—fictional and non-fictional—parables in which historical trauma, structural trauma, and memory interact in different ways in order to convey meaning, identity, or, we could say, an integrating focus. By framing *Maus* and *Watchmen* in the context of the implicit religiosity of their traumatic narratives it is possible also to reframe their processes of canonization and their ongoing relevance as capable of bearing meaning and commitment through time, spaces, and also format different from the original ones.

Notes

1 While the idea of implicit religion and its heuristic capacity has been questioned over time by different scholars (see, e.g., Gauthier 2005) its use seems to fit well with the intricacies of memory, trauma, meaning, identity, existential threats, and

struggles that are at the core of these two narratives and that constitute a crucial element of their cultural relevance.

2 Both *Maus* and *Watchmen* are trauma narratives both thematically—putting front and center plots based on traumatic issues—and stylistically—employing an array of narrative devices typical of trauma literature, such as fragmented narratives, split time, flashbacks, phantasmatic presences. Romero-Jodar has pointed to the "ethical turn" and the trauma turn—along with "the end of the stern censorship code" and "the revamp of the Modernist ethos" that followed—as crucial for the success of this kind of narratives, noting that it was a combination of "historical and aesthetic circumstances" that "allowed the graphic novel to explore the vast field of psychic trauma and collective suffering." Texts that fall into this context include Will Eisner's *A Contract with God* (1978), Alan Moore et al.'s *The Swamp Thing* saga (1983–8), Raymond Briggs's *When the Wind Blows* (1982), Neil Gaiman and Dave McKean *Signal to Noise* (1989), or Frank Miller's *The Dark Knight Returns* (1986).

3 One must be cautious in conflating psychological trauma with cultural trauma. While the point of departure is always some kind of psychological trauma and thus an experience of suffering and pain, some forms of trauma—especially when expressed in collective forms—reverberate in cultural expressions and ways of transmission. Much of the scholarship on trauma has focused on this cultural dimension as able to restage "narratives that attempt to animate and explicate trauma that has been formulated as something that exceeds the possibility of narrative knowledge" (Luckhurst 2008, 79). This is the path that will be followed here too. Theorizing a nexus between traumatic experiences and a form of implicit religiosity intrinsic in them is a delicate step. If applied to individuals, an approach of this kind may have moral implications and presents criticalities such as those highlighted by historian Dominick LaCapra when talking about fidelity to trauma. Applied to cultural collective traumas, to forms of structural traumas, and to the cultural manifestations, representations, and forms of transmission an approach that identifies possible manifestations of some aspects of an implicit religion may nevertheless help us to grasp—as is suggested here—complex and interesting sociohistorical and cultural dynamics.

4 *Maus* has been translated into over thirty languages. Spiegelman himself was often involved in the translation process that encountered various difficulties in terms both of the translatability of the language of trauma and of the cultural impact in countries such as Germany, Poland, or Russia; see for example, Baccolini and Zanettin 2008. It is interesting enough also to make a passing reference to episodes such as the banning of the book from school's curriculum enacted in January 2022 by the McMinn County Schools, TN over "rough language," "unnecessary profanity," nudity (of a cat), and mentions of murder, violence, and suicide.

References

Ataria, Y. (2017), *The Structural Trauma of Western Culture: Toward the End of Humanity*, Cham, Switzerland: Springer International Publishing.

Babcock, J. (2007), "Magic is Afoot: A Conversation with Alan Moore About the Arts and the Occult," *Arthur Magazine*. Available online: https://arthurmag.com/2007/05/10/1815/ (accessed: March 24, 2022).

Baccolini, R., and Zanettin, F. (2008), "The Language of Trauma. Art Spiegelman's Maus and its Translations," in F. Zanettin (ed.), *Comics in Translation*, 99–132, London: Routledge.

Bailey, E. I. (1997), *Implicit Religion in Contemporary Society*, Weinheim, Germany: Deutscher Studien Verlag.

Bailey, E. (1998), "Implicit Religion: What Might That Be?," *Implicit Religion* 1 (1): 9–22. doi: 10.1558/imre.v1i1.9.

Beaty, B., and Woo, B. (2016), *The Greatest Comic Book of All Time: Symbolic Capital and the Field of American Comic Books*, 1st ed. Basingstoke: Palgrave Pivot.

Blake, B. B. (2010), "Watchmen: The Graphic Novel as Trauma Fiction," *ImageTexT* 5 (1). Available online: https://imagetextjournal.com/watchmen-the-graphic-novel-as-trauma-fiction/ (accessed March 24, 2022).

Cooke, Jon B. (2000), "Toasting Absent Heroes. Alan Moore discusses the Charlton-Watchmen Connection," *Comics Book Artist* (9). Available online: https://www.twomorrows.com/comicbookartist/articles/09moore.html (accessed April 4, 2022).

Crome, A. (2015), "Implicit Religion in Popular Culture: The Case of *Doctor Who*," *Implicit Religion* 18 (4): 439–45. doi: 10.1558/imre.v18i4.29085.

Demsky, J. S. (2020), "We are a Long Ways Past *Maus*: Responsible and Irresponsible Holocaust Representations in Graphic Comics and Sitcom Cartoons," in V. Aarons and Ph. Lassner (eds.), *The Palgrave Handbook of Holocaust Literature and Culture*, 529–51, Cham: Springer International Publishing.

Dietrich, B. (2009), "The Human Stain: Chaos and the Rage for Order in Watchmen," *Extrapolation* 50 (1): 120–44. doi: 10.3828/extr.2009.50.1.9.

Dreifus, C. (1989), "Art Spiegelman 'If There Can Be No Art About the Holocaust, There May At Least Be Comic Strips,'" *The Progressive* 53 (11): 34–37.

Evans, E. E. (2019), "'*Watchmen*' is a Powerful Exploration of Black Trauma, and Everyone Needs to Watch," *HuffPost UK*. Available online: https://www.huffpost.com/entry/watchmen-episode-6-hooded-justice-race-trauma_n_5ddc92ece4b0d50f32958d9e (accessed March 24, 2022).

Gauthier, F. (2007), "Orpheus and the Underground: Raves and Implicit Religion—From Interpretation to Critique," *Implicit Religion* 8 (3): 217–65. doi: 10.1558/imre.v8i3.217.

Hirsch, M. (1992), "Family Pictures: Maus, Mourning, and Post-Memory," *Discourse* 15 (2): 3–29.

Hughes, J. A. (2006), "'Who Watches the Watchmen?': Ideology and 'Real World' Superheroes," *Journal of Popular Culture* 39 (4): 546–57. doi: 10.1111/j.1540-5931.2006.00278.x.

Hutcheon, L. (1999), "Literature Meets History: Counter-Discoursive 'Comix,'" *Anglia* 117 (1): 4–14. doi: 10.1515/angl.1999.117.1.4.

Jacobowitz, S. (1994), "'Words and Pictures Together': An Interview with Art Spiegelman," *Writing on the Edge* 6 (1): 49–58. Available online: http://www.jstor.org/stable/43158744.

Kreider, S. E. (2013) "Who Watches the Watchmen?: Kant, Mill, and Political Morality in the Shadow of Manhattan," in J. J. Foy and T. M. Dale (eds.), *Homer Simpson Ponders Politics: Popular Culture as Political Theory*, 97–112, Lexington: University Press of Kentucky.

LaCapra, D. (1998), *History and Memory after Auschwitz*, Ithaca, NY: Cornell University Press.

LaCapra, D. (2001), *Writing History, Writing Trauma*, Baltimore, MD: Johns Hopkins University Press.

Luckhurst, R. (2008), *The Trauma Question*, London: Routledge.

Luoma-aho, M. T. (2014), "'Become Transfigured Forever': Political Transcendence in Alan Moore and David Lloyd's *V for Vendetta*," *Radical Orthodoxy: Theology, Philosophy, Politics* 2 (2): 244–71.

McGrath, J. F. (2015), "Explicit and Implicit Religion in Doctor Who and Star Trek," *Implicit Religion* 18 (4): 471–84. doi: 10.1558/imre.v18i4.29087.

Pärna, K. (2010), *Believing in the Net: Implicit Religion and the Internet Hype, 1994–2001*, Leiden: Leiden University Press.

Phillips, N. D., and Strobl, S. (2013), *Comic Book Crime: Truth, Justice, and the American Way*, New York: New York University Press.

Prince, M. J. (2011), "Alan Moore's America: The Liberal Individual and American Identities in *Watchmen*," *Journal of Popular Culture* 44 (4): 815–30. doi: 10.1111/j.1540-5931.2011.00864.x.

Romero-Jodar, A. (2017), *The Trauma Graphic Novel*, London: Routledge.

Rothe, A. (2016), "Popular Trauma Culture: The Pain of Others Between Holocaust Tropes and Kitsch-Sentimental Melodrama," in Y. Ataria, D. Gurevitz, H. Pedaya, and Y. Neria (eds.), *Interdisciplinary Handbook of Trauma and Culture*, 51–66, Cham, Switzerland: Springer International Publishing.

Self, W. (2021), "A Posthumous Shock," *Harper's Magazine*. Available online: https://harpers.org/archive/2021/12/a-posthumous-shock-trauma-studies-modernity-how-everything-became-trauma/ (accessed March 24, 2022).

Spanjers, R. (2019), *Comics Realism and the Maus Event: Comics and the Dynamics of World War II Remembrance*. PhD Thesis, University of Amsterdam.

Spiegelman, A. (2011), *Meta Maus: A Look Inside a Modern Classic, Maus*, New York: Random House.

Spoliar, L. (2022), "Learning from Laughter: Implicit Religion, Satire, and Power in Two British TV Situation Comedies," *Journal of Beliefs and Values* 43 (1): 68–79. doi: 10.1080/13617672.2022.2005722.

Tabachnick, S. E. (2004), "The Religious Meaning of Art Spiegelman's *Maus*," *Shofar an Interdisciplinary Journal of Jewish Studies* 22 (4): 1–13. doi: 10.1353/sho.2004.0115.

Taylor, M. (2020), "Collective Trauma and the Relational Field," *Humanistic Psychologist* 48 (4): 382–8. doi: 10.1037/hum0000215.

Van Ness, S. J. (2010), *Watchmen as Literature*, Jefferson, NC: McFarland.

Wright, B. W. (2003), *Comic Book Nation: The Transformation of Youth Culture in America*, Baltimore, MD: Johns Hopkins University Press.

9

Manga Pilgrimages: Visualizing the Sacred/ Sacralizing the Visual in Japanese *Junrei*

Mark MacWilliams

Media and religion theorists today argue that popular culture, mediated through TV, video games, movies, and comics is where people today consume culture and, by extension, encounter religion (Hoover 2001, 146–59; Clark 2007, 5–20; Morgan 2007, 21–34). If popular culture is defined as anything "mass produced, widely distributed, and regularly consumed by large numbers of people" (Chidester 2005, 19), what do we find in the case of Japan? In Japan, the major forms of mass media where religion is present are manga or *komikkusu* ("comics") and anime, or animated films. Comics historian Shimizu Isao defines *manga* broadly as drawings with a "satirical or playful spirit." As part of the Japanese pop culture industry, *manga* has been a big business commercially in Japan since the 1960s with, in 2021, overall sales of ¥675.9 billion, making up over 40.4 percent of domestic publishing, the largest segment being digital comics, a new record (Statistica Research Department 2022). *Anime*, which is typically linked to *manga* as part of its "media mix" of shared narrative content with video games, goods, and so on. As a phenomenon of the mass culture industry of corporate conglomerates, which produce and distribute large variety of fan-oriented products, *manga*, and *anime* increasing became a big commercial success beginning in the 1960s (MacWilliams 2008, 7; Seaton and Yamamura 2015, 2; Steinberg 2012). In 2021, the market value strictly for *anime* productions was ¥274.4 billion (about US $2.41 billion) after years of extensive growth of the industry. *Manga* and *anime* are powerful examples of Japanese "soft power" that are a major form of media consumerism in Japan.

So, what does religion, if anything, have to do with it? Stuart Hoover, for example, argues that popular culture, often recycles a stock of religious symbols, ideas, and images as part of its total entertainment package. Whether this "image reservoir" becomes crucial or only incidental to the pleasure popular culture affords its consumers depends on the material. *Manga* and *anime* often are filled with such things (Hoover 2001, 152; Thomas 2012). *Manga* artist, Tezuka Osamu, for example, known as "the god of comics" in Japan, drew comics that often dealt centrally with religion. Tezuka's *Budda* (12 volumes, 1987–8; 2000) is his classic version of the story of the Buddha, while his masterwork, *Hi no Tori* (Tezuka, 12 volumes, 1992; 2020), is a multivolume epic historical/science fiction drama linked together by its major characters' rebirths over the aeons. Both works are replete with images of religious founders, deities, miracles, and themes about the quest for ultimate meaning and purpose in a world of suffering, evil, and ignorance. Both remain decades after Tezuka's death on Amazon.jp's bestseller lists.

This chapter focuses on a subset of comics and animated films directly connected to a major form of modern Japanese religious life, leisure travel, and tourism—pilgrimages (*junrei*). *Junrei* (a combination of two characters meaning "going around" (*jun*) and "worship" (*rei*)) originally refers to going on a circuit of multiple Buddhist temples (Pye 2015, 141–80, Hoshino 1986, 231–72). While there are other terms for it, such as *omairi, môde,* or *henro no tabi, junrei* has become a generic term covering all types of pilgrimages in Japan (see Reader and Swanson 1997, 232–3).

Pilgrimage has a long history in Japan, connected with tourism and leisure travel. Even in the tenth and twelfth centuries, aristocratic women going on pilgrimage to temples like Ishiyama-dera and Hase-dera outside of the capital (Heian-kyô, now Kyoto), did so for both piety and pleasure (Ambros 1997, 301–45). For Victor Turner (1973), whose cross-cultural studies of pilgrimage are seminal to the field, pilgrimage can liberate people from their humdrum existence by traveling to sacred centers out there. Pilgrimage, Turner argues, like modern leisure pleasurable activities such as going to bars, movie theaters, and Mardi Gras, is a "liminoid" phenomenon, taking us beyond the quotidian to places of power, meaning, and even fun. "One works at the liminal, one plays with the liminoid" (Turner 1974, 86–7). Japanese pilgrimage today is often a form of pleasure travel and tourism, even when it is a religious practice.

This essay explores how *manga and anime* are modes of mass media that "positively promote" modern Japanese pilgrimages to sacred centers out there (Reader 2007). What contemporary works promote Japanese pilgrimage? Second, as visual narratives, what role do they play in Japanese pilgrimage? As pilgrimage texts that are also forms of popular culture, how do they reveal something extraordinary, something "sacred" for those who identify themselves as devout pilgrims, or pleasure-seeking tourists, or often both? Here is where caution must prevail. As David Chidester has noted (2005, 12–13), defining religion as practices devoted to a superhuman, transcendent, ultimate reality, separate from the ordinary life and culture, is unworkable for understanding how popular culture can be religious for some people. How can leisure travel and tourism and popular culture associated with it be sacred?

There are two types of comic books and *anime* associated with Japanese pilgrimage. Both use photo-realistic figurative art and caricature to entrance their readers/viewers with fascinating images, ideas, and storylines. One type are *junrei manga,* which are entertaining stories about pilgrimages that provide useful information, and usually are produced for traditionally religious pilgrimage sites. Specific religious organizations, temples, and groups convert *manga* for their own particular proselytizing purposes. My focus here is limited to comics used by religious organizations that use this form of popular culture to communicate information about specific pilgrimages. *Junrei manga* are an entertaining way to convey information about the sacred centers that are the goal of traditional pilgrims.

The second type are *seichi junrei manga* and *anime. Seichi junrei,* meaning "pilgrimage to the sacred land," is a contemporary cultural phenomenon that emerged in the 1990s. It is a form of leisure tourism where fans (sometimes referred to as *otaku* or "geeks," obsessive fans) travel to real-life sites identified as backdrops of popular comics and animated films. These works have content that at best only tangentially deal with traditional religions like Buddhism, Shinto, or Christianity. While traditional religious symbols, ideas, and images from Buddhism, Shinto, or Christianity may appear in them, they seem only incidental to the storyline or pleasure these works afford.

Seichi junrei is a good example of what David Chidester calls popular culture as religion. As he and others have argued, popular culture can create "communities of allegiance" with "symbols, myths and rituals" that people can find fascinating and enjoyable (Chidester 2005, 32). The pleasures of the text that *manga* and *anime* provide are so important to fans that they become pilgrims/tourists, journeying to the real places appearing in their beloved stories. These "sacred lands" can concretize a story's fictional model of reality, offering a real space for fans to play within through all sorts of "religious-like" activities—offering their own handmade votive tablets (called *itaema*), constructing and carrying character-themed portable shrines, eating special foods associated with the stories, and the like. *Seichi junrei* provide liminoid spaces with symbols, extra-natural beings, objects, and ritual activities that create a "sacred land" for fan visitors. Since they are both physical and material in nature—an actual journey, goods purchased, food and activities consumed, *seichi junrei* pilgrimages exist for fans "as a personal domain of sensory, intimate, and desirable experiences" (25). For fan pilgrims/tourists, travel to the sacred land is a way to have a good time, find something meaningful, gain a sense of shared solidarity with other fans, and to experience joy of being on the road.

Junrei Manga

The purpose of *Junrei manga,* which are published by temples and religious organizations, is to proselytize particular pilgrimages. Modern comics about Japanese pilgrimages are usually classified as *kyôiku manga* ("educational comics" or *jōhō manga* ("informational comics"). This particular genre appeared in the 1990s, when the commercial comic book industry generally had reached the height of its postwar popularity. While educational comics are designed for younger people, informational comics aim for older audiences, with a range of topics presented in an entertaining and easily digestible format. Subjects run the gamut from golf, ramen restaurants, biographies of famous people to more arcane academic topics like the Japanese economy, missile defense, and history (Kinsella 2000, 45, 70). Such informational manga, unlike most commercially produced comics, are not purely pleasure leisure commodities. Although visually attractive, graphically easy to scan, and couched in a simple narrative format, they are designed for a serious pedagogical purpose: to teach something.

In the case of *junrei manga,* that something is pilgrimage. Religious organizations or commercial publishers rely on manga's cinematic visuality to inform about, advertise, market, and popularize pilgrimages. They fulfill several purposes: to proselytize a specific spiritual faith, ideas, and practices, to offer practical travel guides about the route, to relate an author's personal experiences on the route, and to highlight particular messages. In terms of the range of modern mass media—print, digital, and audio-visual materials—for popularizing the pilgrimage, *manga* are an important part of the mix.

A good example are informational manga of the Saikoku (or "Western Provinces") pilgrimage. The site is a famous thirty-three temple-circuit located in the Kansai area, roughly centered around the ancient capital of Kyoto. The thirty-three temples, described as places of spiritual power (*reijô* or *reichi*), are devoted to the Buddhist celestial bodhisattva Kannon, a great being of limitless compassion who bestows this- and otherworldly spiritual benefits. Pilgrimages to temples enshrining miraculous Kannon icons were widespread among both the aristocratic lay devotees and Buddhist ascetics, especially in the latter half of the Heian period (794–1185 CE). By the end of the twelfth century, Kannon icon cults developed into what was to become one of the most important pilgrimage circuits in Japan, the thirty-three-temple Saikoku route. Today it begins at Nachi-dera, originally a temple part of the Kumano pilgrimage, and includes famous Kannon temples, such as Ishiyama-dera, Kiyomizu-dera, and Hase-dera. By the Tokugawa period (1600–1868 CE), the Saikoku pilgrimage attracted multitudes of ordinary pilgrims. Although like many pilgrimages, it diminished during the Meiji and Taisho and early Showa periods, the Saikoku route also experienced a "boom" postwar. Major factors for the modern resurgence of pilgrimage were rising economic prosperity, the increasing ease of travel through the development of transportation and tourism infrastructures, and government policies and campaigns encouraging regional tourism and the leisure travel industry. The Saikoku pilgrimage now averages over thirty thousand pilgrims annually, triple the number of the Tokugawa period.

The key to Saikoku pilgrimage's attraction is Kannon's boundless salvific power as a celestial bodhisattva. One can come in contact with that power by worshipping before the thirty-three Kannon icons enshrined there. Pilgrimage texts, from the early modern period to the present, emphasize the faith that Saikoku temples are so supercharged with an abundance of Kannon's numinous power that they become portals through which the Kannon manifests a real presence.

The idea that Buddhist icons are sources of miracles is ancient in Buddhism. An exact likeness of a Buddha or Bodhisattva is not simply a replica, representation, or memory aid of the real thing, but is a *vera icon*, which is "the nature of an apparition and is not just a simulacrum" (Faure 1996, 236). In Japan, where they are called *reizô* or "enspirited or miraculous images." Art historian Dietrich Seckel notes that, in Mahâyâna Buddhism, it was widely believed that images partake "of the bodily presence of the Buddha … and that in extreme cases it can achieve a kind of image magic" (Seckel 2004, 57). Seckel also notes that Buddhist rituals like the "eye opening ceremony" strive "for personification, animation, and the ritually effective presence of the one depicted in the image." Buddhist images often "fuse the Sassurean sign and its signified" revealing, according to David Freedberg, the "traces of animism in our perception of and response to images"—in popular faith, the deity and its image are often interchangeable (Freedberg 1989, 32, 84–6). This "aura" or "real presence" that Kannon icons have is because of their unique existence within the temple's ritual space (Horton 2007, 26–9, Sharf and Horton Sharf 2001). Saikoku Kannon icons typically appear in the miracle tales and temple origin legends as living images. By worshipping them at these temples, pilgrims can receive Kannon's transfer of merit for this and other worldly benefits. This phenomenon is by no means limited to Japanese Kannon icons. In Christian Marian pilgrimage and popular cults from Late Antiquity to popular Roman Catholicism today, worshippers often experience the real presence of saints, the Virgin Mary, and Jesus in relics, icons, and the like (Turner and Turner 1978, 140–71; Orsi 2016, 1–12, 722, 112; see also, Freedberg 1989, 99–135).

To edify and guide pilgrims, Saikoku temples and pilgrimage associations publish a variety of promotional materials. Of these, *junrei manga* are informational comics that teach about the miraculous powers of Kannon. Some are drawn for children, such as the *Nakayama no Kannonsama,* privately published in 1984 by Nakayama-dera, Saikoku temple number twenty-four. With its picture on the cover of a young boy and girl standing before the temple, it is clearly an educational *manga* for children. Others are informational comics published explicitly for adults. An important example is Nagatani Kunio's *Manga Saikoku sanjûsan fudasho Kannon junrei* (Nagatini 1991), a comic sponsored by the Saikoku Sanjûsansho Fudasho Association. This association is a group officially tied to Saikoku temples directly involved in promoting the pilgrimage with YouTube videos, its Facebook page, and a website (https://saikoku33.gr.jp) devoted to that purpose.

The comic book is about an older man's pilgrimage to Saikoku. He is a middle-class salaryman who, after working for a company for thirty years, obtains two months sabbatical and a special bonus to go traveling anywhere he wants. Rather than going abroad with his wife, he decides to do the route alone, dressed in traditional pilgrim's white garb and straw hat, an old-fashioned look that shocks his family when they first see him. He confesses that he has traveled a lot in his life, but "has never once taken a trip to look deeply into his own heart" (Nagatani 1991, 11). The rest of the story has him traveling the thirty-three circuit to find himself. He is a seeker, an individual on a quest to find out who he is as a person.

What information does the *Manga Saikoku sanjûsan fudasho Kannon junrei* offer to guide him, and by extension, pilgrim readers on their quest? The initial impression one has is the comic book's overwhelming conservative character. Like its pre-modern Tokugawa period precursors, it is a typical pilgrimage guidebook. It has illustrations of sacred precincts, temple origin legends, miracle tales, and the like arranged in sequence from temple number one, Nachi-dera to temple thirty-three, Kegonji. This particular content and format have a long history, dating back to pre-modern Saikoku texts of the eighteenth and nineteenth centuries, such as the *Saikoku sanjûsansho Kannon reijôki zue*, an illustrated guidebook of the pilgrimage published by the book dealer Tsujimoto Motosada (1788–1853) in 1803.

All of this is exemplified in the comic book's retelling of a miracle story of Mitake-san Kiyomizu-dera, temple number twenty-seven. This miracle tale, told to the pilgrim by the local priest, takes off on a trip without telling anyone. His dutiful son, an exemplar of Confucian filial piety, gets extremely worried about his father's whereabouts. The young man's mother finally tells him that he had often talked about going on the Saikoku pilgrimage. "That's it," the young man exclaims, "Dad's probably headed to Kiyomizu temple." When the son arrives there, however, his father is nowhere to be seen. After he prays before the enshrined eleven-headed Kannon icon, the son miraculously finds the icon reaching out its arms to him, and clearly hears a voice say, "Go to Harima" (Figure 9.1). He decides on the spot to travel there, and at the base of Mount Mitake near the temple, ten days after his father went missing, he finally reunites with him, who was on his way to Kiyomizu by a different route, from temple twenty-nine Matsuoji. "You're here!," he joyfully cries, and his father apologizes for worrying him so. In the end, both father and son realize that it was Kannon's wonder-working power that brought them back together. The wondrous experience also taught them a

Figure 9.1 The living eleven-headed Kannon icon, enshrined at temple twenty-seven Kiyomizudera, reaching out to console his devotee. Nagatani, Kunio (1991), *Manga Saikoku sanjûsan fudasho Kannon junrei*, Sanshindô, p. 147.

valuable lesson—to vanquish one's selfish heart and transform it into a heart that unselfishly cares for others—as father and son truly do.

As David Morgan has noted, religious iconography has two important functions. Images can be didactic and informational, shaping religious identity by providing "a repository of concepts that characterized a group or tradition," and images can be devotional, providing a direct affective relationship—feelings of tenderness, sympathy, affection—to the person(s) and beings portrayed (Morgan 2005 53). Both functions are displayed here. The comic book emphasizes Kannon's real presence at Saikoku temples, teaches the bodhisattva vow of selfless compassion, and the merits to be acquired by doing the pilgrimage. But it is more than just information, the *manga* visuals also dramatically reveal direct affective relationships—between both father and son, but also Kannon reaching out compassionately to aid his devotees.

Manga and *Anime Junrei—Seichi Junrei*

A second type of pilgrimage that has gained enormous popularity today are *seichi junrei*, a startling new phenomenon in contemporary Japan. These are not tied to traditional pilgrimages like the Saikoku, Shikoku, or Ise pilgrimages. *Manga*, animated TV series, original video animation (OVA), and films produced by commercial mass-media companies create fictional worlds on screen or on the printed page. But these do not remain virtual. Sometimes their fans travel to real world locations associated with their favorite shows and products. Visiting an *anime* or a comic book locale is called a "pilgrimage to the sacred land" (*seichi junrei*). *Seichi junrei* are pilgrimages to real-life locales, which are the background settings or "stages" where the stories fans love fictionally take place. Today, these pilgrimages are a ubiquitous form of Japanese popular culture. One guidebook, for example, "covers one hundred sacred places throughout Japan from *Raki∗Suta* to *Samâuîzu*." (Doriropurojekuto, 2010). Another annual magazine published online by the Anime Tourism Association, *Japanese Anime 88 Spots* (https://animetourism88.com/ja/88AnimeSpot) offers a selected list of 88 top *seichi junrei* sites fans can visit. The number 88 refers to the famous 88 temple pilgrimage associated with Kôbô Daishi in Shikoku. The *seichi junrei* selection was made based on votes from 50,000 anime fans and discussions with local municipalities (Nagata 2017).

Seichi junrei is an important example of a global phenomenon called contents tourism. Generally, contents tourism is any form of media-induced tourism to places associated with films, literature, and the like. It is not specific to Japan, but is a part of the global tourism industry. In the West, for example, there is the online travel site One Travel's "Ultimate Harry Potter UK Pilgrimage," which asks potential customers to "[i]magine exploring the United Kingdom with Harry Potter as your focus." Mandatory sites for Harry Potter fans to visit are locations used in the films, such as King's Cross Station in London and Freshwater West Beach in Pembrokeshire, Wales, where fans have recently built a memorial to Dobby the elf-friend of Harry, who was murdered tragically by the arch-evil wizard Bellatrix Lestrange in *Harry Potter and the Deathly Hallows: Part 1* (Westmoreland Bouchard 2022; Victor 2022).

In Japan, contents tourism is frequently based on a "media-mix" of *anime, manga,* games, toys, and attendant goods dealing with the same characters and their stories, a commercial marketing synergy that took off in the 1990s. By the 2000s, when local communities become increasingly involved in the production and marketing of pop cultural materials, "geographical place and contents get linked together in a commercial partnership" making contents tourism an economically profitable enterprise attracting not only younger Japanese, but an international fan base (Okamoto 2015, 13; 19–21). Key to the development of contents tourism, like the 'Develop your old hometown' campaigns (*furusato zukuri*) in the 1970s and 1980s were supportive government policies and initiatives. Tourism scholar Yamamura Takayoshi notes that in 2005 the Ministry of Land, Infrastructure, Transport, and Tourism and two other government organizations, who coined the original Japanese term, *kontentsu tsûrizumu,* issued a report encouraging local and regional governments to use contents tourism for their economic development (Yamamura 2015, 61). In 2012, the Ministry of Economy Trade and Industry's "Cool Japan Strategy" concluded that marketing content was a vital part of Japan's economic strategy for the next decade (Seaton and Yamamura 2015, 6–7). A similar process is behind the global rise in popularity of traditional pilgrimage routes (Reader 2014). National, local, and regional governments; the travel and tourism industries; and *anime* production companies are all crucial actors for developing and marketing pilgrimages to sacred lands.

The content of these *anime* and *manga* is not about traditional pilgrimages, like the *junrei manga* discussed earlier. Rather, they are based on commercially successful stories so powerful (and marketed so adroitly) that the fictional breaks into the real world. These inspire fans to travel to real-life sites associated with their artists, their stories, and their characters, attracting fan tourists not only in Japan but globally. If a story or series catches on and becomes the rage, chances are fans will travel to the real-life places that are tied to the stories. For example, tourists flock to the small town of Sakaiminato in Tottori Prefecture, hometown of the famous ghost obsessed *manga* artist, Mizuki Shigeru, whose *GeGeGe no Kitaro* is one of the most popular comic book series of all time. Fans get there by a special "ghost train," visit the Mizuki Shigeru museum, and enjoy 150 bronze statues of Mizuki's characters, a "huge stone eyeball in the local shrine, ghost shaped manhole covers, and even eyeball street lights" (Atlas Obscura n.d.). *Seichi junrei* fan tourists to Sakaiminato discover, reexperience, and help construct the "sacred land" of Mizuki Shigeru's comics by experiencing his stories' powerful aura there (see, Greene 2016, 333–56).

A famous example of a *seichi junrei* is the hit TV series *Raki∗Suta* ("Lucky Star" 2007), which has a famous scene where the characters visit Washinomiya Shrine. Washinomiya, located in the small rural town of Kuki City in Saitama prefecture, is the oldest shrine and designated as an important cultural site in the Kanto area. It serves as the model for the *anime* simulacra in the series, Takanomiya Shrine, which is prominently featured in the opening sequence of the show. *Lucky Star* is an animated adaptation of Kagami Yoshimizu's original comedy series serialized in Kadokawa Shoten's *Comptiq* magazine since December 2003. The series inspired a CD drama in 2005, four video games between 2005 and 2009, and, key to the pilgrimage, a twenty-four-episode *anime* TV series produced by Kyoto Animation, which aired on Chiba TV from April 8 to September 16, 2007.

This *anime* is a lighthearted "slice of life" high-school comedy, a genre that is often the inspiration for *seichi junrei* in Japan. The story is about humorous moments in the daily lives of four sailor-dress clad high-school girls in their second year at high school: Izumi Konata, Hiiragi Kagami, Hiiragi Tsukasa, and Takara Miyuki. The IMDb synopsis of the series gives a good idea of the series: "having fun in school, doing homework together, cooking and eating, playing video games, watching anime. All those little things make up the daily life of the *anime* and chocolate-loving Izumi Konata and her friends. Sometimes relaxing but more than often simply funny" (https://www.imdb.com/title/tt1086236/).

It is the real life Washinomiya Shrine, which is the model for the *anime*'s Takanomiya Shrine, that becomes the goal of *Lucky Star*'s *seichi junrei.* Seeing the commercial possibilities of fan tourism, the town initiated a clever marketed contents tourism campaign promoting Washimiya (Kuki) as a fan tourist Mecca. A regional tourism promotion group, the Commerce and Industry Association of Washimiya, Sakata, and Mastumoto was charged with developing *Lucky Star* projects over the years (Yamamura 2015, 67). Local tourism promotions included selling souvenirs, steamed sweet buns with the character "sacred site pilgrimage" stamped on it at the Otori-chaya tea house (another important spot in the series), organizing a "stamp rally" at local shops serving foods associated with the characters, permitting *Lucky Star* fan drawn votive tablets to be festooned at the shrine, and, in 2008, allowing a fan-built portable shrine to participate in the local Hajisai summer night festival (67–9). The 2013 portable shrine was revamped by 120 fan volunteers. Over twelve hundred fans did cosplay for the event (Dong 2013; Okamoto 2015, 149–54). Multiple *Lucky Star* events take place during the year, sometimes as stand-alone events and sometimes merged with the annual cycle of shrine rituals.

The large number of fan attendees also tells a story, both of the success of the *Lucky Star*'s marketing campaigns and its continuing popularity. Its fans became interested in visiting the shrine through Internet fan forums where people pointed out the linkage between the *anime* and the shrine. Large numbers of fans especially visit during New Years. Before it was broadcast in 2007 about 90,000 visited the shrine annually, but in 2008, it tripled to 300,000; in 2010, 450,000; and in 2017, the ten-year anniversary of the series, it had climbed to over 470,000 (Kawashima 2017). The *Lucky Star* pilgrimage became so popular that it appeared on the Japan Travel Bureau's now defunct webpage "Pilgrimage to Sacred Places" along with other manga and *anime* pilgrimages (JTB 2011). It is interesting that this agency, typically interested in advertising the usual staid Zen temples, the imperial palace in Tokyo and the other icons of Japaneseness, highlighted "sacred sites" tied to the fantasy worlds of comics, films and TV shows, and video games. More recently, *Lucky Star* pilgrimage is listed among the Anime Tourism Association's top picks on their "*Anime Seichi* 88 spots" list (2022).

Is *Lucky Star* a good example of how popular culture can be religious? *Seichi junrei* scholar Okamoto Takeshi, for one, is dismissive: "Even though the term 'pilgrimage' has religious connotations, there is no particular link with religion." Fans may call the sites they visit "sacred lands," but, at most, all this means is "places of particular significance to *anime* fans." Okamoto would agree with pilgrimage scholar Ian Reader that *Lucky Star* is at most a "secular pilgrimage," where fans perform only "religious-like," not religious activities (Okamoto 2015, 21). But what does religious-like mean? How are religious-like beliefs and practices different from "authentic" religious beliefs and practices? Can popular culture be a place where people create, generate, and consume something we might call religious?

According to Sakaiminato scholar Barbara Greene, comics and *anime* travel show an "intersection" between orthodox pilgrimage and leisure tourism. The motivations of both are "similar if not identical." Just as the pilgrim in the *Manga Saikoku sanjûsan fudasho Kannon junrei* finds Kannon by going to the actual sites of where the bodhisattva is spiritually present, so too fans go to "the stage" of *Lucky Star* at Washimiya to visualize and reanimate the stories and characters they find so fascinating, fun, and meaningful. As Greene puts it, referencing Mizuki Shigeru tourism to Sakaiminato, "pilgrims undertake their journey in order to have a sublime experience, to connect to their spiritual core, or to transcend their ordinary lives, and to move, even briefly, into the sublime. Tourists also seek to move beyond their everyday lives" (2016, 339). What tourists do, then, is the same kind of "work" (or pleasure) pilgrims do when undertaking their journeys.

What about *Lucky Star*? Clearly, the most obvious religious link the TV show has is to the traditional Shinto shrine, Washinomiya. The opening scene of each episode has the main character, Kagami, walking out of Takanomiya's *torii* gate past a teahouse. This scene looks identical to the real Washinomiya's entrance that also has a tea house called Ôtorichaya next to it, which now is also a major tourist attraction. In the case of *Lucky Star*, the real Washinomiya (literally, Eagle Shrine) is the real locale upon which the show's fictional Takanomiya (literally, Hawk's Shrine) is based.

Using traditional sacred areas as a story setting is a typical trope in *seichi junrei* comics and *anime*. Shinto shrines, Buddhist temples, old pilgrimage routes, and folk religious sites like sacred mountains are often featured in them. Okamoto Takeshi's recent guidebook, *Manga anime de ninki no "Seichi junrei"o meguru Jinja junrei* (Shrine Pilgrimage Traveling Around Sacred Places of Popular *Anime* and *Manga*), for example, notes twenty-eight Shinto shrines associated with fan pilgrimages—just like the *Lucky Star* pilgrimage to Washinomiya. This guide offers a mix of road maps, information on lodging, special foods, and gifts to be had along the way, richly illustrated with images of the *anime* and *manga* characters in *situ*. Of course, what's sacred here are not the actual enshrined deities; the Washinomiya divinity, Amenohohi no mikoto, second child of Amaterasu, the Sun Goddess, who bestows prosperity and luck in love, is not mentioned in the story. What makes Washinomiya sacred is that *Lucky Star*'s story takes place there—it is a place featured in the show and, it occasionally a stage where funny things happen to the main characters.

Lucky Star's amusing stories are, of course, fiction. But while fictional, and neither a sacred text nor officially an institutional religion, do they still do the work of religion? Carole Cusack studies a type of new religious movements she calls "invented religions," which originate neither through divine revelation nor derive from some mysterious unknown past. Many of them, like Jediism or Matrixism, are based on box office films, clearly products of human ingenuity and imagination. Indeed, religion, whether traditional or invented, "is, to a large extent, about narrative and the success of the story." Science fiction movies, like *Star Wars* and *The Matrix*, offer meaning and values for fans greater than anything they have found in traditional religions (Cusack 2010, 4). Films like these, and arguably, *Lucky Star* are "authentic fakes," to borrow David Chidester's term. Like Coca-Cola, "the real thing," and the "church of baseball," Hollywood films and mass media ad campaigns for consumer products can become sacred for fans who find their most important meanings and values in their fictional worlds. Within ordinary leisure, entertainment, and consumer branding, fans can find "traces of transcendence, the sacred, and the ultimate in these cultural formations" (Chidester 2005, 9–10). To their eyes, these texts have authenticity—they offer something central and important for their lives.

To explore this further, let's look at an important link between *Lucky Star* and Washinomiya shrine that occurs in episode twelve of the series (Figure 9.2). In this episode, the girls meet during New Year's at Takanomiya, which is the principal background of its story. Since it is New Year's, the girls, like most Japanese, have gone to the shrine for *hatsumôde,* the first visit in the New Year. Based on this episode, many *Lucky Star* fans also see the New Year's visit to Washinomiya as a key time for their *seichi junrei* tourism. Fan blog posts (both by Japanese and foreigners) typically include their own photos of the real shrine juxtaposed with the exact scenes from episode twelve (Seichi Junrei 2013; Wawawawa 2009).

What the three girls do in episode twelve also seems typically religious in terms of traditional shrine practices. They worship before the enshrined deity and pray for good luck in the new year. They cast their fortunes to see whether they will have good or bad luck in the new year. Kagami and Tsukasa also are doing temporary work as shrine maidens by selling shrine talismans and amulets for their father, who is a shrine priest. All this is very familiar to *Lucky Star*'s Japanese viewers who customarily visit shrines like Takanomiya at New Years'.

Lucky Star reflects typical Japanese attitudes toward religion. As many Japanese religion scholars know well, Japanese often claim that they aren't very religious. So, what do they mean? They see *hatsumôde* more as a customary practice than something based on a deeply held faith and belief. Also, it is important to note worshippers' take on their shrine practices. What most do,

Figure 9.2 Mike Hattsu Anime Journeys Blog about his visit to Washinomiya Shrine on December 7, 2016 comparing *Lucky Star*'s opening scene with its real life version. Courtesy of Mike Hattsu (http://mikehattsu.blogspot.com/2016/12/lucky-star-shrine-revisit.html).

as manga scholar Jolyon Baraka Thomas describes it, is "just in case religion" and "tongue in cheek" religion. The former means doing ritual acts in the oft chance that they might work; even if they seem irrational and probably useless, they do it anyway—a pragmatic and situational approach to being religious. The latter mocks and makes fun of religion, laughing at it while doing it anyway. Not devout believers, they still have fun playing with tradition while maintaining a performative awareness of what they are doing (Thomas 2015).

Episode twelve reflects both attitudes throughout—using New Year's worship at the shrine as an opportunity for some tongue in cheek exchanges. Kagami and Tsukasa, for example, are surprised when Konata appears, full of energy even after being at the *anime* convention all day. She tells them, "January is a new beginning so I have come to build up my good fortune for the coming year." But Konata is forced to admit she really knows nothing about Shinto New Year's rites except what her father just told her. She also points out that her friends adorable shrine maiden outfits are "invigorating." This is an artful and playful turn of phrase given that Shinto New Year's rites are all about revitalizing life's creative energies. Her father's own amorous reaction to the cutely dressed young girls amusingly reflects the mood. He sure seems invigorated when he exclaims, "Female students are so good!" Later on, Konata gets upset when she finds she has received a terribly bad fortune while of course her friends get good ones. Her mood quickly changes though when she decides shrine fortune slips must be like game trading cards, if you get them all—both good and bad—maybe you can win some prizes. The light humor in this scene shows a playful, parodic "just in case" and "tongue in cheek" way of being religious. The episode makes fun of Konata's total ignorance of the meaning of New Year's. Three girls work as shrine maidens but really are in name only, doing it as part time seasonal work, and while all pray before the shrine, they also humorously make fun of it all in the process. As such, episode twelve plays an important role in reflecting but also "in shaping popular perceptions of religion" (Chidester 2005, 30).

While *Lucky Star* is transparently fake—after all it's a TV show featuring fictional *anime* characters—it "can still be doing a kind of symbolic, cultural, and religious work that is real" (Chidester 2005, 30). It can still present an alternative world that, while not authorized by any organized religion per se, is still authentic for fans. Perhaps what's "sacred" in *Lucky Star*'s fictional world differs from the usual Western substantive definition of religion as a belief in some transcendent superhuman being. Isn't what's sacred in *Lucky Star* the world fictionalized in the show, and not some divine world beyond. Moreover, in *Lucky Star*, the main theme seems to be that what's sacred is found in everyday life and personal relationships, in the everyday adventures of Konata with her school friends. Isn't what animates the show and its pilgrimage a profound joy that everyday life in this world can bring—"having fun in school, doing homework together, cooking and eating, playing video games, watching anime"? This pleasure of the text, embedded in real life and found in leisure tourism at places like Washinomiya, where one can reexperience the antics of *Lucky Star*, is a crucial motivation for *seichi junrei*. Maybe what's sacred is immanent rather than transcendent? Maybe *Lucky Star* invents new ways of fictionally visualizing sacred lands—not as "out there," but nearby in the ordinary world we inhabit?

Conclusion

Answering the questions earlier goes beyond the scope of this essay. We have to explore how *Lucky Star*'s content is received by its audience. In what ways do fans treat it as an authentic fake? David Morgan argues we make a serious mistake if we just focus on content, in this case, simply focusing on the anime's story. To go further, we need a practice-centered approach—"to know how people use images to put their worlds together and to keep them working in the face of all the challenges that beset them" (Morgan 2005, 27). Such a study seeks to understand the "sacred gaze," "the particular configuration of ideas attitudes, and customs that informs a religious act of seeing as it occurs within a given cultural and religious setting" (3). This means scrutinizing what goes on in fan's pilgrimages.

Fans play a key role in constructing, imaging, and disseminating *Lucky Star* images. What fan practices are associated with *Lucky Star*? Fans actively promote the pilgrimage's popularity as a mass-media-generated event. Fans inspire others to visit by taking their "laptop computers or mobile phones with them and provide updates and pilgrimage diaries in real time on internet notice boards, and blogs" (Okamoto 2015, 14) and by creating websites memorializing their trips on the internet, uploading pictures of their *Lucky Star* at Washinomiya. As Edgar Axelsson, a scholar in computer-mediated communication, sees it, *seichi junrei* are a form of "digital tourism" (Axelsson 2020).

While designed to offer consumer fans virtual worlds for a pleasurable temporary escape from the quotidian, commercial *anime* like *Lucky Star* have become anchored to the real material world as pilgrimage/tourist sites to reexperience the as if world depicted in the *anime*. Digital blogs by fans disseminate information similar to *junrei manga* of traditional pilgrimages. On their blogs, fans carefully juxtapose scenes from episodes with the actual sacred land they visit. Fans' visual practice on their blogs juxtaposing their own photos with scenes from the show connects *Lucky Star's* virtual world with a real sacred locale. The two coalesce in fans' imaginations while on their pilgrimages and afterward in their blogs.

Lucky Star's fans reveal the extent to which physical travel is largely an imaginative act. They are fictional in that the traveler sees what s/he expects to see, which is often what they read or see on the screen but real because they have become an imaginative way of seeing what's there in the landscape before them. This is really no different from traditional pilgrimages worldwide, where pilgrims draw explicit correspondences between *loci* they visit and the *topoi* of their sacred texts (see Smith 1987, 74–95).

Needless to say, that effort to visualize *Lucky Star* is not just digital. Fans who travel to Washinomiya also do the physical work of making the *anime* real in situ. They visit as tourists, purchase *Lucky Star* goods, take pictures, make story themed shrine palanquins, celebrate at shrine festivals, participate in new *Lucky Star* events, and leave their handmade religious paraphernalia like painted character images on votive tablets at the shrine (Figure 9.3). All these fan activities make their mark, altering the physical, cultural, and religious character of the shrine itself. They make it visible, real, and authentic for the fans who travel there.

In terms of fan ritual practices, one fruitful area of inquiry has been the study of fan-made votive tablets, and fans' own sacred gaze of their beloved "2.5-dimensional" characters on these tablets, which are festooned on Washinomiya's posts for them. As Dale Andrews has argued, characters drawn on these special votive tablets "overcome the restrictions of the two-dimensional anime and enter into a three-dimensional world where the fans themselves exist"

Figure 9.3 Votive table of Lucky Star characters by a recent New Year's pilgrim to Washinomiya. The script says, "I wish happiness in the new year for family, friends and my pet dog. 2023 is the year of the rabbit." Photograph by Mark MacWilliams.

(2014, 222, see also Nobuharu 2010a and 2010b). The prayers to the *Lucky Star*'s main characters, such as "I hope that I can enter the two-dimensional world," echo prayers to gods and bodhisattvas at pilgrimage sites over the centuries. People long to experience that real presence of sacred objects and beings in their own lives, which they find materialized as a real presence on site (see Nobuharu 2010a, 14, Sugawa-Shimada 2020, 124–39).

In closing, *seichi junrei* flip Walter Benjamin's famous notion of the aura. Benjamin believed that "[t]he earliest art works originated in the service of a ritual—first the magical, then the religious kind." The "aura" or the powerful real presence, the authenticity of an art object, he claimed, is lost if detached from ritual, which happens by making mechanically reproduced copies (Benjamin 1968, 225–6). While this *may* be true, for spiritually alive Kannon icons, whose aura is found in situ at temples on the Saikoku route, *Lucky Star* is different. As an *anime,* produced by a leisure-focused culture industry, *Lucky Star* is a fictional world realized through its mass media presence on TV and in its fan produced copies—what Braudillard calls the "hyperreal." These images did not exist originally within a ritual context. But for *Lucky Star* fans, their aura is manifested when they are reproduced in digital media, in fan consumer products, and in fan-generated ritual activities at Washinomiya. The "authentic fake" of fan votive tablets of *Lucky Star* characters is also a copy of traditional ones found at shrines like Washinomiya and at temples like those on the Saikoku route. But don't both the originals and fake copies offer the same potential for fans and pilgrims alike to experience a real presence—to have a sacred gaze of magically or religiously powerful beings—be it Kannon or Konata? Isn't a key part of their aura is because of their potential to assist fans/pilgrims in "to negotiate what it is to be a human," David Chidester's definition of how popular culture works religiously (Chidester 2005, viii). This "negotiating process," however it is defined as a form of religious work or play or both, is what fan/pilgrims do when visiting the centers they deem sacred on their pilgrimages.

References

Ambros, Barbara. (1997), "Liminal Journeys: Pilgrimages of Noblewomen in Mid-Heian Japan," *Japanese Journal of Religious Studies* 24: 301–45.

Andrews, Dale. (2014), "Genesis at the Shrine: The Votive Art of an Anime Pilgrimage," *Mechademia* 9 (2014): 217–33.

Anime Tourism Association. (2022), *Anime seichi—otozurete mitai Nihon no anime seichi 88.* Available online: https://animetourism88.com/ja/88AnimeSpot (accessed June 26, 2022).

Atlas Obscura. (n.d.), "Yokai of Mizuki Shigeru Road, Sakaiminato, Japan." Available online. https://www.atlasobscura.com/places/yokai-hunt-mizuki-shigeru-road (accessed October 27, 2022).

Axelsson, Edgar. (2020), "Digital Tourism: Building Experience for Seichi Junrei 'Anime Pilgrimage,'" Master's Thesis, Malmö University.

Benjamin, Walter. (1968), "The Work of Art in the Age of Mechanical Reproduction," in Walter Benjamin (ed.), *Illuminations*, 217–52. New York: Schocken Books.

Bowman, Glen. (1991), "Christian Ideology and the Image of the Holy Land," in John Eade and Michael J. Sallnow (eds.), *Contesting the Sacred: The Anthropology of Christian Pilgrimage*, 98–121. London: Routledge.

Cusack, Carole M. (2010), *Invented Religions: Imagination, Fiction and Faith*, Burlington, VT: Ashgate.

Chidester, David. (2005), *Authentic Fakes: Religion and American Popular Culture*, Berkeley: University of California Press.

Clark, Lynn S. (2007), "Why Study Popular Culture? Or, How to Build a Case for Your Thesis in a Religious Studies or Theology Department," in Gordon Lynch (ed.), *Between Sacred and Profane: Researching Religion and Popular Culture*, 5–20, New York: I. B. Tauris.

Dong, Bamboo. (2013), "New & Improved Lucky Star Portable Shrine Welcomed by 1,200 Cosplayers," *Anime News Network*, last modified September 6. Available online: https://www.animenewsnetwork.com/interest/2013-09-06/new-and-improved-lucky-star-portable-shrine-welcomed-by-1200-cosplayers (accessed June 26, 2022).

Doriropurojekuto. (eds.). (2010), *Anime to kommiku seichi junrei NAVI*, Tokyo: Asuka Shinsha.

Faure, Bernard. (1996), *Visions of Power: Imagining Medieval Japanese Buddhism*, Princeton, NJ: Princeton University Press.

Freedberg, David. (1989), *The Power of Images: Studies in the History and Theory of Response*, Chicago: University of Chicago Press.

Greene, Barbara. (2016), *Furusato* and Emotional Pilgrimage: *Ge Ge Ge no Kitarō* and Sakaiminato, *Japanese Journal of Religious Studies* 43: 333–56.

Hoover, Stewart. (2001), "Visual Religion in Media Culture," in David Morgan and Sally M. Promey (eds.), *The Visual Culture of American Religions*, 146–59. Berkeley: University of California Press.

Horton, Sarah. (2007), *Living Buddhist Statues in Early Medieval and Modern Japan*, New York: Palgrave Macmillan.

Hoshino, Eiki. (1986), "Aruki shûkyô to meguri shûkyô," in Yamaori Tetsuo (ed.), *Yugyô to hyôhaku*, 231–72, Tokyo: Shunjûsha.

JTB. (2011), "Pilgrimage to Sacred Places Map." Available online:. http://www.jnto.go.jp/eng/indepth/cultural/pilgrimage/ (accessed 1 October, 2011).

Kawashima, Taro. (2017), "Raki Suta hôsô jûshûnen seichi junrei ima mo daininki." *Yahoo Japan nyûsu*. Last modified August 18, 2017. Available online: https://news.yahoo.co.jp/byline/kawashimataro/20170818-00074646 (accessed June 26, 2022).

Kinsella, Sharon. (2000), *Adult Manga: Culture and Power in Contemporary Japanese Society*, London: Routledge.

MacWilliams, Mark. (ed.) (2008), *Japanese Visual Culture: Explorations in the World of Manga and Anime*, Armonk, NY: M. E. Sharpe.

Morgan, David. (2005), *The Sacred Gaze—Religious Visual Culture in Theory and Practice*, Berkeley: University of California Press.

Morgan, David. (2007), "Studying Religion and Popular Culture: Prospects, Presuppositions, Procedures," in Gordon Lynch (ed.), *Between Sacred and Profane: Researching Religion and Popular Culture*, 21–34, New York: I. B. Tauris.

Nagata, Kazuaki. (2017), "Anime Group Launches Tourism Pilgrimage Inspired by Shikoku Henro," *The Japan Times*, August 26, 2017. Available online: https://www.japantimes.co.jp/news/2017/08/26/national/anime-group-launches-tourism-pilgrimage-inspired-shikoku-henro/ (accessed April 14, 2023).

Nagatani, Kunio. (1991), *Manga Saikoku sanjûsan fudasho Kannon junrei*, Tokyo: Sanshindô.

Nobuharu, Imai. (2010a), "'Anime 'Sacred Pilgrimages': The Potential for Bridging Traditional Pilgrimage and Tourism Activities through the Behavior of Visitors to Anime 'Sacred Places'—An Analysis of 'Votive Tablets' (*ema*) at Washinomiya Shrine, Saitama Prefecture." Translated by Isaac Gagne. Kokugakuin Digital Museum. Available online: http://jmapps.ne.jp/kokugakuin/det.html?data_id=52874 (accessed August 1, 2022).

Nobuharu, Imai. (2010b), "Kontentsu ga motarasu basho kaishaku no henyô," *Kontentsu bunkashi kenkyû* 3: 69–86.

Okamoto, Ryosuke. (2015), *Pilgrimages in the Secular Age: From El Camino to Anime*, trans. by Deborah Iwabuchi and Enda Kazuko, Tokyo: JPIC.

Okamoto, Takeshi. (2014), *Manga anime de ninki no "seichi junrei"o meguru jinja junrei*, Tokyo: Kekusunarejji (xknowledge).

Okamoto, Takeshi. (2015), "Otaku Tourism and the Anime Pilgrimage Phenomenon in Japan," *Japan Forum* 27: 12–36.

Orsi, Robert. (2016), *History and Presence*, Cambridge, England: Harvard University Press.

Pye, Michael. (2015), *Japanese Buddhist Pilgrimage*, Bristol, CT: Equinox.

Reader, Ian. (2014), *Pilgrimage in the Marketplace*, New York: Routledge.

Reader, Ian. (2007), "Positively Promoting Pilgrimage: Media Representations of Pilgrimage in Japan," *Nova Religio* 10: 13–31.

Reader, Ian, and Paul Swanson. (1997), "Editors Introduction, Pilgrimage in the Japanese Religious Tradition," *Japanese Journal of Religious Studies* 24: 225–70.

Sharf, Robert and Horton Sharf. (2001) *Living Images: Japanese Buddhist Icons in Context*, Stanford CA: Stanford University Press.

Seaton, Philip, and Yamamura Takayoshi. (2015), “Japanese Popular Culture and Contents Tourism—Introduction,” *Japan Forum* 27: 1–11.

Seckel, Dietrich. (2004), *Before and Beyond the Image*, trans. by Andreas Leisinger, Zürich: Artibus Asiae.

Seichi Junrei. (2013), “RakiSuta butai tanhô.” *(Touring Lucky Star’s Stage Settings) Available online:. http://blog.livedoor.jp/seichijunrei/archives/51979645.html (accessed October 6, 2022).

Shimizu, Isao. (1996), *Manga no rekishi*, Tokyo: Kawade Shobō Shinsha.

Smith, Jonathan Z. (1987), *To Take Place: Toward Theory in Ritual*, Chicago: University of Chicago Press.

Statistica Research Department. (2022), *Manga Industry in Japan—Statistics and Facts.* Statistica. Last modified January 31, 2022. Available online: https://www.statista.com/topics/7559/manga-industry-in-japan/#topicHeader__wrapper (accessed June 26, 2022).

Steinberg, Mark. (2012), *Anime’s Media Mix: Franchising Toys and Characters in Japan*, Minneapolis, MN: University of Minnesota Press.

Sugawa-Shimada, Akiko. (2020), “Emerging ‘2.5-dimensional’ Culture: Character-oriented Cultural Practices and ‘Community of Preferences’ as a New Fandom in Japan and Beyond,” *Mechademia* 12 (Spring, 2020): 124–39.

Tezuka, Osamu. (1987–8; 2000), *Budda.* 12 Volumes, Tokyo: Ushio Shuppansha.

Tezuka, Osamu. (1992; 2020), *Hi to Tori* 12 Volumes, Tokyo: (originally Kadokawa Bunko) Asahi Shimbun Shuppan.

Thomas, Jolyon Baraka. (2012), *Drawing on Tradition: Manga, Anime and Religion in Contemporary Japan*, Honolulu: University of Hawaii Press.

Thomas, Jolyon Baraka. (2015), “Tongue in Cheek, Just in Case.” *Sacred Matters*, edited by Gary Laderman. Available online: https://sacredmattersmagazine.com/tongue-in-cheek-just-in-case/ (accessed October 21, 2022).

Turner, Victor. (1973), “The Center Out There: Pilgrim’s Goal,” *History of Religions* 12: 191–230.

Turner, Victor. (1974), “Liminal to Liminoid, in Play, Flow, and Ritual: An Essay in Comparative Symbology,” *Rice Institute Pamphlet—Rice University Studies* 60 (3), 53–92. https://hdl.handle.net/1911/63159.

Turner, Victor and Edith Turner. (1978), *Image and Pilgrimage in Christian Culture*, New York: Columbia University Press

Victor, Daniel. (2022), “Dobby’s Grave Can Stay on a Beach in Wales, but Please Stop Giving Him Socks,” *New York Times*, November 2, 2022. Available online: https://www.nytimes.com/2022/11/02/world/europe/dobby-grave-beach-wales.html?smid=url-share (accessed April 14, 2023).

Wawawawa. (2009), “*Seichi junrei wa RakiSuta jinja 4th*, Available online:http://www.nyanmilla.net/b_cat/wawawawa.htm (accessed October 6, 2022).

Westmoreland Bouchard, Jen. (2022), "The Ultimate UK Pilgrimage That True Harry Potter Fans Need to Take!," *OneTravel Going Places*. Available online: https://www.onetravel.com/going-places/ultimate-uk-pilgrimage-true-harry-potter-fans/ (accessed October 28, 2022).

Yamamura, Takayoshi. (2015), "Contents Tourism and Local Community Response: *Lucky Star* and Collaborative Anime-Induced Tourism in Washimiya," *Japan Forum* 27 (March 2015): 59–81.

10

Comics and Meaning Making: Adult Comic Book Readers on What, Why, and How They Read

Sofia Sjö

Introduction

To comprehend contemporary meaning making we need to explore how people engage with popular culture. Since the turn of the millennium, the research area of religion and popular culture has grown extensively. Though the focus has often been more on popular cultural texts than on the reception of these texts, several studies have underlined the existential potential of engagement with popular culture (Axelson 2008, 2014, 2017; Blom 2021; Lyon and Marsh 2007).

While scholars have extensively studied some forms of popular culture, such as films (Knauss 2020), other areas are still in need of research. This is the case with comic books. Not only have religious aspects of comic books seldom been explored (de Rooy 2017; Koltun-Fromm 2020), making this volume noteworthy, but generally there has also not been a lot of research conducted with a focus on comic books and meaning making. There are studies of how children (Norton 2003) and adults (Botzakis 2011) understand comics and what they mean and mean to them, about comic book fans and fandom (Orme 2016), and comic book collecting (Woo 2011), and many studies do mention how fans have received comic books. However, few studies have explored what reading, collecting, and talking about comic books can mean to people.

This chapter wishes to do something about the partial lack of explorations of comics and meaning making. The focus is on what six avid readers of comic books and graphic novels have to say about what they get out of reading comics and how their reading relates to meaning making. The participants are between thirty-seven-and sixty-three years old and live or have lived in Finland. They read different kinds of comic books and graphic novels and they have all been asked to talk about their personal engagement with comic books and graphic novels: what do they read, how do they read, why do they read, and how has their reading changed over time.

Theoretically, this project builds on the notion of lived religion and meaning making in contemporary life (McGuire 2008). The basic argument of lived religion is that we need to move beyond traditional forms of religious expressions to capture aspects of contemporary meaning making. This is thus a perspective that often incorporates a wide and functional understanding of religion—religion as meaning making. The perspective is practice focused; what is explored is what people do and find meaning in (Ammerman 2021, 15–20). One important area of exploration has been how individuals engage with popular culture (Blom 2021; Cloete 2017; Crome 2019; Winston 2009) and this study contributes to this field.

Previous Research and Frameworks

In exploring aspects of contemporary meaning making, this project relates to and builds on previous research regarding meaning making and popular culture. It engages with earlier findings and explores how well earlier models and frameworks work to capture how the participants in this project relate to comics. Below, the main conversation partners are introduced.

Meaning Making and Comic Books

The fact that comic books are important for some people is well known. Bonny Norton (2003), among others, has illustrated what children get out of reading comic books. Norton highlights a common thread in comic book reception research: finding that comic books do something useful (Dorrell, Curtis, and Rampal 1995; McGrail et al. 2018). This is not least prevalent in studies with a focus on education. Stergios Botzakis (2006, 2009, 2011) has asked the same question I have: what do adults get out of reading comic books? His findings are noteworthy, though somewhat restricted due to his goal of seeing the usefulness of comic books.

Botzakis has interviewed adult comic book readers in their twenties and early thirties about their reading and identified several reasons for reading. In his doctoral thesis (2006), Botzakis discusses five reasons and in a later article (2009), he presents the following four reasons: Reading as study; reading as appreciation and ownership; reading as friendship; and reading as search for meaning. In discussing this final reason more in-depth (2011), Botzakis has illustrated how reading comics can have moral, critical, and connective/validative dimensions. In this study, I primarily engage with the four reasons for reading that Botzakis discusses in his 2009 article and the aspects of meaning making presented in his 2011 article.

Botzakis's findings are an essential reference point for this study. However, it also highlights the need to consider the context and the participants. As is discussed in this study, there are obvious differences in the findings of this and Botzakis's study, differences related to both context and participants.

Film and Meaning Making

Botzakis's study touches on aspects of meaning making, but this is an area of research in which other forms of popular culture have been explored more. Tomas Axelson has in several projects studied film and meaning making. In his doctoral thesis (2008) he offers a detailed exploration of what is meant by meaning making; a concept that is often used without much discussion. Meaning can be understood as relating to different levels. Axelson builds on Jos van der Lans (1987), according to whom meaning making on a first level, refers to naming objects and events. On a second level, meaning is constructed in the understanding of more complex phenomena and the social setting, relating to social adaptation and commitment. On a third level, meaning is constructed in relation to one's own identity and questions such as "Who am I?" and "What is the purpose of my life?" Finally, on a fourth level, meaning is understood in a more abstract and philosophical way concerning ultimate concerns and metaphysical questions.

In later studies (2014, 2017), Axelson has further explored the meaning making process in relation to films. The focus is here on individuals' engagement with films that they have been moved by. Axelson has identified several ways in which individuals engage with films (2017, 12; 2014, 127). These dimensions of engagement open up for comparisons with other forms of popular culture. Not all of the varied dimensions are prevalent among the participants in Axelson's study, and neither are they in the material for this study. However, they indicate not only the diverse ways in which one can engage with popular culture but also possible differences depending on the form of popular culture. The most essential dimensions are introduced in the analysis part on in this chapter.

Television Fandom and Meaning Making

Several studies have illustrated that being a part of fandom is meaningful (Jenkins 2018). Minja Blom (2021) has in her doctoral thesis explored how meaning making in fandom can incorporate mythical and ritualistic aspects. Her focus is on fans of vampire television series and the material has been gathered from online discussion forums. Building on William Doty's mythography (Doty 2000), Blom first presents a mythological fandom framework. The first aspect of this framework is Metaphors: the series work as metaphors for fans and suggest something essential about life. The second aspect is Heroic Models: the series offer models for the fans that they live by, models that can both challenge and confirm prevalent norms.

In understanding fan rituals, Blom uses Johanna Sumiala's (2010) comprehension of media rituals. Blom writes about her fan ritual model:

> Fan practices function as communal fan rituals that connect people with imagined communities via the media, but also with communities formed by close friends and family. The communal aspects of rituals are central in fan rituals, but fans also use viewing practices to break free from their everyday life and find new strength. (Blom 2021, 2)

Blom encourages the reader to test her models in relation to other forms of fandom. She also highlights how concepts from the study of religion can be used in interpreting meaning making in a secular setting. In addition, her study, just as this one, looks at fan practices from the perspective of lived religion and contemporary meaning making (Blom 2021, 16). For these reasons, Blom's study is a useful conversation partner, and particularly her explorations of rituals are highlighted here.

By providing important comparisons and valuable understandings of meaning making, the studies presented earlier aid in answering the main questions of this study: what do adults get out of reading comic books and what forms of meaning making do their engagement with comic books relate to?

Methodology

In finding participants for this study, snowball sampling was used. I reached out to colleagues in academia and acquaintances in Finnish science fiction and fantasy fandom, who put me in touch with possible participants. Consequently, three of the participants are academics and five are active in some form of science fiction and/or fantasy fandom. There was thus an overlap of the academic and fandom-related participants.

All of the participants were interviewed via Zoom and the interviews took from forty-five minutes to one and a half hour. The participants were sent the interview questions in advance. The questions focused on memories of reading comic books, reading comics during different times of their lives, how they generally read comic books, what reading comic books means to them and has meant to them during their life, and fandom activities. The interviews were conducted in Swedish or Finnish.

All interviews have been transcribed and the quotes used in this study have been translated into English by the author. In analyzing the interviews, a combination of a thematic and a critical comparative analysis was used. Themes highlighted in previous studies of popular culture and meaning making were identified and these were then explored in more detail bringing forth both similarities and differences. In presenting the findings, the focus is on dominant features and on giving the participants a voice via quotes from the interviews.

Participants

Four of the participants identify as males and two as females. They all have families in the form of partners and/or children. Their families do not always share their interest in comic books, but they also generally do not seem to mind it. Several of the participants at some point used the word *nerd* to describe themselves:

> Nerd [laughs] in general.
>
> I was very nerdy as a kid as well.
>
> A kind of typical nerd.

The word *nerd* was not used in a derogatory way. Instead, the participants seemed at home as nerds and active fans of some form of popular culture.

The participants all own comic books and regularly purchase comic books, but few of them see themselves as collectors. As one participant puts it:

> It's not that I consciously collect … they [comic books and graphic novels] just accumulate, if you put it like that … I don't know if you could say that I am a comic book collector, as I buy them to read them myself.

Here is a difference in relation to the readers Botzakis (2009) interviewed. There is a clear appreciation of ownership among the participants of both studies; all the participants enjoy owning comics that are important to them. However, while some of Botzakis' participants highlighted the potential to make money of comic books (Botzakis 2009, 54–5), this is mentioned by none of the participants in this study.

All of the participants mainly read comics on paper, but online reading is also engaged with. Apart from an interest in comic books and graphic novels, the participants also have in common a general interest in reading. None of them thus only read comic books or graphic novels rather they engage with many forms of literature and many forms of popular culture. In this way they resemble Botzakis's participants for whom reading is "an intertextual activity, involving a variety of texts and a variety of media" (2009, 54). In this study though it is the participants interest in comic books and graphic novels that is the main focus.

Analysis

During the interviews the participants together mentioned over seventy different comic books, comic strips, or graphic novels, in addition to talking about publishers such as DC, Marvel, and Egmont, genres such as *mangas*, science fiction, fantasy, and westerns, and websites such as Webtoons. Despite this richness, they all had comic books and graphic novels that were more important to them, and these were the publications the interviews focused on.

For two of the participants, *Donald Duck* was a favorite that they had read since childhood and continued to read today.[1] Two had a similar relationship with *The Phantom*.[2] For one of the participants *Teenage Mutant Ninja Turtles* held a special place and for another the same was true for *Batman*. Three mentioned Neil Gaiman's *The Sandman* series and for one this was the clear favorite. Two mentioned regularly reading *mangas*.

Reading for the Stories

The participants reasons for reading were many faceted. This is something that Botzakis (2006, 2009, 2011) also clearly shows in his study. A main reason the participants in this study gave for reading comics was the stories:

> I focus on stories. I do not have a reason to collect a whole [comic book series] ... I'll buy until a storyline ends.
>
> It is not the case that I read comics only when I'm tired and do not have the energy for something else, it is the stories.
>
> It doesn't have to be very well drawn all of it or like visually appealing, it can be grotesque sometimes, that doesn't matter either as long as it has a story.

There is thus a love of reading and stories driving these participants, but this, as already highlighted, is not combined with an idea of profit as it is for the readers in Botzakis's "Reading as Appreciation and Ownership" (2009, 54–5).

Reading as a Break

A recurring topic brought up in the interviews is the contemplative side of reading comics, an aspect also central in Axelson's study, where the participants often reported viewing films to relax (2014, 2017). The participants in this study very often read to relax and to take a break from the everyday.

> It's kind of that little break. From the everyday I guess. It comes and I have done my part of whatever it may be, doing the dishes, and then I go and lie down and read.
>
> Those [*Donald Duck* pocket books] I read when I just want to zero my brain a bit. If you want to press the reset button and detach from the everyday- without having to think a lot.

Comic books and graphic novels can of course also be challenging and provide food for thought, but this does not take away from the fact that reading also can mean getting away from the everyday for a while.

Reading Rituals

This contemplative dimension of reading comics is connected to other dimensions we find in Axelson's study (2014, 2017) and also in the work of Blom (2021). Reading comic books for several participants has a ritual dimension to it, in the sense that it is something that is done in a certain way and at a certain time and "forms regularity in everyday life" (Axelson 2017, 12).

> I bought them when the work week had ended, right after work I would walk down to the store and buy a comic book and then it was kind of done, then I had a break.

> It has kind of become a routine for me. Simply at the beginning of my lunch break I read my comic strips.
>
> You shouldn't sit and be like, you should preferably be lying down when you read them, because they are relaxing. There are these routines that I have... It is the same ... if I buy a comic book at an antiquarian then you open it at a café with a coffee and a bun or a sandwich. So you enjoy it, the thing becomes a whole.

The last quote highlights another aspect that is connected to the contemplative dimension—the role of the body and the material side of comic books.

The Material and Corporeal Side of Reading

Axelson talks of a senso-motoric dimension that refers to how films generate physical responses in viewers (2017, 12), but this is not quite the point here. Rather, the readers I have interviewed highlight how reading is often related to relaxing the body by lying down or reading in bed or by combining reading with the joy of, for example, Saturday morning coffee. Or, in the case of one participant, other more or less regular and bodily aspects:

> I have a really dumb ritual and this is a bit embarrassing but I'll tell you anyways. I only read mangas on the toilet.

The material dimension of physical comic books is also specifically highlighted and related to bodily sensations by some of the participants, specifically touch and smell.

> That first time when you open it [the comic]. It's the same as when you buy a new novel. When you open it the first time, it's an, I like the feeling when the paper breaks for the first time.
>
> I like this holding it in my hand and to lie down on the sofa or the bed to read ... To be able to like open up a new comic book and like that. That is cool in itself.
>
> There is nothing that smells as good as a new comic book.

There is thus a clear corporeal-material dimension to reading comic books that refers to the bodily sensations that are both brought on by the physical object of the comic book and the rituals of relaxing the body or combining reading with consuming things you enjoy. Though the body is also a part of engaging with other forms of popular culture, reading comic books would seem to include the body and the material as a more prominent feature.

Reading as a Not-So-Social Act

Rituals are in Blom's study (2021) highlighted as something that brings people together in real or imagined communities. The fans in Blom's study feel connected both to other fans and to the characters on the TV screen (2021, 135–65). Botzakis in turn discusses reading as friendship and highlights how his readers feel a connection to the comic book characters they love (2009, 55–6). For film viewers, watching films have a social dimension; you can do it together and it stimulates conversations (Axelson 2017, 12).

The participants in this study do mention that they like talking about comic books with others; however, this is not something that comes across as an essential aspect.

> I kind of don't have a great need to discuss it.

Most do mention that it can be nice to talk about comic books, but it does of course have to be with the right people—others who have read what they have read. As the readers in this case are somewhat older, they do point out that they had more people to talk to when they were younger and also more of a need for it then.

> It was more important for me when I was younger.
>
> There is this fandom and all these others that you can be a part of and discuss but people the same age and like that, there isn't much of that.

What the participants mostly seem to wish to get out of talking about comic books are recommendations of things to read. However, this they can also get from fanzines and online reviews, so actually talking to someone is pleasant, but not that important.

Comparing the participants of this study to the ones in Botzakis's study (2009), there seems to be an age aspect here. While several of Botzakis's participants are still looking for their place in life, my participants are more settled and do not generally turn to comics for friendship or to other readers to find a social dimension. Reading is for them more of a solitary affair, but this does not make it less important to who they are.

Reading as Identity Work

Building on James Paul Gee (1996), Botzakis (2009, 52) highlights how reading can be seen as a part of identity work; what we read says something about who we are and how we see ourselves. Watching films and engaging in television fandom also tie into aspects of identity. Axelson talks of the self-reflexive dimension of watching films (2017, 12), while Blom highlights how fans can find meaningful metaphors and models in what they watch (2021, 87–114). As pointed out, the participants in this study are avid readers in general, so their identity is not captured only via comic books or graphic novels, but it is an aspect of it.

For the participant who loves Neil Gaiman's *The Sandman*-series (1988–96), the graphic novel series is something she has come back to over and over again in her life. She has also engaged with *The Sandman* in her academic career, but it is the way the series has fascinated her personally that is most essential for her.

> I found it when I was in high school, my high school boyfriend was a big fan and I started reading it then, the whole series had not come out yet, but there was something in it, probably the myths and architypes used in it. It was something that connected very deeply with me.

Though she found the series close to thirty years ago, it is still important to her and just last year she even got a tattoo inspired by the series.

The identity connected aspects of comic books and graphic novels is naturally particularly related to the comic books and graphic novels that have been especially important to the participants. One of the participants who collects *Donald Duck* reflects in the following way on why he engages with this comic book.

> There must be something in these stories, in these characters as well, okay the characters yes, Donald Duck himself. So yes, I have always kind of identified myself with him because he is this kind of normal guy for whom things do not always go that well, but who still has the energy to go on [laughs].

However, for others the aspect of identity is related to being a comic book reader in general.

> Yes, for me comic books are important, they are a part of me. I have grown up with them, they have become like a part, they have been and will always be a part of me.

Several of the participants mention that reading comic books and collecting comic books they have read as children or since they were children has a nostalgic aspect to it, in the sense that it brings them back to their past but also connects them to this past in an important way. As one participant puts it:

> It's like going back to the holy script.

In a way it allows them to accept themselves and who they are. They keep reading what they have always read because they enjoy it.

> It gives you something, it gives, it keeps you young, and childish.

Reading as Learning

By engaging with popular culture, you can of course also learn a lot. This is clear in Botzakis's study in the notion of reading for study (2009, 53–4) and it also comes through in many of the dimensions Axelson has identified regarding engaging with films, such as the problem-solving dimension, philosophical-existential dimension, political dimension, and symbolic-nomic dimension (2017, 12; 2014). The participants of this study do highlight this potential to learn via comic books as well. One participant mentions learning about the experiences of trans people via comic books:

> Because it's an unknown topic for me I like to learn more about it.

Another discusses how comic books can relate to and comment on what is going on in society.

> It is not like I read a certain comic book because it is political. I would rather say that it has a satirical link so that it touches on what is going on in society, it can read it [society].

However, for most it is not the learning aspect of reading comics that is highlighted. This again might be related to age. As one participant discusses, he learned a lot about history via comics as a kid, but now the situation is different.

> Nowadays I don't feel that I learn that much by reading *The Phantom*, it's more just something fun. Maybe not anything more special than that. But that is something nice in itself.

Reading as Visual Pleasure

A final dimension that needs to be highlighted is the aesthetic dimension. Films offer viewers audiovisual pleasures (Axelson 2017, 12). For readers of comic books, the audio part is missing, but the visual aspect is highlighted by all the readers I talked to for this study. Yes, it is the stories that are important, but there is no denying the important role of the visual—the pictures and art works—as well.

> If they can't draw according to my brain, according to my taste, then I don't buy it. No matter how good the story is, if it isn't well drawn you cannot read it.
>
> It is important, more than you might think. When I think about the web-series I read … I've gone through a whole lot of series before I have found the ones I have stayed with, it's like if the art, the drawings, the visual, if it doesn't please me, then I easily leave it.

> I like well-drawn [comic books], the kind that create a certain mystique.

Even the one participant who says she is not a visual person still, to her own surprise, keeps getting back to the visual and how beautiful some of the comic books she loves are:

> It is very realistic and absolutely shockingly beautiful.

The participants in this study thus discuss many reasons for engaging with comic books. We see similarities with the ways in which fans engage with other forms of popular culture, but also differences. Reading comic books is thus obviously meaningful. But how does reading comic books more precisely relate to aspects of meaning making?

Reading as Meaning Making

Going back to Van der Lans's levels of meaning making (1987), the interviews for this study highlight how comic books can be a noteworthy aspect of who you are or who you see yourself as. The participants are comic book readers, they are aware that reading comic books is not that typical for their age group, but this does not matter. They read for all the different reasons highlighted earlier. Comic books do give insights into the world as well—Van der Lans's second level—and can no doubt also highlight thoughts related to ultimate concerns - Van der Lans's fourth level - but these are not very central aspect brought up by the participants in this study.

Regarding meaning as it is discussed by Botzakis (2011)—meaning as something with moral, critical, and connective/validative dimensions—we can also recognize these in the material of this study. One reader of *Donald Duck* likes the moral dimension in the comic book:

> In the heart these stories, they are like family stories in a way, you stick together and help each other and, in that way, they have these positive values that I think are good.

Another reader highlights how some comic books inspired critical reflections about society when he and his friends were in their teens:

> You debated. It was fun. And we were this generation in senior high that said we get this kind of humor. In contrast to the grown up's society.

The readers interviewed in this study also clearly recognize themselves in comic books and graphic novels and find validation.

> Yes [laughs], if I put it like this, in *Asterix* I have always identified with the druid Miraculix a bit . . He's a real nerd and no one really listens to him. And then he is a bit of a know-it-all … That feels right.

Still these are not the main meaning making features that reading comic books has for the participants in this study. Rather, this study highlights the ritual dimension that engaging with popular culture can provide. This is, as mentioned, a dimension that for Blom (2021, 135–65) primarily brings the participants in connection with others. For the participants in this study, it has a lot more to do with taking a break from the everyday, awarding yourself, and recharging by relaxing your body and enjoying something to eat. These are perhaps not aspects that are traditionally connected to concepts such as meaning making and ritual, but there is no doubt that this makes comic books meaningful for the participant of this study. And it is a feature of comic books that can perhaps be recommended for others as well. As one participant puts it:

> Actually, if you would ask someone, it would suite everyone … It is what it's for [the comic book]. That break. In that way it suits everyone. It's just that everyone doesn't enjoy reading comic books.

Conclusion

This study has explored what adult readers of comic books and graphic novels get out of reading and compared the types of engagement and meaning making aspects brought up by the participants with the findings of previous studies of popular culture and meaning making. There are several reasons for why one can enjoy reading comic books and graphic novels. For the participants in this study, the stories are essential, but reading also provides a break from the everyday and a ritual framework that highlights the material and bodily aspects of reading. Reading also connects to identity work and how the readers see themselves.

In line with, among others, Blom's study (2021), the meaning processes involved in reading comic books and graphic novels can well be related to the study of lived religion. The participants in this study do not relate to a great extent to existential questions such as why we live or die, the nature of existence or whether there is a god (Axelson 2008, 38), but their thoughts on why and how they read does underscore how meaning making is related to lived experiences;

what we do and what gives us pleasure, peace, or the energy to live our lives to the best of our abilities are important aspect of contemporary meaning making and lived religion.

The study highlights many similarities with how people engage with other forms of popular culture, but also differences that point to the need to explore varied kinds of popular culture and varied participants. The participants in this study express some similar ideas as the young adults Botzakis interviewed (2006, 2009, 2011), but also differences that relate both to the participants age and the contexts they are a part of. Studies of popular culture do tend to focus on young people. This study underlines that popular culture can be meaningful for all, independent of age.

There are limitations to this study. The group of participants is small and doing the interviews via Zoom was not ideal, though it did make it possible to carry out this project during a pandemic. However, no doubt sitting down with the participants and discussing their favorite comic books and graphic novels face-to-face would have brought more depths to the interviews. Still, the material does provide noteworthy perspectives and hopefully this chapter can inspire more studies of this kind.

Notes

1. Toivanen (2001) has discussed the popularity of the *Donald Duck* comic book in the Nordic countries and particularly Finland. In comparison to the United States, *Donald Duck* has for long been a Nordic favorite and in Finland not only among children but also among older readers.
2. As with *Donald Duck*, *The Phantom* has had a much greater success in the Nordic countries, particularly Sweden, than in the United States, the country of its origin (Aman 2018). The two participants who mention reading *The Phantom* both read it in Swedish.

References

Aman, R. (2018), “When the Phantom Became an Anticolonialist: Socialist Ideology, Swedish Exceptionalism, and the Embodiment of Foreign Policy,” *Journal of Graphic Novels and Comics* 9 (4): 391–408.

Ammerman, N. T. (2021), *Studying Lived Religion: Contexts and Practices*, New York: New York University Press.

Axelson, T. (2008), *Film och mening: En receptionsstudie om spelfilm, filmpublik och existentiella frågor*, Psychologia et sociologia religionum: 21, Uppsala: Acta Universitatis Upsaliensis.

Axelson, T. (2014), *Förtätade filmögonblick: Den rörliga bildens förmåga att beröra*, Stockholm: Liber.

Axelson, T. (2017), 'Movies and the Enchanted Mind: Emotional Comprehension and Spiritual Meaning Making among Young Adults in Contemporary Sweden," *Young—Nordic Journal of Youth Research* 25 (1): 8–25.

Blom, M. (2021), *Fanius muutti elämäni: myytit ja yhteisölliset fanirituaalit televisiosarjojen Buffy vampyyrintappaja, True Blood ja Vampyyripäiväkirjat faniudessa*, Doctoral Dissertation, University of Helsinki.

Botzakis, S. (2006), *Reading when They Don't Have to: Insights from Adult Comic Book Readers*, Doctoral Dissertation, University of Georgia. Available online: https://getd.libs.uga.edu/pdfs/botzakis_stergios_g_200608_phd.pdf (accessed April 13, 2023).

Botzakis, S. (2009), "Adult Fans of Comic Books: What They Get Out of Reading," *Journal of Adolescent & Adult Literacy* 53 (1): 50–9, doi: 10.1598/JAAL.53.1.5.

Botzakis, S. (2011), "To Be a Part of the Dialogue: American Adults Reading Comic Books," *Journal of Graphic Novels and Comics* 2 (2): 113–23, doi: 10.1080/21504857.2011.631023.

Cloete, A. L. (2017). "Film as Medium for Meaning Making: A Practical Theological Reflection," *HTS Teologiese Studies/Theological Studies* 73 (4): 1–6. https://doi.org/10.4102/hts.v73i4.4753.

Crome, A. (2019), "Cosplay in the Pulpit and Ponies at Prayer: Christian Faith and Lived Religion in Wider Fan Culture," *Culture and Religion* 20 (2): 129–50.

De Rooy, R. (2017), "Divine Comics," *European Comic Art* 10 (1): 94–109. doi: 10.3167/eca.2017.100108

Dorrell, L. D., Curtis, D. B., and Rampal, K. R. (1995), "Book-Worms Without Books? Students Reading Comic Books in the School House," *Journal of Popular Culture* 29 (2): 223–34.

Doty, W. G. (2000), *Mythography: The Study of Myths and Rituals*, 2nd ed., Tuscaloosa: University of Alabama Press.

Gee, J. P. (1996), *Social Linguistics and Literacies: Ideology in Discourses*, 2nd ed., Philadelphia: Routledge Falmer.

Jenkins, H. (2018), "Fandom, Negotiation, and Participatory Culture," in P. Booth (ed.), *A Companion to Media Fandom and Fan Studies*, 13–26, Hoboken: Wiley Blackwell.

Knauss, S. (2020), "Religion and Film: Representation, Experience, Meaning," *Theology* 4 (1): 1–102.

Koltun-Fromm, K. (2020), *Drawing on Religion: Reading and the Moral Imagination in Comics & Graphic Novels*, Pennsylvania: Pennsylvania State University Press.

Lyon, C. H., and Marsh, C. (2007), "Film's Role in Contemporary Meaning Making," in S. Knauss and A. D. Ornella (eds.), *Reconfigurations: Interdisciplinary Perspectives on Religion in a Post-Secular Society*, 113–26, Vienna: Lit.

McGrail, E., Rieger, A., Doepker, G. M., and McGeorge, S. (2018), "Pre-Service Teachers' Perspectives on How the Use of TOON Comic Books during Guided Reading Influenced Learning by Struggling Readers," *SANE Journal: Sequential Art Narrative in Education* 2 (3): 1–28. https://digitalcommons.unl.edu/sane/vol2/iss3/1

McGuire, M. B. (2008), *Lived Religion: Faith and Practice in Everyday Life*, Oxford: Oxford University Press.

Norton, B. (2003), "The Motivating Power of Comic Books: Insights from Archie Comic Readers," *Reading Teacher* 5 (2): 140–7.

Orme, S. (2016), "Femininity and Fandom: The Dual-Stigmatisation of Female Comic Book Fans," *Journal of Graphic Novels and Comics* 7 (4): 403–16, doi: 10.1080/21504857.2016.1219958.

Sumiala, J. (2010), *Median rituaalit: johdatusta media-antropologiaan*, Tampere: Vastapaino.

Toivanen, P. (2001), *En serietidning på fyra språk*. Acta Wasaensia No. 88, Vaasa: University of Vaasa.

Van der Lans, J. (1987), "Meaning Giving Behavior. A Neglected but Urgent Research-Task for the Psychology of Religion," in O. Wikström (ed.), *Religionspsykologi nu: Nordiskt religionspsykologiskt symposium, Sigtuna, 13–14 Jan 1987. Religionspsykologiska skrifter 2*, 3–10, Uppsala: Uppsala universitet.

Winston, D. (2009), "Introduction," in D. Winston (ed.), *Small Screen, Big Picture: Television and Lived Religion*, 1–14, Baylor: Baylor University Press.

Woo, B. (2011), "The Android's Dungeon: Comic-Bookstores, Cultural Spaces, and the Social Practices Of Audiences," *Journal of Graphic Novels and Comics* 2 (2): 125–36, doi: 10.1080/21504857.2011.602699.

Part 4

Learning from Comics

11

The Magic of the Multiverse: Easter Eggs, Superhuman Beings, and Metamodernism in Marvel's Story Worlds

Sissel Undheim

Popular culture provides a fertile ground for a host of narratives, symbols, and characters known from history of religions. Dispersed and consumed on a multitude of new emerging media platforms, these narratives, symbols, and characters become ingredients in artistic processes of imagination and adaptation where religion can be played with in a variety of ways. In these processes of production, consumption, and engagement, there are high stakes, but they also create new room for exploring and combining humor and playfulness with awe and "great mystery" in ways that resonate with, but also contribute to contemporary cultural production of religion. Comics has been a very prolific medium in these processes (e.g., Chireau 2019; Clements and Gauvain 2014; Lewis 2014; Salazar 2020; Thomas 2012). In this chapter, I will look at three recent TV series from the Marvel Cinematic Universe (MCU). Like other MCU products, these series engage in complex intertextual story worlds based on the Marvel Comics where the protagonists originated. How do various narrative and literary devices, such as "Easter eggs," multiverses, and contemporary cultural tendencies categorized under the term *metamodernism*, provide means for engagement and social bonds that are reminiscent of contemporary religious engagement? I am particularly interested in how these fictive story worlds open for larger narratives that explore non-empirical "truths" in a post-postmodern universe.

Marvel and Awe in the Cinematic Universe

While the world was in pandemic lockdown, Disney+ and Marvel provided the perfect distraction and entertainment in peoples' own living rooms through their new format: the TV series. Launching what is called the "Fourth Phase" of MCU—the stories that picks up after the closure of one epic cycle with *Avengers: Endgame*—*WandaVision*, *Loki*, and *Moon Knight* marked a new era with a new stage and a new mode of storytelling in the expansive narrative. In addition to the TV-series format available for streaming, the story world of the Fourth Phase is simultaneously developed in comics and in movies for the big screen, such as in *Spiderman—No Way Home* (2022), *Dr Strange and the Multiverse of Madness* (2022), and *Thor, Love and Thunder* (2022).

In the following, I have chosen to focus on three of the first Disney-Marvel TV-series, *WandaVision*, *Loki*, and *Moon Knight*, emphasizing the complex intertextuality and creative productivity that the transmedia story world of Marvel provides and that these three narratives tie into on many different levels.

One of the perhaps most striking aspects of these three TV series (at least for scholars of religion) is how so many of MCU's main characters fit the category "superhuman agents" (Gilhus 2016). In *Moon Knight*, the protagonist is an avatar of the ancient Egyptian God Khonshu,[1] while Loki is the Norse god of mischief himself. Wanda Maximoff, the protagonist of *WandaVision*, is in the course of the nine-episode long series revealed to be a witch—the Scarlet Witch, known from Marvel's comics. Her powers are no longer explained to be merely the result of scientific experiments, as in her previous MCU appearances, but are now overtly caused by magic (Dagsland 2022).

All three protagonists are popular characters in Marvel's comics series, and like most other products from MCU, the TV-series work in an intertextual yet independent relationship with the comic books. The levels of realities, characters, and cross-references are almost overwhelming. The combination of comedy, puns, and apocalyptic as well as relational drama take viewers on emotional roller coasters, with new spectacular reveals at almost every turn. One of the things that unites the three examples is the way that these adaptations for a new media format not merely build on and refer to the original comic books characters, but creatively and playfully adapt in sometimes quite innovative ways.

WandaVision

WandaVision was the first of the MCUs and Disney+ move from big screen movies to TV-series format, and much anticipation had been built up among fans prior to its release. The first episode was released on January 15, 2021, and then a new episode was released once a week regularly for nine weeks in total, until March 5. Episode 1 begins as an unmistakably recognizable black-and-white episode of a 50s show, like *I love Lucy,* or *Dick van Dyke*, heavily nodding at the rich self-referentiality of contemporary pop culture. According to Jane Barnette:

> To call *WandaVision* "meta" underestimates the levels of self-conscious reflexivity that abound within the larger Marvel Cinematic Universe (MCU), where referentiality and citation form the very foundation upon which stories are told. Not only do the films pick up on storylines from one another, but they exist within a universe—a multiverse—that includes decades of comic-book iterations of these characters and their backstories (and retcons). (Barnette 2022, 41)

While the format of following episodes was modelled after popular TV-series formats from the subsequent decades, something was still clearly off in Wanda's world. Not before episode four, however, does the "outside world" break into the television-like life of small-town Westview, or the "Hex," which turns out to be Wanda's making. Though not excluding viewers unfamiliar with the comics, small hints along the way rewarded the fan community as bits and pieces were folded into an increasingly more coherent explanation of all the weird things that apparently rubbed against the otherwise so harmonious atmosphere in Wanda's Westview. Looking at representations of witches in the Scarlet Witch comics from the 1960s and onward, alongside other famous witches from popular culture, Sophie Dagsland has demonstrated how traditional as well as neo-pagan movements and Wicca have influenced the representations of Wanda and Agatha in the original comics, and then have been further elaborated in the TV series (Dagsland 2022).[2] Powerful, subversive, and, in the comics, difficult to assign to either side of a divide between good and evil, MCUs Wanda from *WandaVision* (and later *Dr. Strange: Multiverse of Madness* 2022) is portrayed as a highly complex woman. No prototypical villain, her emotional pain and humanity is portrayed in ways to make the audience empathize and even side with her. Unaware of her own immense magical powers, it is her grief and pain that cause her to bewitch the town and everyone in it, in order to recreate her best childhood memories. The viewers learn that in her war-ridden childhood, American TV series provided a calming comfort because her parents put them on to deflect from the loud noise of bombs and fighting. The TV-series format is thus not a funny format gimmick but explained as a result of Wanda's trauma and emotional pain.

Barnette points out how the late-nineteenth-century discourse linked hysteria to witchcraft: "Both seen as afflictions affecting primarily women, witchy and hysterical behaviors have noticeable overlaps as they are described in scientific studies. Even for those unfamiliar with this scholarship, however, the extreme physicality of the [scene where Wanda creates the Hex] communicates the emotional intensity of conjuring the Hex and especially the Vision for Wanda" (Barnette 2022, 50).

When Agatha (the "evil witch") and Wanda are confronted in the last episode, Wanda points out one important distinction that somehow redeems her: "You see, the difference between you and me, is that you did this on purpose" (S1, E9).

Even the fake commercials that are inserted into the "fake" TV shows that still structure the "fake" world of Wanda and her family, convey this post-ironic, emotional trauma.

> Voiceover: Feeling depressed? Like the world goes on without you? Do you just want to be left alone? Ask your doctor about Nexus. A unique anti-depressant that works to anchor you back to your reality. Or the reality of your choice.
>
> Side effects include feeling your feelings, confronting your truths, seizing your destiny, and possibly more depression. You should not take Nexus unless your doctor has cleared you to move on with your life. Nexus. Because the world doesn't revolve around you. Or does it? (*WandaVision* S1E7, 14.10–50)

The commercial adds yet another level to the made-up world of Wanda's Westview, blending the magic and the "real" by adding even more layers and complexity to Wanda's emotional and cognitive confusion.

In many ways, Marvel's Wanda echoes discourses about contemporary witches and their focus on power and magic, but also on the role of emotion, suffering, and healing as central to the often immense and dangerous powers witches can (or attempt to) control. Emotions, be them love, loss, pain, or jealousy, are often depicted as cause, as what unleashes the magical powers, and they can be too powerful even for the witch herself to control. The tension between the good witch/bad witch stereotypes plays out in the final battle between Wanda and Agatha Harkness, in the last episode of the season. Even then, though, the question of Wanda's intentions and control of her powers remain unsettled in the final scene. In the apocalyptic battle between Agatha and Wanda, exposing the frail postmodern, constructed. and hyperreal ontology of Wanda's Hex, and in extension the reality of everything else, only her emotions—her love, pain, and grief—can be trusted as real.

Loki

While the Scarlet Witch taps into numerous aspects of modern paganism and New Age spirituality, as well as traditional conceptualizations of "evil witches" and dark magic, Loki at first sight appears to be fully at home in Norse religion—an apparently more distant tradition than that of contemporary witches. Ancient Norse religion and culture have in recent years provided a treasure trove for pop cultural production. Marvel's Thor, of which Loki has been a central character to now become protagonist of his own show, is perhaps the most well known, yet by no means the only one (cf. Skjoldli 2019).

Unlike many other games and TV series that aim for a somewhat historical authenticity in their portrayal of the Vikings and the gods, Marvel's Asgard is placed in the Sci-Fi universe as a planet among countless others. Though the gods have retained many of their characteristics known from Norse mythology, they interact with people and other heroes and villains in narratives set in our contemporary world.

The plot of *Loki* is no less complicated than previous MCU narratives. Diverging timelines create a bewildering number of deviants that the Time Variance Authority (TVA) tries to regulate, sometimes quite violently. Loki is arrested "for crimes against the sacred timeline" and forced to collaborate with the TVA to hunt down variants of himself who cause trouble on diverging timelines. Loki's role as the god of mischief plays on some of the same ambivalence that Wanda Maximoff's witch identity did in *WandaVision*. The constant doubt about whether he is the villain or the hero—whether he is evil or eventually on "the good side"—takes an even larger role in this narrative. He simply cannot be trusted, and this character trait has already been well established in the comics and in previous MCU productions. The writers thus have an even richer intertextuality, from the story world of Marvel as well as that of Norse mythology, to play on.[3] The Loki trapped by the TVA seem, however unlikely, to develop and even express genuine heartfelt emotions for the other characters, Sylvie and Mobius. They are however not easy to convince. In a key scene at the end of time (and their quest), with He who remains, there is the following exchange:

Sylvie: I don't believe you!
Loki: Sylvie. The Universe is in the balance. Everything we know to be true. Everything …

…

Sylvie: What was I thinking, trusting you. Has this whole thing been a con?
Loki: Really? That's what you think of me … After all this time. Sure. Why not. Evil Loki's master plan comes together. Well, you never trusted me, did you. What was the point? Can't you see? This is bigger than our experience.
Sylvie: Why aren't we seeing this the same way?
Loki: Because you can't trust … And I can't be trusted.
Sylvie: Then I guess we're in a pickle. (S1 E6)

Trusting and giving in to emotions comes with a high risk for both Loki and Sylvie, but only Loki is the one who choses trust. Mobius, whose friendship with Loki develops throughout the episodes, becomes a trustworthy anchor to Loki. When the season comes to an end, Loki realizes that he is back in another timeline where Mobius does not know even him.

Kim Bell commented on the finale of the season:

> What, after all, does it mean to "survive," if in the memory of the people for whom you care most, you never even actually existed? What's more, when Mobius casually asks, "Who are you?," Loki is left with the realization that, having lost the one person by whom he felt truly seen, Loki is the only one who might be able to answer that question. It's the kind of universally harrowing realization that makes a viewer feel not just for the god, but also for anyone who's ever struggled to come to terms with who they are, and what exactly their purpose and place is in this world—in other words, just about everyone. (Bell 2021)

In the end, despite being a god, it is Loki's humanity and his emotions that ground him and win the viewers over. Despite the lies, betrayal, and selfishness—not to mention the apocalyptic chaos that follows him everywhere—the affective connection that is created between Loki and the viewers becomes, as Bell points out, real on an emotional level, as his pain, compassion, and love conveyed on the screen evoke recognition and empathy. The very fact that we don't know—that the audience, as well as Loki himself, know he can't be trusted, makes the stakes of engagement in how he and the story develops next even higher. As a classic cliffhanger ended the season, Marvel left the audience wanting to know more.

Moon Knight

In the first episode of season 1 that premiered on Disney+ on March 30, 2022, the viewers were introduced to museum shop clerk Steven Grant, a shy and seemingly goodhearted man. As in *WandaVision*, however, there are hints that complicates the identification of the protagonist as either good or bad in this narrative, too. Later episodes reveal that Steven has a dissociative identity disorder (DID). His other personality, Marc Spector, has a much more complicated and violent life as the *Moon Knight*, the avatar of the Egyptian moon god Khonshu. In the Comic series (1974), Spector is also called "The fist of Khonsu," hinting to a kind of violence that would seem incompatible with Steven's personality. Other Egyptian gods are included in the MCU narrative, most importantly Ammit and Tawaret, but gods like Isis, Osiris, and other central deities appear as well.[4] Steven/Marc's antagonist is Arthur Harrow, a former avatar of Khonshu, now a devout disciple of Ammit. Harrow is a complex villain portrayed as a religious sect leader obsessed with a twisted idea of divine justice. Ethan Hawke, the actor who portrays Harrow, has in interviews revealed that among his inspirations for the role was David Koresh, leader of the religious group Branch Davidians, who after long conflict was killed under siege by Texas police: "I liked the idea of playing a cult leader, you know, I always find those kinds of figures fascinating .... Someone who thinks of themselves as a spiritual guru, someone who considers themselves enlightened beyond the rest of humanity" (Lang 2022).

In addition to the unstable epistemology caused by the shifting perspectives of Marc/Steven's DID, there are also shifts between different levels of realities. The last episode of the season, episode 6, is called "Gods and monsters." Here, the conflict between Khonshu and Ammit and their avatars Steven/Mark and Harrow culminates in spectacular battle scenes in Kairo city and on the slopes of the great pyramids of Giza. Securing victory, Marc/Steven refuses to kill Harrow, as Khonshu demands.

Returned in a flash to the psychiatric ward, Steven and Marc alternate in a dialogue with Harrow as head doctor (a reality level we have encountered also in earlier episodes):

Steven: So this is what reality looks like.
Harrow: The imagination is very real. This chair, desk, the light were all first created in the imagination.
Steven: But do you believe that Khonshu and Ammit are real?
Harrow: Do I? No.
Marc: What if we disagree, Doc?
Harrow: Marc…
Marc: What if we believe something different?
Harrow: Then our work here continues.
Steven: For how long?
Harrow: For how long is a piece of string?

[We see blood-stained footprints as Harrow walks to his chair, picking up on the opening scene of the series, where he filled the soles of his sandals with broken glass before he stepped into them, thus making two of the different levels of "reality" align: the one where Harrow is the disciple of Ammit and the one where he's the doctor in charge of the psychiatric ward.]

Marc: Hey, you see that, don't you?
Steven: Oh yeah. I see it. I see it.
Harrow: Why am I bleeding?
Steven: Yeah, I don't – don't think you know as much as you think you do
Marc: And while it is tempting to accept our diagnosis, Doc.
Steven: We'd rather go save the world. Laters gators. (*Moon Knight* S1E6. 33.44–35–10)

The scene fades and Steven wakes up in his own bed in his own apartment, where the first episode started, only this time he knows about Marc. The same music, Engelbert Humperdinck singing "Everyday I wake up" in the song *A Man Without Love* intensifies the repetitiveness of Steven's reality, and yet something fundamental has evidently changed.

The layers of different realities that we have encountered in *WandaVision* and *Loki* are even darker and more destabilized in *Moon Knight* because they so explicitly may or may not be a result of Marc's dissociative identity disorder, caused, as the viewers have learned, by a terrible childhood trauma. Similarly, Wanda's pain and grief stem from the traumatic loss of her parents as a child, and then her brother and Vison in adulthood, and the realization that instead of the future she and Vison had planned together, she only has loneliness left.[5]

Even Loki's mischievous personality is partially explained in terms of guilt and childhood trauma. These complicated heroes/villains thus become recipients of the audiences' sympathy as they emotionally invest and engage with these traumas that are also the cause of flawed, and even immoral, behavior.

Destabilizing the set narrative of heroes and villains, neither *The Scarlet Witch*, nor *Loki* or *Moon Knight* will settle as either good or bad characters. Their appeal is rather enhanced by the fact that the audience never quite knows where they stand, or what their next move will be. This is also what encourages the audience to engage, both online and on fan forums, where fans present and discuss their theories while they wait for the next episode.

Hunting Easter Eggs

The addition of TV series to the Marvel universe, where new story lines are drawn up and characters further developed, further emphasizes what Sarah Iles Johnston calls "serial narratology." She stresses the importance of "episodes" in mythological narratives: "audience members continue to think about the story in between installments" (2015, 202). This, according to Johnston, allows for the audience to get to know the characters better, and to engage and invest more in their fates. Further, such episodic narration, Johnston points out, allow for longer and more complex story arcs.

This is seen in another favorite feature on Marvel (as well as the *Star Wars* Universe and a number of other big franchise pop cultural products), namely crossovers. Crossovers occur when a character who is familiar from one context appears in another, such as when Iron Man suddenly appears in a Thor movie, or Bruce Banner and Captain Marvel enters a scene in *Shang Chi and the Legend of the Ten Rings* (cf. Johnston 2018, 139–40). According to Johnston:

> Crossovers may also reward audience with a sense of having special knowledge, which makes them feel complicit with the narrator and thus further encourages them to buy into the narrative—somewhat like the "Easter Eggs" that contemporary viewers spot in movies and television show. (Johnston 2018, 142)

The audience thus become actively engaged in the story as they are invited to interpret the clues and fill holes in the narrative. Crossovers in Marvel thus not only appear when a character from one narrative arc enters another but also across media, from comics to the cinematic universe (and back). Johnston further explains:

> Crossovers, in sum, can do a number of things very efficiently: establish the existential, ethical, and operational rules of a new story; lend it credibility and authority by their mere presence; and establish a particular climate or mood by gesturing towards other stories." (Johnston 2018, 142)

We are now in the world of hyperserials (Johnston 2018, 134–40), endless narratives that intersect and interweave, which also allow for the introduction of new characters and plots. For Marvel, this is of course very profitable business, but these complex narratives also play with ontologies and epistemologies that we recognize from contemporary religion.

Dictionary.com defines Easter eggs (Movies, television) as "a hidden message, as a cryptic reference, iconic image, or inside joke, that fans are intended to discover in a television show or movie." They presuppose and play on common knowledge, most often about characters and previous stories leading up to the one in question. As such, the comics play an important role for everyone hunting Easter eggs in MCU. Easter eggs originated in video games in the 1980s, but have by now become almost mandatory features in any big production. They are thus puns, jokes, and messages that are intentionally hidden for audience to spot or even actively look for.[6]

As *WandaVision*, *Loki*, and *Moon Knight* so clearly exemplify, narratives and characters are weaved together, picked up again and elaborated in an endless weave of self-referencing, rewarding those who have done their "research" or have invested in the larger mythology, and leave room for engagement and speculation. The comic books are perhaps the richest source for such Easter eggs (Dagsland 2022). Fans turn to them to look for "prefigurations" and hints that can help resolve some of the mysteries that are woven into the narratives to keep the audience hooked. The hunt for, and online discussions interpreting these Easter eggs, further engage and create communities where fans can present their exegeses and develop them with peers who are equally engaged. As several scholars have pointed out, these fan communities can have many traits that are similar to religious communities, and sometimes they may overlap (cf. Anker 2017; Davidsen 2016a). In her study of so-called Otherkin, Danielle Kirby pointed out that active extension of narrative is a shared feature: "Such narratives may involve continuing narrative for favorite characters, new characters continuing within a familiar secondary world, or perhaps mash up approaches to texts where multiple separate narrative worlds are combined" (2013, 119–20).

To sum up, narratives, and particularly narratives that traverse modes and media, allow for ubiquitous hidden clues and "treasures" that are meant to be discovered by the audience, as a means of engaging and making the audience invest in the narrative (or episodic instalment). These stories and characters are again weaved into even larger and more complex narratives. The comics play an important part here, not only as providers of intertextuality and Easter eggs, but as some kind of flexible developing canon against which new narratives relate, whether it is as extensions, developments, or contradictions, contrasts, and rewritings. The richer the narrative becomes, with characters, symbols, and storylines, the more material there is to play with for writers, directors, and producers.

Multiverse

Interviewing spiritual seekers in Sedona, Arizona, in her recent book, Susannah Crockford noted how notions of multiverse were part of the worldviews of many of her interlocutors. According to them, they had access to portals that allowed them to transcend realms and universes, not unlike Dr Strange and several other pop cultural story worlds from companies like, for instance, Marvel, Lego, and Disney.[7]

Crockford notes how the idea of multiple universes, or multiverse, seems to correspond to current scientific interest in quantum physics, not unlike how Big Bang theories correspond to (or respond to) theological concepts of creation *ex nihilo* (2021, 79):

> God is no longer required to create the Universe, God *is* the universe. Peter's innovation was to describe the individual within this self-contained oneness as a simulation, analogous to a computer program or video game, a way of having different experiences. Portals were his way through from this universe to other universes in the infinite multiverse. (Crockford 2021, 79)

There appears then to be a connection between the scientific of pseudo-scientific theories about multiverses and the fictional fascination for the multiverse in comic superheroes' transmedia narratives.

As Danielle Kirby explains, the notion of the multiverse, referring to the coexistence of seemingly endless parallel realties, has been popularized since the 1960s. What she points out that may be of particular interest here, "is the way in which the idea of the multiverse opens up the potential for massive intertextuality, and to a degree paves the way for a macro structure that interweaves disparate worlds without damaging the integrity of each individual constructed reality" (Kirby 2013, 116; cf. Johnston 2018). The multiverse idea has opened up to thought experiments that seem to appeal to a metamodern cultural sentiment, precisely because it exposes the fragile postmodern reality, subject to so many deconstructions that it constantly falls apart. The idea of a multiverse where reality hinges on emotions and belief, thus appears to be the perfect setting to explore the metamodern as a contemporary cultural trend. (Cardenas 2021; Dember 2022; Undheim 2019).

Metamodernism, Emotions, and Realities

These almost exhausting shifts between different ontological levels in the *WandaVision*, *Loki*, and *Moon Knight* narratives, and the role of human emotions in grasping for "the real" in all these unstable realities may echo some aspects of the post-postmodern sentiment described by Timotheus Vermeulen and Robin van den Akker as "metamodernism" and developed in religious studies by Linda Ceriello (2018a, 2018b; Undheim 2019). Metamodernism in this sense is a term meant to describe a yearning for modernity's sincerity and the sublime, one that is unattainable due to postmodern ontologies and the impossibility of "undoing" postmodernism. This leaves the metamodern in an existence of constant oscillation:

> A continuous oscillation, a constant repositioning between attitudes and mindsets that are evocative of the modern and postmodern but are ultimately suggestive of another sensibility that is neither of them. A discourse that negotiates between a yearning for universal truths but also an (a)political relativism, between a desire for sense and a doubt about the sense of it all, between … sincerity and irony, knowingness and naivety, construction and deconstruction. (Van den Akker and Vermeulen 2010, quoted in Ceriello 2018)

In an analysis of the TV series *Buffy the Vampire*, Linda Ceriello points to enhanced "reflection on their epistemic situatedness, … and a reliance on relationships to evince something 'true'" (2018b, 217) as characteristic of metamodern sentiments. The scenes from *Loki*, *WandaVision*, and *Moon Knight* discussed above also dwell on and explore these issues. When the worlds around Loki, Wanda, and Steven as they know it fall apart and their perception of reality destabilized, it is their emotions and relationships with others that recenter their sense of identity and self in this new reality. When Wanda learns that her TV-series' perfect world, even her husband and children, are constructs of her own magic, when Loki realizes that his sometimes even more mischievous variants are causing new branches in the sacred timeline, or when Steven has to come to terms with Marc as part of himself, it is their relationships to others and the emotions (however painful) that grow out of these that still give them purpose and hope. They (and the viewers) cannot ever be certain that this will be enough, though, because "new storylines will emerge that could render anyone capable of evil" (Ceriello 2018b, 225).

When Wanda, Loki, and Steven's realities become destabilized, what seems to keep them going, may sound like Timotheus Vermeulen's quote from the TV show Girls: "Just because it's fake doesn't mean I don't feel it" (Vermeulen 2015). This aspect of metamodern affect, the relationship between reality and feelings, is also discussed in the anthology *Metamodernism. Historicity, Affect and Depth after Postmodernism*. Gry Rustad and Kai Hanno Schwind argue that:

> Unlike in postmodern equivalents, metamodern sitcoms use devices such as irony, pastiche and parody to articulate emotive affect. Irony clashes with authenticity to render characters as flawed and complex subjects; a hyperreal style such as animation is used not to flatten the characters (and confine them in viewers' eyes to performers) but to render emotional depth. Unlike the cool, flat, unemotive postmodern sitcom, metamodern sitcoms have … a "warm" tome, urging viewers to vicariously connect with the social, human situation they depict and empathise with the characters therein." (van den Akker, Gibbons, and Vermeulen 2017, 86)

This, Rustad and Schwind stress, is derived from a very particular cultural logic in Western societies, where we now see metamodern sentiments in increasingly more sitcoms. "It is here that a clash between irony and authenticity emerges, reconciling audiences with flawed and complex, but ultimately loveable characters" (2018, 145).

Combining pop cultural nostalgia and self-referentiality with a post-postmodern, post-ironic sense of humor, being both tongue-in-cheek and utterly sincere, the metamodern jokes of *WandaVision*, *Loki*, and *Moon Knight* likewise tend to leave a bittersweet aftertaste. Is this because they make the audience really want *to believe* their realities? (cf. Undheim 2019). Just like we want to believe that even the trickster can be trustworthy when it is needed the most? Or is it because the seemingly mad person with DID, actually is a neoromantic prophet for the gods, a messenger of a deeper, a more real truth hidden behind the surface of the multiverse? (cf. Johannsen 2016). The direct impact of popular culture on contemporary religious ideas and practices is, of course, difficult to measure. A number of scholars have however demonstrated how popular culture inspires religious ideas and practices, and supply the feedback loop between the cultural production of religion and the production of popular culture (e.g., Clark 2003; Cusack 2016; Davidsen 2016a, 2016b; Hjarvard 2011; Possamai 2012).

As Crockford describes one of her interlocutors: "Media provided him with clues through which he constructed his own narrative of individual messianism" (2021, 82). It may seem like finding the truth is all about finding and deciphering the Easter eggs, and for some, this is also where fiction, or fantasy, and the real-world merge.

So, where can we end such an ever-expanding narrative of gods, witches, Easter eggs, and multiverses? Carol Cusack (2010) has pointed out, and rightly so, that playfulness also was a large part of fiction-based religion in the 1960s and 1970s, like the neo-pagan Church of all worlds. Yet it seems that playfulness, as well as the "lack of sense of it all" has speeded up considerably in our new digital media age, and not least because of the multiple platforms and the multiverse of multiple realities. When it all seems to fall apart, though, and there are too many realities in the multiverse to keep track of, the metamodern solution will be flawed human relationships and the emotions they generate.[8] The metamodern oscillation in the MCU multiverse, between deconstruction and construction, between apathy and emotion, and between relativism and the characters' desires for universal truths, is what eventually allow you to believe in the gods and the reality that make you feel.

Notes

1 Divergent spelling, but evidently inspired by the ancient Egyptian god Khonsu.

2 For contemporary Wicca, see, for example, Magliocco 2004; Urban 2015; Hutton 2019; and Quilty 2022.

3 In many ways, Loki's urge to always stir things up make him seem like the perfect god for groups like Discordianism and The Church of SubGenius, where humor and culture jamming is central to their "creed" (Cusack 2010).

4 An aspect of the series that has also gained a lot of attention from fan communities, is the fact that Marc Spector is one of very few Jewish protagonists in MCU. This is for instance clear in the scenes depicting his mother's shiva, where he wears a kippah, but is even more present in the comics, where his father is a rabbi. (ref.)

5 *WandaVision* S1 E6, 23.40–24.25: Pietro: "How'd you even do all this?" Wanda: "I don't know how I did it. I only remember feeling completely alone. Empty. I just … Endless nothingness."

6 A quite well-known example, and perhaps not so secret anymore, is how "insiders" can tell those who know (that is, the MCU) from those who don't, by watching who leaves their seats in the movie theatre when the end credits start. Those who know will remain seated, because Marvel (as well as increasingly more entertainment movies) inserts one or more small scenes in the end credit, loaded with references and hints as to what might happen next. There are YouTubers and TikTok-personalities who specialize in producing "Easter eggs" videos, where they identify and analyze the hidden clues and try to predict how the plot will develop.

7 Multiverse narratives have appeared in a number of pop cultural story worlds, such as DC (e.g., *Flash*), *Lego* (cf. Undheim 2019), and *His Dark Materials* (Feldt 2016). The Academy Award winning animation movie *Spiderman—Into the Spiderverse*, is another example.

8 This is interestingly also very much the tone of *Thor, Love and Thunder* (2022).

References

Barnette, J. (2022), "What is Wanda but Witches Persevering? Palimpsests of American Witches in *WandaVision*." *Theatre Journal* 74 (1), 41–57. doi: 10.1353/tj.2022.0003.

Bell, K. (2021), "The Saddest Loki Episode 6 Moment according to Fans Will Surprise You." *Looper*. Available online: https://www.looper.com/461245/the-saddest-loki-episode-6-moment-according-to-fans-will-surprise-you/?utm_campaign=clip (accessed April 13, 2023).

Cardenas, J. (2021), "'You're Like Me'—A Metamodern Reading of Spider-Man: Into the Spider-Verse." In *What Is Metamodern?* Available online: https://whatismetamodern.com/film/spider-man-spider-verse-metamodernism/ (accessed April 13, 2023).

Ceriello, L. (2018a), "Toward a Metamodern Reading of Spiritual but Not Religious Mysticisms," in W. B. Parson (ed.), *Being Spiritual but Not Religious Past, Present, Future(s)*, 200–18, New York: Routledge. https://doi.org/10.4324/9781315107431-13.

Ceriello, L. (2018b), "The Big Bad and the Big 'Aha!'. Metamodern Monsters as Transformational Figures of Instability," in Michael E. Heyes (ed.), *Holy Monsters, Sacred Grotesques: Monstrosity and Religion in Europe and the United States*, 207–33, Lanham, MD: Lexington.

Chireau, Y. (2019), "Looking for Black Religions in 20th Century Comics, 1931–1993." *Religions* 10 (6: 400): 1–17. https://doi.org/10.3390/rel10060400

Clark, L. S. (2003), *From Angels to Aliens: Teenagers, the Media and the Supernatural*, New York: Oxford University Press.

Clements, J., and Gauvain, R. (2014), "The Marvel of Islam: Reconciling Muslim Epistemologies through a New Islamic Origin Saga in Naif al-Mutawa's The 99." *Journal of Religion and Popular Culture* 26 (1): 36–70.

Crockford, S. (2021), *Ripples of the Universe: Spirituality in Sedona, Arizona* (Class 200, New Studies in Religion), Chicago: University of Chicago Press.

Cusack, C. M. (2010), *Invented Religions: Imagination, Fiction and Faith*, Farnham, England: Ashgate.

Cusack, C. M. (2016), "Fiction into Religion: Imagination, Other Worlds, and Play in the Formation of Community." *Religion* 46 (4): 575–90.

Dagsland, S. K. (2022), Religion og Film: Wanda Maximoff (Scarlet Witch) og Agatha Harkness i WandaVision (2021). *En utforskning av den moderne heksen i populærkulturen*, MA thesis, University of Bergen.

Davidsen, M. A. (2016a), "The Religious Affordance of Fiction: A Semiotic Approach." *Religion* 46 (4): 521–49.

Davidsen, M. A. (2016b), "From Star Wars to Jediism: The Emergence of Fiction-Based Religion," in Hemel E. van den, Szafraniec A. (eds.), *Words: Religious Language Matters. The Future of the Religious Past*, 376–89, New York: Fordham University Press. Available online:https://scholarlypublications.universiteitleiden.nl/access/item%3A2837728/view (accessed April 13, 2023).

Dember, G. (2022), "Everything Metamodern All at Once." *What Is Metamodern?* Available online: https://whatismetamodern.com/film/everything-everywhere-all-at-once-metamodern/.

Endsjø, D. Ø., and Lied, L. I. (2011), *Det folk vil ha: Religion og populærkultur* [What People Want: Religion and Popular Culture]. Oslo, Norway: Universitetsforlaget.

Feldt, L. (2016a), "Contemporary Fantasy Fiction and Representations of Religion: Playing with Reality, Myth and Magic in *His Dark Materials* and *Harry Potter*." *Religion* 46 (4): 550–74.

Feldt, L. (2016b), "Harry Potter and Contemporary Magic: Fantasy Literature, Popular Culture, and the Representation of Religion." *Journal of Contemporary Religion* 31 (1): 101–14.

Gibbons, A., Vermeulen, T., and van den Akker, R. (2019), "Reality Beckons: Metamodernist Depthiness Beyond Panfictionality." *European Journal of English Studies* 23 (2): 172–89, doi: 10.1080/13825577.2019.1640426.

Gilhus, I. S. (2013), "'All Over the Place': The Contribution of New Age to a Spatial Model of Religion," in S. J. Sutcliffe and I. S. Gilhus (eds.), *New Age Spirituality: Rethinking Religion*, 35–49, Durham, NC: Acumen.

Gilhus, I. S. (2014a), "Medialisering og refortrylling: Religiøs endring i Norge [Mediatization and Re-enchantment: Religious Change in Norway]," *DIN: Religionsvitenskapelig tidsskrift* 2014 (1): 9–26.

Gilhus, I. S. (2016), "What Became of Superhuman Beings? Companions and Field Guides in the Study of Religion," in P. Antes, A. W. Geertz, and M. Rothstein (eds.), *Contemporary Views on Comparative Religion: In Celebration of Tim Jensen's 65th Birthday*, 375–88, Sheffield: Equinox.

Gilhus, I. S., and Sutcliffe S. (2013), "Conclusion: New Age Spiritualities—'Good to Think' in the Study of Religion," in S. J. Sutcliffe and I. S. Gilhus (eds.), *New Age Spirituality: Rethinking Religion*, 256–62, Durham, NC: Acumen.

Hjarvard, S. (2011), "The Mediatisation of Religion: Theorising Religion, Media and Social Change," *Culture and Religion: An Interdisciplinary Journal* 12 (2): 119–35.

Hutton, R. (2019), *The Triumph of the Moon: A History of Modern Pagan Witchcraft* (New ed.), Oxford: Oxford University Press.

Johannsen, D. (2016), "On Elves and Freethinkers: Criticism of Religion and the Emergence of the Literary Fantastic in Nordic literature," *Religion* 46 (4): 591–610.

Johnston, S. I. (2019), *The Story of Myth*, Cambridge, MA: Harvard University Press.

Karthauser, K. (2011), "The Awesome, or the Metamodern Sublime," *Notes on Metamodernism*. Available online: http://www.metamodernism.com/2011/10/28/the-awesome-or-the-metamodern-sublime/ (accessed April 13, 2023).

Kirby, D. (2013), *Fantasy and Belief: Alternative Religions, Popular Narratives and Digital Cultures* (Approaches to New Religions), Sheffield: Equinox.

Kirby, D. (2012), Readers, Believers, Consumers, and Audiences: Complicating the Relationship Between Consumption and Contemporary Narrative Spiritualties," *Australian Journal of Communication* 39 (1): 119–31.

Lang, B. (2022), "Moon Knight's Ethan Hawke Says Harrow is the Show's True 'Good Guy'," cbr.com published April 14, 2022. Available online: https://www.cbr.com/moon-knight-ethan-hawke-arthur-harrow-hero-mcu/ (accessed April 13, 2023).

Lewis, A. (2014), *American Comics, Literary Theory, and Religion: The Superhero Afterlife*, Basingstoke: Palgrave Macmillan.

Magliocco, S. (2004), *Witching Culture: Folklore and Neo-Paganism in America* (Contemporary Ethnography), Philadelphia: University of Pennsylvania Press.

Possamai, A. (2012), *Handbook of Hyper-Real Religions*, Leiden: Brill.

Quilty, E. (2022), "Witchlife: Witchy Digital Spaces," *Journal of Contemporary Religion* 37 (1): 29–49. https://doi.org/10.1080/13537903.2021.2018801

Salazar, M. (2020), "One with the Universe: The Construction of Doctor Strange's Magic in 1973," *Journal of Religion and Popular Culture* 32 (3): 163–82.

Skjoldli, J. (2019), "Guder til salgs (støvete, men pent brukt). Hva formidler Thor, Vikings og American Gods om norrøne guder?" *Chaos – Skandinavisk tidsskrift for religionshistoriske studier* 71 (1): 29–64.

Thomas, J. (2012). *Drawing on Tradition: Manga, Anime, and Religion in Contemporary Japan*, Honolulu: University of Hawaii.

Undheim, S. (2019), "Made Up Prophecies: Metamodern Play with Religion, Spirituality and Monomyth in the LEGO Universe," in R. C. Hains and S. R. Mazzarella (eds.), *Cultural Studies of LEGO: More than just bricks*, 97–121, Cham: Springer International Publishing.

Urban, H. (2015), *New Age, Neopagan, and New Religious Movements: Alternative Spirituality in Contemporary America*, Oakland: University of California Press.

Van den Akker, R., Gibbons, A., and Vermeulen, T. (2017), *Metamodernism: Historicity, Affect, and Depth after Postmodernism*, London: Rowman & Littlefield International.

Vermeulen, T, and van den Akker, R. (2010), "Notes on Metamodernism," *Journal of Aesthetics Culture* 2 (1): 1–14.

Vermeulen, T. (2015), "The New Depthiness," *E-Flux Journal* 61, Available online: https://www.e-flux.com/journal/61/61000/the-new-depthiness/ (accessed April 13, 2023).

Woodhead, L. (2016), "Intensified Religious Pluralism and De-Differentiation: The British Example," *Society* 53: 41–6.

Zogbi, Emily. (2022), "Moon Knight: Why Ethan Hawke Wanted to Play the MCU Cult Leader," *cbr.com*. Available online: https://www.cbr.com/moon-knight-why-ethan-hawke-wanted-play-mcu-cult-leader/ (accessed April 13, 2023).

12

Comics and Religious Studies: *Amar Chitra Katha* as an Educational Comic Series

Line Reichelt Føreland

How can comics be used in religious studies? The main example in this chapter is a comic series created for educational purposes, but it is important to note that comics not created for such purposes can be as suitable. As pointed out by Jeffrey M. Brackett, the use of comics in religious studies creates opportunities for the teacher to meet pedagogical goals and course outcomes. This is not necessarily dependent on the popularity of the specific comics used (Brackett 2015, 493) or whether they are intended for educational use. I still chose a popular comic series that has been promoted as a series with an educational value to illustrate the possibilities and difficulties that can arise in religious studies.

The series *Amar Chitra Katha* (*ACK*) was created by Anant Pai in 1967/1969 to present Indian religious and historical stories to children. From early on, it was used in schools, and the publishers directly promoted the series as a valuable teaching tool for educators. The publisher has recently initiated a storytelling program using these stories as part of the curriculum in Mumbai schools using principles of storytelling in the education system (India Education Diary Bureau Admin 2021). *ACK* is part of multimodal media franchises that are widely used and popular, explicitly targeting educators and branding the series as educational. If stories from the comic series are used in the regular curriculum, the narrative and visual choices in the comic series will potentially have an impact on the educational content. I will not, however, discuss whether the comic series truly had a pedagogical impact in school curricula in India, but use it to illustrate both the potential and the more problematic sides of using comics specifically targeted at education in religious studies.

I will look closely at the use of comics in education, with particular attention given to their possible functions in religious studies. Here, religion must be understood in a broader context, comprising religious and ethical topics and direct depictions of religious themes and interpretations. I will discuss literature on comics in the classroom, specifically in religious studies, as well as literature on visual literacy and language. When discussing the *ACK* series, I have supplied additional literature on the role of the image in Hinduism.

Comics, Media, and Religious Studies

Using comics in the classroom is not a new phenomenon, and in an international setting, comics have been used in the classroom since at least the 1920s. This includes both the use of comics created for educational purposes and comics that are not created for such a purpose (Tilley and Weiner 2020, 358). One comic series intended for educational purposes that was used quite early and had a broad reach was *Classics Illustrated*, which began in 1941, and included adaptations of well-known Western literary works. In classrooms, they were used both to ease the reading of literary works and to compare with the original. "Teachers wanted to show the readers what they missed by reading the abridged comics-format version of literature" (359).

In the case of *ACK*, the comparison with the *Classics Illustrated* and similar series is quite interesting since *ACK* contains adaptations of Hindu mythology and religion. However, many *ACK* readers would not be able to read the original manuscripts and stories because they lack the required language skills. At the same time, giving visual access to mythological and religious stories may be considered especially valuable considering visual culture's place in India and the Hindu religion. This also provides the student of Hinduism with access to adaptations of authoritative texts, even though one should read the comic issues critically as adaptations and not as authoritative texts.

Even though there is a growing literature on comics in the classroom, there is not, until now, much material covering the use of comics specifically in religious studies. Books such as *Graphic Novels and Comics in the Classroom: Essays on the Educational Power of Sequential Art* (Syma and Weiner 2013) cover a wide range of uses, such as the use of comics to teach language, multimodality, intertextuality, literature, art, history, and feminism. Other books cover subjects such as math, social studies, and science (Jaffe and Hurwich 2019). Several books and studies focus on how to use comics to improve oral skills, reading and writing, and to teach or improve literacy (Bakis 2014; Bowkett and Hitchman 2012; Jaffe and Hurwich 2019).

In *The Graphic Novel Classroom* (Bakis 2014), the author discusses comics related to religious studies. Two relevant examples are used. One is Will Eisner's *A Contract with God;* the other is Marjane Satrapi's *Persepolis*. The classroom examples mostly focus on an analytical reading of the elements of the story, such as artwork and epilogue. Only one among the sixteen discussion points is directly related to the depiction of God or religion in the comic book: "On page 25 are three individual images separated by space from top to bottom. How is God represented on this page? Is this the kind of page you pictured when you thought you'd be reading graphic novels?" (Bakis 2014) Instead of giving space to further discussion about the depiction of God, it directs the attention toward discussion expectations on comic books themselves. When it comes to *Persepolis*, there is a question regarding the split of religious values and modernity, but mostly the attention is on *Persepolis* as a memoir and coming-of-age story. However valuable these perspectives are, the lack of discussions and questions about relevant topics for religious studies is quite indicative of the lack of such a discussion in the otherwise rich literature on the use of comics in the classroom.

Visual Literacy and Language

Visual literacy can be understood as "the ability to critically read, interpret, and persuasively relay content … through images or visual messages. It is the ability to understand an image's (concrete and inferential) message, its use of symbols, and the rationales for the artist's various compositional choices" (Jaffe and Hurwich 2019, 26). Contemplating visual elements in a frame or panel may require a certain level of visual literacy. When studying religion, visual elements and icons play an important role, which means that it is also important to have good visual literacy. Using comics in religious studies can demand visual literacy and aid in developing the students' visual literacy levels.

In the book *Worth a Thousand Words: Using Graphic Novels to Teach Visual and Verbal Literacy* (Jaffe and Hurwich 2019), there is a chapter on how to read pictures in comics, which is relevant for understanding comics in religious studies. The chapter focuses on how one can critically read an image and thereby enhance visual literacy. The use of comics in religious studies is not mentioned specifically, but if using comics in religious studies, one must be able to critically read an image. Presenting religious topics through a visual medium will be significant in understanding the topics.

Comics are written in a visual language but can comprise of both visual and written language. When reading a comic, the reader needs to pay attention to the form and how the form presents meaning. Comics are sequential and therefore the perceived connection and sequence are meaningful. The process of decoding forms, visual meaning, and sequence can be quite complex (Cohn 2013, 2, 7–8).

The content of comics is expressed visually and often verbally and, therefore, comics can aid in the comprehension of abstract and multifaceted phenomena. Several studies also indicate that "visual educational content aids memory and comprehension while making content more meaningful and accessible" (Jaffe and Hurwich 2019, 12). A comic or picture book presents the possibility of reflecting on specific content or constructing meaning and interpretations. This possibility is a distinct advantage of using a comic series where the reader can reflect and meditate on the content, making room for interpretations, and reflections valuable in religious studies.

Educational Comics and Comics in Education

Educational comics are comics created for a specific educational purpose. As the educational content is the most important aspect of these comics, there is a certain risk that purpose is valued higher than content and aesthetic experience. When using texts created for a specific purpose, it is of utmost importance to read critically, with special attention given to who has produced the text, the explicit or implicit values presented, and the use of rhetorical techniques. Some educational texts can have a certain agenda besides being suitable for educational purposes. Comics can be preaching or critical, and their creators can be purely commercially motivated, religious with a commercial agenda, or trying to present a certain conviction or worldview as more correct (Undheim 2020, 21). For example, the Kingstone comics and the Kingstone Bible Trilogy are Christian comic books and graphic versions of the bible, respectively (Kingstone Comics n.d). Kingstone comics are both religious and have issues that directly thematize Christian topics, but even though they deal with religion, the comic issues also have an outspoken mission to appear convincing on Christian beliefs and must therefore be regarded as religious comics or media. Analyzing the purpose of the text should therefore be a part of the reading itself.

Comics created for a different purpose but with content that is deemed suitable for religious studies can be used to give insights into different religions, mythologies, and ethical questions. At the same time, the use of comics in religious studies or in general can be used to distribute, generalize, and reformulate religions and worldviews. Endsjø and Lied even argue that these expressions can create religious expressions (Endsjø and Lied 2011, 15). The mediatization of religion can take on the character of belief leading not to a new kind of religion but "rather a new social condition in which the power to define and practice religion has changed" (Hjarvard 2014, 27). The use of comics in religious studies can therefore aid in the dissemination of knowledge and simultaneously be a part of the cultural production of comics using religious expressions. Eidhamar presents a categorization of religious teaching into four categories that can be valuable in this context. Perspectives presented or used can give an outside perspective that is either personal or academic or an inside perspective that is either personal or academic. Using an outside perspective means approaching a religion one does not believe in oneself, whether this is approached personally or academically. Of course, it is also possible to approach religious studies from an inside perspective, both personally and academically (Eidhamar 2019). Comics used in religious studies can therefore be regarded as representations (Undheim 2020, 21) that can inform the reader of certain religious topics and the existence of these topics in a cultural context whether the approach is personal or academic.

The use of comics in education is by no means limited to educational comics. *ACK* is presented as an educational comic, but this might well be a marketing strategy to reach a wider audience and legitimize the use of comics in an educational source (Chandra 2008). As described earlier, the use of a comic book such as *Persepolis* might be as useful as using *ACK* in religious studies depending on the thematic context and how the comic is used.

When considering the use of comics in an educational context, it is almost unavoidable to disregard the reputation of comics in a historical context. This reputation has changed since Fredric Wertham published *Seduction of the Innocence* in 1954, in where he argued that there was a connection between reading comics and youth crime (Duncan, Smith, and Levitz 2016, 25). Still, when using comics in an educational system, prejudices concerning the value of comics might still have a certain influence. These prejudices might be both positive and negative. The use of comics in education have long been described by many teachers as motivational (Wallner 2020, 47). Even though there might be some truth to the description of comics as motivational, at least to some readers, it is problematic to describe comics as only motivational.

Creating comics in the classroom can also be used as a creative method to teach specific content. Creating such comics is closely connected to educational comics as they both have an educational purpose. This method is a valuable tool in religious studies, as in other subjects. Making comics can be a creative outlet that furthers collaboration and integrated use of technology that can enhance the students' writing skills and other skills and subjects (Maliszewski 2013, 234, 236). Nevertheless, the writing of comics as part of religious studies will not be dealt with in this chapter.

Amar Chitra Katha

ACK was initiated by Anant Pai and is one of the most defining Indian comic series. The word *chitrakatha* means picture stories, and in large part, the term originated from Anant Pai himself. Choosing the word *chitrakatha* to describe the series might have played a part in legitimizing the comics for educational use and trying to secure it as part of India's cultural heritage.

ACK has been an important overall influence on the Indian comic industry. Even though comic books in India must be understood both as a continuation of "a larger social context of visual culture" and as part of an international comic book scene, the *ACK* transformed the comics culture by offering a series that was created locally (Stoll 2017, 88–9). In 2011, at the first Comic-Con India in New Delhi, attended by more than fifteen thousand people, Anant Pai received a Lifetime Achievement Award (93). Anant Pai and his series have both influenced the comic book scene in India and represented Hindu and Indian identity to a large readership, which is often a reason to include elements or issues from the series in religious studies.

The first publications of *ACK* started in 1967 with translations of Western illustrated classics, largely based on Western fairytales such as *Jack and the Beanstalk* and *Cinderella*, into Indian languages. The first ten issues did not sell well, and the eleventh issue, titled *Krishna*, is often considered the first issue of the series. *Krishna* was published in 1969 in English, written by the founder Anant Pai and illustrated by Ram Waeerkar. The transition from Indian languages to English was motivated by Pai's knowledge of the growing English-speaking urban middle class (McLain 2009, 25, 28). *Krishna* is a landmark in India's comic book market: "It was the first indigenous Indian comic book, created in India and featuring an Indian hero and an Indian storyline" (25). The format is quite linear, with six rectangular boxes on each page. Each comic is typically made up of twenty-eight or thirty-two pages featuring Hindu mythological and religious stories (Chandra 2008, 13).

Krishna focuses on central episodes in the life of the Hindu God Krishna, and according to Pai, the Sanskrit mythological text, the *Bhāgavata Purāṇa*, is used as a source. McLain also points to *Harivaṃśa* and popular renditions of both *Bhāgavata Purāṇa* and *Harivaṃśa* as sources (McLain 2009, 25–6). With the eleventh issue of *Krishna*, the formula for the *ACK* series was established. "The comic establishes the formula for this series by focusing its narrative on one hero who is featured on the cover and whose dramatic action centers the narrative." (26). The story also established the biographical model that was used for the mythological narratives. "The mythological stories were told by keeping a mythic-heroic individual at the center of the narrative, and by building sequential momentum through a deliberate parsing of the mythological story into a *bildungsroman*" (Chandra 2018, 12). If one were to use the comic series as part of religious studies, it is worth noting that the established biographical model can interfere with the rendition of mythological and religious stories. Chandra has explicitly criticized *ACK* for obliterating variation both because of the format and the visual style being modelled after popular versions of stories (Chandra 2008).

In the "first" issue of *Krishna*, Pai avoided presenting miraculous events but rendered them so that it was possible to read both miraculous and scientific explanations into the scene. Later, in accordance with the rise of Hindu communalism in India's popular culture in the 1970s and 1980s, miraculous events were explicitly depicted without ambiguity. Pai has described that he understood that readers considered the comic series as something sacred, and that *ACK* was a "legitimate source of these sacred stories" (McLain 2009, 29, 35). Because of the role of the image in the Hindu religion, "even comic book images of a deity would be considered sacrosanct by most Hindus" (31). If the stories depicted in the comic book series were understood as something sacred and as a legitimate source of sacred stories, the series can have a central position in religious education and a personal religious practice.

ACK is influenced by both Western artistic and storytelling traditions and Indian visual and literary culture, originally being published in English. *ACK* combines mythology and mythological gods with history, historical leaders, and sacred and secular elements. Drawing from the American archetype of the superhero, the series then establishes a form of a national canon of Indian heroes. After gaining a wider audience, some of the popular issues were also published in other regional Indian languages. This allowed the publisher to reach an even wider audience. It was thus not only reaching an urban middleclass but was distributed to urban cities, small villages, and an increasing number of school libraries. The *Krishna* issue was one of several made available in at least four languages—Bengali, Malayalam, Kannada, and Assamese (McLain 2009, 3, 44).

The *ACK* series is targeted at a quite wide age group but specifically at schoolchildren. With the recent developments, however—using YouTube and making apps—they are targeting an even wider age group and children who are not old enough to attend school. The ACK company Tinkle has created a junior app with an age rating of 3+ in addition to the app where one can buy comics to read online. The YouTube channel has videos based on the comic series in several languages (Amar Chitra Katha Pvt. Ltd. n.d.; 2021). What type of impact these new developments have on the comics' influence and reach in an educational context is outside the scope of this article. It is still interesting to note that the YouTube channel is active and continues to publish videos with animation stories, still pictures from the comics, and contributions from people participating in storytelling events.

Learning about Hindu religion and mythology from an academic approach these stories can be valuable for an older audience, but it is vital to have a somewhat critical approach as the stories are not neutral. Using a biographical model might make the stories more available both for unexperienced readers and those who are not familiar with the source material. There are always selections being made when creating adaptations, both story-wise and visually, which shows the importance of working with visual literacy in religious studies and otherwise.

ACK as a Source of Indian and Hindu Mythology and Culture

Since its beginning, at least 480 titles in thirty-six national and international languages have been published in the *ACK* series. *ACK* is viewed as "foundational texts for the religious and national education of their young readers" (McLain 2009, 3–4) and has played an important role for people who are unable to read the original Hindu scripture in Sanskrit and instead rely on popular media expressions. *ACK* is so influential that it has reinforced certain stereotypical representations of Hindu nationalism, (Amin 2017) being described by some as "Hindu-centric" (Mannur 2000) and as a series with a "strong 'great man' bent and a decided Hindu chauvinist bias" (Bakshi 1983).

ACK follows a trend in the Indian comic book market where mythological texts continuously are represented in new interpretations and renditions. This trend is so influential on the Indian comic book scene that it can be difficult for new comic book artists to get publication deals if they do not create the same type of narratives (Rajendran 2014, 11). A tendency among mythological narratives in the Indian comic book market is that "many of these representations focus only on some aspects on the narratives they study (such as the war in the *Mahabharatha*) thus glamorizing and commoditizing that theme, and further reinforce normative and hegemonic value systems" (4). If using *ACK* in religious studies, one must pay attention to the narrative structure and the visual and narrative elements that are included or left out. Using biographical stories as sources can be problematic considering, among other things, the richness of the source material and the limited number of pages in the comic adaptations. They can be valuable sources precisely because of the accessibility, but both the use of a biographical method and the criticized representations in the comic series shows that it should not be an easy read if used in an academic context.

The image has played an important role in Hindu religion, and still does: "The images and myths of the Hindu imagination constitute a basic vocabulary and a common idiom of discourse. Since India has 'written' prolifically in its images, learning to read its mythology and iconography is a primary task for the student of Hinduism." (Eck 2007, 17). *Darśan* means seeing. It refers to seeing in a religious context and is an important ritual activity. "Since, in the Hindu understanding, the deity is present in the image, the visual apprehension of the image is charged with religious meaning" (3). *ACK* was not intended for ritual worship. To avoid religious controversy, its founder Anant Pai has described how the gods on the covers originally looked away from the reader to avoid a darsanic gaze. Inside the comic books, there are still many occasions where a darsanic experience is possible. The series can therefore be understood as sacred, depending on the reader, giving space to inside perspectives, and personal approaches in religious studies. *ACK* can, along with other Indian comic books and pop-cultural expressions, both function as a sacred text and give insight into modern understandings of religion and Indian identity.

The founder of *ACK*, Anant Pai himself, answered accusations of placing Hindu religion at the forefront at the expense of other religions. He claimed that epics such as "the *Ramayana* and the *Mahabharata* were the heritage of all Indians" and adds that he since included "titles like *Babur*, *Humayun*, a title on Jesus Christ, and tried to make the series more secular." (Pai 2000). *Babur* was the first comic book to include a Muslim protagonist (McLain 2005). Ẓahīr al-Dīn Muḥammad, or Bābur, was a descendant from Genghis Khan, who invaded India in 1525–6 (Faruqui 2012). He was the founder the Mughal dynasty in the northern part of India, and Humāyūn or Nāṣir al-Dīn Muḥammad was his son and the second Mughal ruler in India (Spear 2022). The other Mughal rulers have also received their own issues in the *ACK* series: *Noor Jahan* in 1977 (no. 148), *Akbar* and *Shah Jahan* in 1979 (no. 200 and 204), *Jahangir* in 1980 (no. 221), and *Dara Shukoh and Aurangzeb* in 1981 (no. 231). According to Chandra, it is typical for the series that Muslims are portrayed in stereotypical terms as gruesome invaders in the comic series (Chandra 2008).

The cover photo of the issue *Babur* is quite indicative of the representation of Bābur. In the background, one can see images of what must be understood as an ongoing battle. The stories of Bābur and Humāyūn can be of value, and depicting them as invaders is not necessarily incorrect, but the problem arises if Muslim invaders are the only or most of the representations of Islam or Muslims in the series, which scholars claim to be the case (Pritchett 1995). The depiction of these invaders can also be understood as a glorified representation of war. In fact, in the introduction of the comic issue, Bābur is described as a good soldier, an able general, a wise and just ruler, and a generous person with good humor (Amar Chitra Katha 1977). In an interview with McLain, Pai commented on the use of invaders as heroes with the example of the comic issue *Akbar* (Humāyūn's son):

> Yes. Take the example of Akbar. After the Battle of Panipat, Hemu was defeated. Akbar was very young, just thirteen years old, and he ordered Hemu's headless body to be hung at the gate for all to see. This is disturbing, but it is a historical fact, it can't be avoided. Yet it need not be emphasized. So I chose to have this shown in long shot, not in close-up. That way, you see, Akbar stays a hero … This is the motto that I work under: "One must tell the truth, one must tell what is pleasant; but don't tell what is unpleasant just because it is true." In Sanskrit this is "satyam bruyāt priyam bruyāt mā bruyāt satyam apriyam." You see, Indians have a generally good view of Akbar. He was a good king, very accommodating. Not in his youth, but he changed. You know, we promote integration through *Amar Chitra Katha*. So why show bad things about Akbar—why not show that he was a good king? (interview from 2000, quoted in McLain 2005, 217)

The *ACK* series has been marketed as an accurate and authentic source on Hindu mythology and religion:

> They [Pai and his team] insist that in their recasting of sacred Hindu scriptures no symbolic meanings have been altered; no new interpolations have been inserted, and no facts have been left unchecked. Parents, educators, students, and other consumers can therefore rest assured that when they purchase these

> comic books, they get the real thing, only better—the "original" Indian story, now in a fun, short, and colorful format. (McLain 2009, 87)

The example clearly shows how the comic book format is used to present stories in a particular way and from a particular point of view. When the producers place themselves as an authoritative source appropriate for use in educational contexts, the series must be read critically, keeping in mind that all adaptations will add or remove something from the original. It adds to the complexity that "Hinduism is notoriously difficult to define as a unified and systematic religion due to its multiplicity of sacred texts, historical teachers, philosophies, and regional and sectarian tradition" (McLain 2009, 113). This makes the attempt to retell the Hindu stories in a unified narrative even more complex. The series, read with caution, can still be valuable in religious studies both in presenting adaptations of religious stories and myths and in giving insight into the society believing in and consuming these stories. *ACK* can be valuable in religious studies, both from personal and academic approaches.

Conclusion

Even though *ACK* is created for an educational purpose, its use in religious studies is not without its challenges, perhaps precisely because of this pronounced purpose. The editorial team has, as mentioned, described the series as an authoritative source that follows the original manuscripts closely. This means that it is important for the user of these comics in religious studies to be especially critical of the choices that have been made. These choices will be both visual and narrative. When reading a comic book as a part of religious studies, it is perhaps even more important to consider what part of the narrative is presented and from which perspective, how the characters and events are depicted, and what visual and narrative sources are used and not used. If *ACK* is used in religious academic studies—no matter if it is from an inside or outside perspective—the need for a certain visual literacy becomes apparent.

Even though the series is not necessarily a Hindu series, the stories are often presented from a Hindu perspective. As such, they give insight into both Hindu stories and mythology and Hindu perspectives, in addition to presenting narrative intended for a Hindu audience—or at least an Indian audience. The Hindu perspectives are not only present in the selected narrative but also in the visual vocabulary and how the series both avoids and gives opportunities for a darsanic experience. Therefore, focusing on the visual aspects of the stories gives plenty of opportunities for both personal and academic approaches in religious studies.

References

Amar Chitra Katha. (1977), "Babur." India Book House. Available online: https://digital.amarchitrakatha.com/id005835186/Babur (accessed April 13, 2023).

Amar Chitra Katha Pvt Ltd. (2021), "Amar Chitra Katha Junior App." Google Play. November 26, 2021. Available online: https://play.google.com/store/apps/details?id=com.ns.ackjunior&hl=no&gl=US (accessed April 13, 2023).

Amar Chitra Katha Pvt Ltd. (n.d.), "Amar Chitra Katha—YouTube." YouTube. Available online: https://www.youtube.com/channel/UCaymvCOGWUB4kcOh0bXPZZg (accessed October 18, 2022).

Amin, Shaan. (2017), "The Dark Side of the Comics That Redefined Hinduism." *The Atlantic*. December 30, 2017. Available online: https://www.theatlantic.com/entertainment/archive/2017/12/the-comics-that-redefined-hinduism/539838/ (accessed April 13, 2023).

Bakis, Maureen. (2014), *The Graphic Novel Classroom: Powerful Teaching and Learning with Images*, New York: Skyhorse publishing.

Bakshi, Rajni. (1983), "ACKs: Distorted History or Education?" *The Telegraph Sunday*, November 13, 1983. Available online: https://jan.ucc.nau.edu/~sj6/AmarChitraKatha%201983.pdf (accessed April 13, 2023).

Bowkett, Stephen, and Tony Hitchman. (2012), *Using Comic Art to Improve Speaking, Reading and Writing*, New York: Routledge.

Brackett, Jeffrey M. (2015), "Religion and Comics," *Religion Compass* 9 (12): 493–500. https://doi.org/10.1111/rec3.12167.

Chandra, Nandini. (2008), *The Classic Popular: Amar Chitra Katha, 1967–2007*, New Delhi: Yoda Press.

Chandra, Nandini. (2018), "The Fear of Iconoclasm: Genre and Medium Transformations from Comics to Graphic Novels in Amar Chitra Katha, Bhimayana, and Munnu," *South Asian Review* 39 (1–2): 11–33. https://doi.org/10.1080/02759527.2018.1515801.

Cohn, Neil. (2013), *The Visual Language of Comics: Introduction to the Structure and Cognition of Sequential Images*, London: Bloomsbury Academic.

Duncan, Randy, Matthew J. Smith, and Paul Levitz. (2016), *The Power of Comics: History, Form and Culture*, London: Bloomsbury Academic.

Eck, Diana L. (2007), *Darśan: Seeing the Divine Image in India*, Delhi: Motilal Banarsidass Publisher.

Eidhamar, Levi Geir. (2019). "Innenfra eller utenfra, faglig eller personlig? Perspektiver i religions- og livssynsundervisningen belyst ut fra internasjonal debatt," *Prismet* 1: 27–46. https://doi.org/10.5617/pri.6855.

Endsjø, Dag Øistein, and Liv Ingeborg Lied. (2011), *Det folk vil ha: religion og populærkultur*, Oslo: Universitetsforlaget.

Faruqui, Munis D. (2012), *The Princes of the Mughal Empire, 1504–1719*, Cambridge: Cambridge University Press. https://doi.org/10.1017/CBO9781139135474.

Hjarvard, Stig. (2012), "Three Forms of Mediatized Religion. Changing the Public Face of Religion," in Stig Hjarvard and Mia Lövheim (eds.), *Mediatization and Religion: Nordic Perspectives*, 21–44, Gothenburg: Nordicom.

India Education Diary Bureau Admin. (2021), "Jasudben ML School Introduces Teaching via Tales in Its Curriculum; Ties Up with India's Favourite Storyteller 'Amar Chitra Katha.'" *India Education | Latest Education News | Global Educational News | Recent Educational News* (blog). April 26, 2021. Available online: https://indiaeducationdiary.in/jasudben-ml-school-introduces-teaching-via-tales-in-its-curriculum-ties-up-with-indias-favourite-storyteller-amar-chitra-katha-2/ (accessed April 13, 2023).

Jaffe, Meryl, and Talia Hurwich. (2019), *Worth a Thousand Words: Using Graphic Novels to Teach Visual and Verbal Literacy*, San Francisco, CA: Jossey-Bass.

Kingstone Comics. n.d. "Kingstone Bible Comic Collection." Kingstone Comics. Available online: https://kingstonecomics.com/collections/kingstone-bible-comic-collection (accessed March 28, 2022).

Maliszewski, Diana. (2013) "The Benefits of Writing Comics," in Carrye Kay Syma and Robert G. Weiner (eds.), *Graphic Novels and Comics in the Classroom: Essays on the Educational Power of Sequential Art*, 233–44. Jefferson, NC: McFarland.

Mannur, Anita. (2000), "'The Glorious Heritage of India': Notes on the Politics of Amar Chitra Katha," *Bookbird: World of Children's Books* 38 (4): 32–3.

McLain, Karline. (2009), *India's Immortal Comic Books: Gods, Kings, and Other Heroes*. Contemporary Indian Studies, Bloomington: Indiana University Press.

McLain, Karline Marie. (2005), "Whose Immortal Picture Stories?: Amar Chitra Katha and the Construction of Indian Identities." Doctoral Dissertation University of Texas. https://repositories.lib.utexas.edu/handle/2152/1631 (accessed April 13, 2023).

Pai, Anant. (2000), "Mythology in Pictures," *Gentleman* February: 38–40.

Pritchett, Frances W. (1995) "The World of Amar Chitra Katha," in Lawrence A. Babb and Susan Snow Wadley (eds.), *Media and the Transformation of Religion in South Asia*, 95–6. Philadelphia: University of Pennsylvania Press. https://doi.org/10.9783/9781512800180-007.

Rajendran, Aneeta. (2014), "Narrative, Public Cultures and Visuality in Indian Comic Strips and Graphic Novels in English, Hindi, Bangla and Malayalam from 1947 to the Present." Avilable online: https://gargicollege.in/wp-content/uploads/2018/12/MRPmonograph-april5-.pdf (accessed April 13, 2023).

Spear, T. G. Percival. (2022), "Bābur Mughal Emperor." Britannica. 2022. Available online: https://www.britannica.com/biography/Babur (accessed April 13, 2023).

Stoll, Jeremy. (2017), "Comics in India," in Frank Bramlett, Roy T. Cook, and Aaron Meskin (eds.), *The Routledge Companion to Comics*, 88–97, New York: Routledge.

Syma, Carrye Kay, and Robert G. Weiner. (eds.) (2013), *Graphic Novels and Comics in the Classroom: Essays on the Educational Power of Sequential Art*, Jefferson, NC: McFarland.

Tilley, Carol L., and Robert G. Weiner. (2020), "Teaching and Learning with Comics," in Frank Bramlett, Roy T Cook, and Aaron Meskin (eds.), *The Routledge Companion to Comics*, 358–66. New York: Routledge.

Undheim, Sissel. (2020), "Helt Seriøst!? Om Populærkultur i KRLE og Religion og Etikk." *Religion og Livssyn* 2022 (2): 20–9. Available online: https://www.religion.no/_files/ugd/6972da_c91310a7f6c74775baa3059e13c70948.pdf (accessed April 13, 2022).

Wallner, Lars. (2020), *Det Rutiga Klassrummet: Serier, Multimodalitet och Litteracitet*, Lund: Studentlitteratur.

13

A Contract with God or a Social Contract?

Christophe Monnot[1]

Introduction

This contribution takes a sociological look at a monument of the comic strip. *A Contract with God* by Will Eisner (1978) is often described as the first graphic novel. This album, however, is part of an emerging new wave in comics. The launching of the Belgian magazine *(À suivre)* by Casterman in 1978 underlines the fact that this emergence is not due to a single individual, but that Eisner's album is part of an adult turning point in world comics. This new wave takes comics out of the world of humor or superheroes and into a more intellectual dimension with complex narratives.

Thus far, analyses of Eisner's graphic novels have mainly focused on their graphic innovations or their relation with Judaism. The issue of immigration from Europe and the settlement in Jewish neighborhoods in large American cities have been discussed, but few analyses (Parker Royal 2011b) have been interested in the narrative material from a sociological perspective. This chapter aims to show how the title story of *A Contract*, despite the eminently religious aspect of its narrative, remains profoundly social Eisner, in putting his tales into pictures, never neglects this dimension. Although Eisner is not a sociologist, his narratives of human lives offer some important sociological insights. They feature characters with individual life trajectories that are not only made up of personal choices but also of surprises or misfortunes. These choices and incidents underline that individual destinies are embedded in a complex social framework. Dauber (2006) and Parker Royal (2011c) stress the social character of the other three stories of the volume. We would like to point out here that even if we only deal with the first story—the one that titles the volume—some deeply sociological features can be singled out.

After a summary of the story and the introduction of the author, we will describe some specific features of *A Contract*. We will then examine the narrative on three intertwined perspectives. We will untangle these perspectives in three distinct parts to emphasize the importance of each of them in understanding the sociological significance of Eisner's story. We will conclude by stressing that under the guise of a simple story, *A Contract with God* shows that a (religious) life trajectory is not only individual, but depends on a cultural and religious context that it is also a *social contract.*

The Story: Fleeing the Russian Pogroms

A Contract tells the tragic story of a teenager, chosen by his Jewish community, to flee the late nineteenth-century pogroms in Russia. Before his flight to the United States, he signed a pact with God engraved on a flat rock that he kept in his pocket. On his arrival in New York, he became a member of the Hasidic community. He was widely recognized for his piety and was anonymously given a pram with a little girl in it, whom he adopted and named Rachele.

Everything seemed to work out according to the terms of the contract until the day when a serious illness took the adopted girl away. This situation led the hero to rebel against God and to throw the flat stone of the contract out the window. From then on, the pious man's life turned into "the proverbial slumlord. He raises the rents, cuts the heat, stops repairs, gets rich, and takes a beautiful Gentile mistress" (Klingenstein 2007, 85). However, a taste of unfinished business drove the rich man to the synagogue to ask the rabbis to prepare a new contract with God. After much palaver, he obtained this document. Holding it in his hands, he was dreaming of starting a family and having offspring when he was suddenly thrown out of his thoughts by a sharp pain in his chest, the sign of a heart attack that took him away in a matter of minutes.

Three perspectives of analysis will be drawn out to underline that a social process presides over the various return trips to the synagogue. The story of *A Contract* summarizes newcomers' oscillations between the sociocultural and religious heritage of the country of origin and the dominant culture in the United States in the 1930s.

This story is especially interesting because the author is a second-generation immigrant and tells stories from the previous generation. While putting into images how this generation remembers the difficulties that they encountered, Eisner also brings in the point of view of the second generation of migrants, who have been able to leave the ghettos or to acquire enough distance to the tribulations of the first generation. By recounting the turpitude of the inhabitants of the Jewish ghettos in the United States, Eisner synthesizes the narratives that constitute the memory of this diaspora.

The author has highlighted the social life in the Jewish ghetto in several stories, such as "The Name of the Game" (2003). But what is interesting about *A Contract* is that its sociological dimension is little discussed and overshadowed by the religious dimension stemming from Eisner's rather unique topic for this narrative. The human dimension as well as the story of the memories of a first-generation migrant have been recounted, which is why this chapter focuses exclusively on the first story of the volume.

Will Eisner

This graphic novel marks the return of the comic book maverick, Eisner, previously known for his successful antihero, *The Spirit*. Like many comic-strip artists in the United States, he is the son of Jewish immigrants from Europe (Buhle 2004; Parker Royal 2011a; Schlam 2001). He was born in 1917 in New York City, where he lived in Jewish Brooklyn (Dauber 2006). Artistically, the 1940–52 years are known as Eisner's golden period, with the publication of his hero, *The Spirit*, in twenty daily newspapers' Sunday editions, building his potential readership up to five million (Grant 2005).

In the 1970s, the comic book world was in full swing and rediscovered *The Spirit*'s very avant-garde stance (Andelman 2005). Eisner was rescued from oblivion and began a new career at the age of almost sixty. With his pioneering "spirit," he sought to make albums with a realistic narrative that read like a novel (Harvey 2001). Although not entirely autobiographical, the story that opens his first so-called graphic novel is nevertheless closely linked to the author's biography. Eisner had lost a daughter, Alice, about ten years earlier, at the same age as Rachele, the daughter of the hero of the story (Roth 2007, 467; Tuusvuori 2017, 17). This information was not disclosed by the author until 2001, in the preface to the reprint of the album (Eisner 2001; Schumacher 2010, 314–15).

A Contract that Signs a Covenant

This dense narrative is accessible in many ways. Of these, we propose to focus on the narrative, deliberately leaving aside many graphic aspects (Eisner 1985). This story can be examined on three intertwined perspectives. These perspectives correspond to the focal points raised by sociology of religion and migration sociology, namely, the character of the religious heritage in the migration process; the requirement to maintain a tradition and finally, the accommodations the migrant must concede with the host culture. We will untangle these three perspectives present in the story to show one or another characteristic of the issues raised by Eisner's work.

In evoking the pact of a young Jew, one cannot help but refer to the great story of the covenant of the Jewish people with God. However, the signing of the pact concentrates on the three perspectives mentioned earlier, namely, the religious roots of the young Jew fleeing the pogroms, the issue of maintaining a "pure" lineage and the barrier to minimize accommodation with the host culture that will lead the young Jew to "naturally" join the Hasidic community in New York. The contract crystallizes on its flat stone a core of values that the immigrant is keen to retain from his culture of origin in his migratory journey.

The first perspective of analysis consists of the references to the Bible that the author scatters throughout the story. The tale begins with a man walking in a torrential rain—an initial reference to the flood in which the hero thinks that building fifty-five on Dropsie Avenue is about to rise and go with the tide "like Noah's arch" (Eisner 1978, 92[2]) (Figure 13.1). The journey offered to the young Jew evokes the Abrahamic tradition. We see, for example, a man shaking hands with the leaving young man, saying: "You will go with Reb Lipshitz to the North. There is a seaport where you can buy a passage on a ship!" Another added: "Do not worry Frimmeleh, God is with you. You will go to America" (21). The first penciled version even mentions that the youngster was "chosen by God" (Lind 2018, 32 [comic strip plate 16]).

The flat stone used for the contract then refers to the tablets of the law carved on stone by Moses at Mount Sinai. This stone with the inscription *A Contract with God* is the title panel of the story (comic strip plate 1), underlining the explicit reference to the tables of the law.

The hero's virtuous conduct and its consequences are other aspects that recall the Torah's teachings. Young Hersh was chosen because he behaved virtuously. The elders say to him, "God will reward you (bold in the text)" (Eisner 1978, 20). In the forest, before young Frimme writes his contract, in a dialogue with the elderly who accompanies him, the elderly will say to him, "if justice is not in God's hands—where would it be?" (21). Frimme is good and just and will commit himself faithfully to the Hasidic community.

Like a modern Job, the Jewish hero will do everything possible to fulfill his part of the contract. The adoption of a daughter, Rachele, dumped on

Figure 13.1 Will Eisner, *A Contract with God and Other Tenement Stories*, W.W. Norton, p. 18. By courtesy of W.W. Norton.

his doorstep, will be seen as a sign that God was also fulfilling his part of the contract. It is when Rachele dies that everything shifts. The balance is broken, and the covenant is called into question. As in the story of Job, the pious Hersh has nothing to reproach himself for. In a peculiar way, the story reverses the logic of the biblical book of Job. It is by breaking with God that Hersh finds success in all his endeavors and quickly becomes wealthy.

However, this rise to fortune is fraught with persistent malaise. The breaking of the covenant implies a denial of part of the immigrant's Jewish identity.

It is then that Hersh approaches the synagogue to ask for a new pact to be prepared for him. For this second contract, the author takes care to provide a modern religious setting (characterized by a synagogue, rabbis, and Talmudic discussions), far from the allusions to the biblical grand covenant. The rabbis emphasize the "private" character of the requested contract and, finally, it is by offering a building to the synagogue that Hersh facilitates the rabbis' agreement to propose a new contract. A contract in the purest American way. Business is business, God seems to be far removed from all these dealings, until the moment of the heart attack. The human being is reminded of his finiteness, he is not the one who lays down the rules of the contract of life (Figure 13.2). There is a grain of sand in the great American commercial machinery.

Tuusvuori argues that "Eisner's work ought to be called 'two contracts with God'" (Tuusvuori 2017, 25). Susanne Klingenstein (Klingenstein 2007) mentions, "the long roots of Eisner's quarrel with God." For her, the story of this contract with God must be placed in the Jewish tradition. Even though, in Jewish thought, the individualism of the covenant is the opposite of the idea of covenant that is contracted with a community (85), this covenant is an explicit reference to the covenant concept in Judaism.

For the author, the lesson to be drawn from this first perspective of analysis is that fidelity does not change the covenant. One always remains a Jew, a member of the covenant's people. The covenant transcends everything else to the point that even when Hersh manages to negotiate a new contract, American style, the rules of the covenant for life and death prevail (see Deuteronomy 29 and 30). Human beings cannot set the rules of the covenant between God and man. The fact is that no human being is completely in control of his or her destiny; he or she may even die at the moment of his or her new start in life.

A Contract to Continue a Line of Tradition

The second perspective is the long tradition, the cultural baggage that one generation seeks to pass on to the next (Parker Royal 2011b). The author shows the extent to which, in a diaspora situation, the maintenance of the cultural heritage is essential. In an illustrative way, he underlines what several studies in the sociology of migration have shown: in seeking to maintain a tradition in their host country, migrants must adapt it and thus unwittingly transform it (Baumann 2009; Knott 2009). The author illustrates this through two of the hero's biographical moments, represented by the two contracts. The death of a

Figure 13.2 Will Eisner, *A Contract with God and Other Tenement Stories*, W.W. Norton, p. 44. By courtesy of W.W. Norton.

daughter, which is the pivot of the story, puts an end to the line of tradition he had been commissioned for by his home village in Russia. It was to carry out this elective mission that he had signed the pact engraved on a flat stone. Breaking the lineage leads to breaking the contract. That death means more than a human loss. It also signifies the collapse of a fragile branch of the Jewish heritage tree.

This point is not to be minimized: when Hersh has negotiated a new contract, it is indeed on a new lineage that he places his hopes. He says: "And, and after all—I am not too old to marry. I shall have a daughter" (Eisner 1978, 55) (Figure 13.3). Producing offspring and continuing the memory is a central issue in diaspora populations. For the hero of the story, it is when the hope of being able to transmit his heritage is reborn that he dies of a heart attack, putting a definitive end to the chain of tradition! We are here at the heart of a strong

Figure 13.3 Will Eisner, *A Contract with God and Other Tenement Stories*, W.W. Norton, p. 31. By courtesy of W.W. Norton.

tension in Eisner's work in reference to the Shoah. One can observe here that in the narrative of the memories of the first generation recompiled by the author are linked to later events. The baggage of a diaspora's tradition in seeking to make memory necessarily transforms its meaning in the light of more recent events.

Following the first contract, the young Jew will seek a pious life by taking refuge in the Hasidic community. Yet, ironically, Hersh will leave no religious legacy in New York, only an economic and real estate heritage, partly bequeathed to the Dropsie Avenue Synagogue … And his legacy to the Jewish community will be the fruits of a theft from the synagogue's treasury, the start of his life of fortune in breach of Jewish tradition.

In this perspective, the other aspect to be dealt with is that of the reconfiguration of tradition in a diaspora situation, which the author raises in two ways. The first is young Hersh's involvement in the Hasidic community, a community that provides security through orthopraxy. The author does not address this issue head-on and limits himself to underlining the hero's piety, acknowledged by all. The second is that of religious leaders in a diaspora situation: the rabbis reinterpret the tradition to formulate the (second) contract.

Two panels, one of them on a full page, present their scruples and fears of disobeying and blaspheming God until an elder suggests that their service is to "abbreviate" the law rather than "deviate" (Eisner 1978, 51). The terms of the new contract they propose are thus the result of a negotiation and reinterpretation of the Torah. But again, the author treats these teachers of the law's palavers ironically. In the story, the new negotiated contract will not produce any tradition. Instead, the tradition will "appoint" an unknown young Hasidic to take over the contract, as will be shown below.

As Jeremy Dauber (2006, 291) points out, "In telling this story, then, Eisner is also creating a metaphor for American Jewish existence and the issue of violating tradition as well as maintaining it, both speaking to his own autobiographical experiences and creating an ethnic-national narrative." The protagonists' hesitations, (de-)conversions, are possible points of rupture or renegotiation of tradition. However, through the story, we read that the religious tradition does not bother much with human beings' moods. It is maintained, transformed, and resumed on the basis of forgotten details. It should also be noted that, for the author, it is a case of the Jewish tradition after the Shoah, even if his drawn heroes are set in the New York of the interwar period.

A Contract to Secure a Cultural Heritage

The third perspective of interpretation is that of the arrangements that migrants are constrained to make between the values of their culture of origin, which they wish to preserve, and those they would like to share with their host society. In Eisner's account, young Hersh seeks to faithfully maintain the tradition as promised by the village elders (Figure 13.3). To this end, he joins the Hasidic community. By throwing away the pact, he denies his origins and fully integrates into the American way of life. The second pact will only be an assimilated American's attempt to reconnect with Jewish tradition. The author thus underlines migrants' ambivalence in their assimilation process, prey to doubts regarding their culture of origin as well as their host culture.

In the Hasidic community, the hero is in fact not fully immersed in American culture. He is distanced from it by communal rules and social ties centered on synagogue life. He remains sitting on a fence between two places, far from his home village, but far from New Yorkers' reality. He strives to keep the principles of Jewish piety, physically close to American life, but socially far removed from its values. By breaking with the pact, Hersh broke into American life head-on. He met with dazzling economic success. He is one of those self-made men that American society is so fond of feeding its dream

Figure 13.4 Will Eisner, *A Contract with God and Other Tenement Stories*, W.W. Norton, p. 28. By courtesy of W.W. Norton.

with. This is a critical allusion by the author to this valorization of first-time immigrants' entrepreneurial success in—and thanks to—twentieth-century America. For Eisner, this assimilation cannot be achieved without lies, deals, and heartbreaks.

The section of the story that shows Hersh's success, however, is the most negative part of the narrative. In recounting Hersh's extraordinary fortune, the author deliberately dwells on the points that stump the reader: his hero becomes harsh and stingy with his tenants, he treats them only as sources of income to be maximized. Only on one page (panel 41) does the author relate Hersh's success with his banker giving him good news. In contrast, the description of his daily life with his mistress and her questions takes up four pages. With his story, the author also seeks to question the doxa of the host society.

Success, the American dreams, only produce dreams! No one will inherit Hersh's fortune, and no one will survive it. Ironically, it is the synagogue that will benefit from Hersh's (non-traditional) wanderings by living off the income from the building on Dropsie Avenue that Hersh traded for the contract. This is the author's way of showing that, despite the hero's deviations and oscillations in the story, the tradition endures, it continues, unchanged (Figure 13.5).

As an epilogue, a second irony in the story: The rejected contract stone is found by a young Hasidic. With this, the author shows that the thorny issue of

Figure 13.5 Will Eisner, *A Contract with God and Other Tenement Stories*, W.W. Norton, p. 61. By courtesy of W.W. Norton.

assimilation for American immigrants is not over. Each generation has to take up the work again to integrate into American society. Thus, from this perspective, the story *A Contract* can be read as a reminder "that the Jewish subject, in the process of assimilation, faces threats to his or her identity" (Parker Royal 2011b, 157). Laurence Roth (2007, 466) proposes to understand this story as "a visual critique of the American exceptionalism—the cultural chauvinism—that fueled the rise of superhero comics, and of a Jewish exceptionalism hard-pressed by the immigrant experience."

A Sociological Reading of the Narrative

It is important to note that the issue of settling into an American immigration context is the common thread running through this creative period. The different stories that Eisner offers provide a panorama of life situations for these newcomers who have come to settle on Dropsie Avenue in the Bronx: "Eisner's graphic cycle underscores the ambivalence felt by many ethnic Americans (in this case, first- and second-generation Jewish Americans). On the one hand, it represents the split of the Jewish subject, torn between the lure of cultural integration and the ethnic community's demands. That is what Werner Sollors describes as tensions between relations of "consent" and "descent," which he sees as "the central drama in American culture" (1986, 6). For Parker Royal, "the hybrid nature of *A Contract with God* … is an apt form for a kind of ethnic writing that struggles with questions of assimilation and identity. As an in-between text … Eisner's graphic cycle underscores the ambivalence felt by many ethnic American (in this case, first- and second-generation Jewish Americans)" (2011b, 153).

Eisner uses these threatening features to remind readers that many aspects of the American dream are just hot air and do not lead to much. Thus, the first- or second-generation Jew in America is, for Eisner, a being caught between two contracts, that of his home culture and that of his host culture. Both have their share of (unfulfilled) promises and constraints. Jewish tradition (whether synagogue or Hasidic) continues to run its course despite defections and betrayals, and the American dream must go on sparkling despite its false promises.

In this story, "the subject matter … could easily stand alongside more 'traditional' narratives as illustrative representations of Jewish American life in the twentieth century" (Parker Royal 2011b, 151). He implicitly refers to the literature on migration and the city in the American sociological tradition that began in early twentieth-century Chicago with Robert E. Park, comparing the growing city of Chicago to a living organism (Park, Burgess and McKenzie 1925) or the city to a laboratory of human life (Park 1915). Specifically relevant is Louis Wirth on migration in his book *The Ghetto* (1928). Eisner sketches in his own way the Jewish diaspora's life in New York. Religious affiliation is treated as one of the components of the ghetto's social environment.

It is known from several studies that migration favors the arrivals' conversion or deconversion (Hirschman, 2004; Rambo, 1993; Snow and Machalek 1984). The hero of the story illustrates many migrants' ambivalence to the United States (Jews in Eisner's stories), torn as they are between two cultures. This is even more interesting as the author focuses on the concrete consequences of religion such as the lifestyle and social changes of the protagonists he draws. The one in *A contract* underlines the difficulty of newcomers from the diaspora to reconstruct themselves in the American context.

The author's strength also lies in staging the flaws of the American dream, that of the self-made man, who quickly achieves fortune. This gap gives weight to tradition, that is, the cultural and religious heritage acquired in the country of origin. Eisner shows the back-and-forth movements in the process of newcomers to the United States' accommodation between the culture of origin and the host culture.

The contract and its questioning in the narrative make it possible to highlight two major perspectives in sociology. Firstly, that of life trajectories, which for newcomers are made up of oscillations between commitment and questioning. Secondly, that of the contingencies of a social environment that influences belief and its misgivings.

In this story, the idea of questioning a contract with God made by a young Jew shows that a religious history, however individualized, is always embedded in a social context. He follows social science observations that show that the context of migration fosters young arrivals' conversion to the Hasidic community, in order to maintain a strong link with a "pure" tradition. This context also favors the assimilation of others like Hersh who reject the contract and turn away from Judaism or distance themselves from religion to forge a strong bond with the host society. Hersh's revolt, and then his appeasement, illustrate the ambivalence of many migrant arrivals in the United States, torn between two cultures and undergoing a slow accommodation juggling between newcomers' cultures of origin and acceptance of the new one.

Interestingly in these stories, Eisner depicts ghetto life as an *insider*, while Louis Wirth (1928) portrays it as an outsider. Eisner is not a sociologist and the Chicago School cannot have been of much significance to him. Nor does he work solely on field observations, but collects stories, observations that constitute a memorial corpus of the Jewish diaspora in New York. He then stages them as if they were unfolding before the reader's eyes. However, he offers the readers narratives that compile the Jewish ghettos' (hi)stories. He stages them with caricatured heroes. In each of these stories, these cartoonistic figures concentrate a kind of Weberian idealtype. They do not actually exist, but their stories closely mirror these ghetto populations' lives. In the *Contract*, however, Frimme's story differs from the others, because Eisner then does not focus so much on the neighborhood's social issues. Rather, he depicts an immigrant's entire journey, from his home region—complete with all its attendant beliefs—to New York City and its American dream. He does this through a religious analogy, which has been of particular interest to commentators and scholars so far (Eisner usually treats religion only as a backdrop to his comic adventures).

Obviously, Eisner met with a number of criticisms: these characters were much closer to caricature than to description, the scenes favored humor, and so on, which made the story sometimes inappropriate (Lund 2021) . He himself admitted the latter. The scenarios, even if some sociological interpretations can be drawn from them, as in this case, face the difficulty that they are first and foremost at the service of a story and not of a sociological issue. And even if this were the case, comics imply shortcuts and ellipses, which means that they are not the best medium to transcribe sociological terrain. The French comic by the sociologist Valérie Amiraux tells the life of the Hasidic Jews in her neighborhood through the questions of her daughter Salomée (Amiraux and Desharnais 2015). It is through her daughter's questions and remarks that the sociologist can make the field observations accessible to the readers, in this case, with the assumed limits of the child's gaze and naivety.

In a recent issue of *Sociologica* (vol. 15 (1), 2021), several authors analyzed the relationship between social sciences and comics (for an overview, see: Hague 2021). In France, a project launched by four young sociologists aims to integrate documentaries from research fields in a new and specific collection called *Sociorama*. This collection of albums is "meant to fill an original position in the social field of realistic graphic novels" (Berthaut, Bidet, and Thura 2021, 268). However, this kind of work does not satisfy the instigators of the collection. As they note in their recent paper, "from these reflections stems the understanding that these comic books have not entirely fulfilled their dual objective of scientific dissemination and editorial success" (288). Other initiatives include the successful *Portraits of Violence* album by Evans and Wilson (2016) is an exercise in comic book writing to be put somewhat into perspective according to the author. “I see the book as an accompaniment and not a replacement for the original texts, which the volume draws upon” (Evans 2021, 260).

In telling the story of *A Contract*, it is not clear that Eisner was aware of the different levels of analysis that his story would produce. Of the three perspectives we have identified here, we note that they are all intertwined around the theme of the contract, which thus takes on multiple levels of analysis. If we untangle the threads of the religious contract, we actually observe sociological patterns of the first generation migrant individual. One point where the sociological analysis joins those that discuss the Jewish characteristics of the narrative is that of religion as an important memory and cultural baggage in the life of the migrant. Eisner was so skilled at putting the profound dilemmas of first-generation migrants into a narrative that few have seen the sociological dimension beyond the religious dilemma of his narrative.

The three perspectives we have distinguished can all be related to the sociology of religion or, more broadly, sociological literature on migration. The first perspective shows how a first-generation migrant arrived with a cultural baggage where religion played a paramount role. Louis Wirth has emphasized how fundamental the role of the synagogue was for these Jewish arrivals fleeing persecution in Eastern Europe and Russia. At the same time, he showed how necessary the renegotiation of tradition was (second perspective) with the arrival of the different immigration waves. However, the third perspective is that maintaining a cultural heritage in another society cannot be achieved without a trade-off with the original values and identities that one would like to uphold. We therefore realize that while Eisner tells us the story of *A Conctract*, he is not telling us anything other than how difficult it is for the first-generation migrant to work out a social contract. If Eisner is not a sociologist, we can underline sociological dimensions in his human stories. In putting his tales into pictures and caricatures, the author never neglects the human dimension and the possible social interactions. Although by showing the ambivalence of a Jew with his religious tradition, Eisner underlines the ambivalence of migrants toward the culture of origin and the culture of the host society. It highlights and depicts in a caricatured way the cost of assimilation or the price of remaining confined to one’s ghetto.

Conclusion

The richness of Eisner’s story *A Contract with God* is multilevel. Here, we have presented three of them that seemed most relevant to us. The first is the religious references of the covenant with God. The cultural anchoring of the Jewish tradition will not allow the hero of the story to completely cut himself off from his roots.

> Yet, as Eisner shows in ["To the Heart of the Storm" (1991)], being Jewish is far more complicated than just a religious matter, and conversion will not change who a person really is. As Aunt Goldie's husband puts it, after converting to Catholicism, Goldie is "not entirely" Jewish but "underneath … she's still a Jew… Y' can't change the stripes on a zebra!" (Eisner 2007, 245–6). (Dong 2011, 28)

Despite the individual nature of the process, the author emphasizes the extent to which the tradition remains collective and embedded in a cultural heritage, which refers to the second perspective, namely the chain of memory.

The idea of *A Contract* that was meant to safeguard the memory of a village (which will disappear following the pogroms) by means of a community member enables the author to recall how much a person is part of a chain of transmission. In this story, "The Heart of the Storm" (Eisner 1991) stems from the hero's inability to ensure the proper transmission of his cultural and religious heritage because of his only daughter's death. This gap is experienced as a personal tragedy while having an impact on the religious community he belongs to (one can see an implicit reference to the Shoah here). However, for Eisner, tradition, a primordial concern of the early arrivals, could not care less about human beings' piety, as it is only concerned with continuing its long journey. Forgotten residues can thus be relays to perpetuate the tradition for the next generation, which will reinterpret it in its own way.

The third and final perspective we have described, in a sociological perspective, in this narrative is that of a cultural pact that the migrant has to deal with in his or her migration trajectory. The pact represents the will to preserve one's culture of origin. Now, migrants must also deal with the host society. Eisner points out that assimilation cannot take place for newcomers without questioning certain aspects of the cultural contract with the culture of origin. Their soul-searching implies possible and probable oscillations for migrants, who must also take into account their life trajectories and status changes in the new society. Conversion or deconversion is here necessary in the trajectory toward the migrant's assimilation.

To conclude, we would argue that Eisner's work reminds us of several basic tenets of sociology. In particular, the individual in his or her life trajectory is always dependent on a social context. Even if this trajectory is told in an individual way, Eisner reminds us that it must be placed in the social situation in which changes appear. Strangely, in the sociology of religion, religious variables, such as belief, practice, and belonging, are only individual variables. It is important to have individual dimensions, but Eisner reminds us here that the individual is not isolated from a context. By excessively individualizing the research on conversion and deconversion, the scholar no longer perceives the social and contextual contingencies in which these phenomena emerge. Eisner takes a fundamental stance for sociology: (de-)conversion is not only individuals, it emerges in a life trajectory, within a specific social context. The questioning of *A Contract with God* is therefore very much in line with the ambivalence and hesitation that a first-generation migrant encounters in a social contract. Eisner's narrative of contract discussions reminds sociologists that a negotiation, even a highly religious one, is always deeply embedded in a social background and context.

Notes

1 The author would like to thank the *Centre interfacultaire d'histoire et de sciences des religions* of the University of Lausanne for financial support and Dominique Macabies for the English version.

2 The page numbers refer to the comic strip plate/panel number independent of the book version and not the actual page in the book.

References

Amiraux, Valérie, and Desharnais Francis. (2015), *Salomé et les Hommes en Noir*, Montréal: Bayard Canada.

Andelman, Bob. (2005), *Eisner: A Spirited Life*, Milwaukie: M Press.

Baumann, Martin. (2009), "Templeisation: Continuity and Change of Hindu Traditions in Diaspora," *Journal of Religion in Europe* 2 (2): 149–79. doi: 10.1163/187489209X437026.

Berthaut, Jérôme, Bidet, Jennifer, and Thura Mathias. (2021), "Making Sociologically-Grounded Fictions. A Review of the Sociorama Collection Experience," *Sociologica* 15 (1): 265–90. doi:10.6092/issn.1971-8853/12777.

Buhle, Paul. (2004), *From the Lower East Side to Hollywood: Jews in American Popular Culture*, London: Verso.

Dauber, Jeremy. (2006), "Comic Books, Tragic Stories: Eisner's American Jewish History," *AJS Review* 30 (2): 277–304. doi: 10.1017/S0364009406000134.

Dong, Lan. (2011), "Thinly Disguised (Autobio)Graphical Stories: Eisner's Life, in Pictures," *Shofar* 29 (2): 13–33.

Eisner, Will. (1978), *A Contract with God and Other Tenement Stories*, New York: Baronet Press.

Eisner, Will. (1985), *Comics and Sequential Art*, New York: Poorhouse Press.

Eisner, Will. (1991), *To the Heart of the Storm*, Princeton: Kitchen Sink Press.

Eisner, Will. (2001), *A Contract with God and Other Tenement Stories*. 3rd edn 1985. Reprint, Burbank, CA: DC Comics.

Eisner, Will. (2003), *The Name of the Game*. 2nd edn 2001. Reprint, Burbank, CA: DC Comics.

Eisner, Will. (2005), *The Contract with God Trilogy*, New York: W. W. Norton.

Eisner, Will. (2007), *Life, in Pictures: Autobiographical Stories*, New York: W.W. Norton.

Evans, Brad, and Wilson Sean Michael (2016), *Portraits of Violence: An Illustrated History of Radical Critique*, Oxford: New Internationalist.

Evans, Brad. (2021), "Portraits of Violence. Critical Reflections on the Graphic Novel," *Sociologica* 15 (1): 241–63. doi: 10.6092/issn.1971-8853/12283.

Grant, Steven. (2005), "The Spirit of Eisner," *Comics Journal* 267 April-May: 104–10.

Hague, Ian. (2021), "Social Sciences/Comics: A Commentary on Sociologica's Exploration of Comics," *Sociologica* 15 (1): 305–10. doi: 10.6092/issn.1971-8853/12780.

Harvey, Robert C. (2001), "The Graphic Novel, Eisner, and Other Pioneers," *Comics Journal* 234 (June 2001): 92–7.

Hirschman, Charles. (2004), "The Role of Religion in the Origins and Adaptation of Immigrant Groups in the United States," *International Migration Review* 38 (3): 1206–33. doi: 10.1111/j.1747-7379.2004.tb00233.x.

Kitchen, Denis. (2017), "The Art, Tools and Techniques of Eisner," in John Lind (ed.), *Eisner. The Centennial Celebration*, 15–19. Milwaukee: Dark Horse Comics & Kitchen Sink.

Klingenstein, Susanne. (2007), "The Long Roots of Eisner's Quarrel with God," *Studies in American Jewish Literature* 26: 81–8.

Knott, Kim. (2009), "Becoming a 'Faith Community': British Hindus, Identity, and the Politics of Representation," *Journal of Religion in Europe* 2 (2): 85–114. doi: 10.1163/187489209X437008.

Levitz, Paul. (2015), *Eisner: Champion of the Graphic Novel*, New York: Abrams Comicarts.

Lind, John, ed. (2018), *A Contract with God: Curator's Collection. Volume One: Pencils*, Milwaukee: Kitchen Sink Books/Darks Horse Comics.

Lund, Martin. (2021), "Eisner: A Contract with God," in Domsch Sebastian, Hassler-Forest Dan, and Vanderbeke Dirk (eds.), *Handbook of Comics and Graphic Narratives*, 431–50. Berlin, Boston: De Gruyter, doi 10.1515/9783110446968-024.

Park, Robert Ezra. (1915), "The City: Suggestions for the Investigation of Human Behavior in the City Environment," *American Journal of Sociology* XX, 5 (March 1915): 577–612.

Park, Robert Ezra, Ernest Watson Burgess and McKenzie, Roderick Duncan. (1925), *The City*, Chicago: University of Chicago Press.

Parker Royal, Derek. (2011a), "Jewish Comics; Or, Visualizing Current Jewish Narrative," *Shofar: An Interdisciplinary Journal of Jewish Studies* 29 (2): 1–12.

Parker Royal, Derek. (2011b), "Sequential Sketches of Ethnic Identity: Eisner's *A Contract with God* as Graphic Cycle," *College Literature* 38 (3): 150–67.

Parker Royal, Derek. (2011c), "There Goes the Neighborhood: Cycling Ethnoracial Tensions in Eisner's Dropsie Avenue," *Shofar: An Interdisciplinary Journal of Jewish Studies* 29 (2): 120–45.

Rambo, Lewis R. (1993), *Understanding Religious Conversion*, New Haven: Yale University Press.

Roth, Laurence. (2007), "'Drawing Contracts: Eisner's Legacy.' Review of *The Contract with God* Trilogy: Life on Dropsie Avenue, Eisner; The Rabbi's Cat, Joann Sfar; Klezmer. Book One: Tales of the Wild East, Joann Sfar; Megillat Esther, J. T. Waldman," *Jewish Quarterly Review* 97 (3): 463–84.

Schlam, Helena Frenkil. (2001), "Contemporary Scribes: Jewish American Cartoonists," *Shofar: An Interdisciplinary Journal of Jewish Studies* 20 (1): 94–112. doi: 10.1353/sho.2001.0075.

Schumacher, Michael. (2010), *Eisner: a Dreamer's Life in Comics*, New York: Bloomsbury.

Snow, David A., and Machalek, Richard (1984), "The Sociology of Conversion," *Annual Review of Sociology* 10: 167–90.

Sollors, Werner. (1986), *Beyond Ethnicity: Consent and Descent in American Culture*, New York: Oxford University Press.

Spiegelman, Art. (1986), *Maus: A Survivor's Tale*. 2 vols. Vol. 1, New York Pantheon.

Spiegelman, Art. (1991), *Maus: And Here My Troubles Began*. 2 vols. Vol. 2, New York: Pantheon.

Tuusvuori, Jarkko. (2017), "Philosophy in the Bargain: *A Contract with God* (1978) by Eisner," in Jeff McLaughlin (ed.) *Graphic Novels as Philosophy*, 17–40. Jackson: University Press of Mississippi.

Vinklarek, Petr. (2013), "The Interplay of Text and Image in Comics: A Linguistic Interpretation of Eisner's *A Contract with God*," in Gregory Jason Bell, Katarina Nemcokova, and Wojcik Bartosz (eds.), *From Theory to Practice*, 135–43. Zlin: Thomas Bata University in Zlin.

Wirth, Louis. (1928), *The Ghetto*, Chicago: University of Chicago Press.

14

Comics as a Way of Doing, Encountering, and Making Religion

Kees de Groot

How does the study of comics contribute to our understanding of religion in contemporary societies, which are sometimes characterized as liquid, that is, having floating boundaries between the institutional spheres, including the religious (de Groot 2018)? This concluding chapter collects the insights that have been gained and formulates questions for further research. Comics allow us to learn about society, about culture, and, above all, about the presence of religion in society. The study of comics and religion demonstrates that comics are a way of encountering, doing, and making religion in different social contexts.

Doing Religion

For participants in religion, reading religious comics, looking at the pictures, talking about them, or using them as guides to visit sacred sites, have become part of the repertoire of religious practice. Religious groups, motivations, expressions, and teachings have been involved both in protest against, and in the promotion of comics. While participants in traditions as diverse as Christianity, Hinduism, and Zoroastrianism enjoy seeing their familiar stories and imagery in the visual language of comics, others have rejected the medium of comics for the portrayal of persons who are held sacred—or have at least rejected certain portrayals of the sacred. The integrated appearance of text and image seems to have a sacred power of its own, which provokes responses ranging from veneration and awe to indignation and hurt. In between, there is the moderate criticism mentioned earlier by those who appreciate how comics present the sacred tradition to the uninitiated, but question the validity of how this is done, as some Zoroastrian respondents do.

Visual language has been used in various religious traditions. An early Christian example is the *Annunciation* (1333) by Simone Martini and Lippo Memmi, where the words spoken by the Archangel Gabriel, who is depicted alongside Mary, are included in the picture (Vermassen 2018). Religious comics are related to these examples, although it is important to note that the popular status of comics differs considerably from these high-status sacred images. Three chapters in this volume (by Häger and Kauranen, by MacWilliams, and by Reichelt Føreland) have shown the delicacy of dealing with the sacred gaze in comics.

The flip side of veneration is outrage. There is a high sensitivity in religions to visualized criticism, parody, and satire, for example, in cartoons. Comics also tend to be considered provocative by those who regard offending instances as a violation of a sacred order. Several traditions have even prohibited images altogether or certain images in particular (van Asselt et al. 2007). The medium matters.

On the supply side of religion, the impact of the medium is evident in two categories: classic religious comics for children, such as those studied by Trysnes, and contemporary religious comics for adults such as those studied by Häger and Kauranen. The first category shows religion as it negotiates the conditions of the new modern medium in the twentieth century: the traditional message is presented in the language of the time. Comics designed for the religious education of children radiate the ideals cherished by organized religion, but at the same time reflect the surrounding culture of the time. Thus, comics culture influenced the portrayal of young Christians as private investigators. The second category, adult comics, is even more deeply indebted to contemporary culture. Lived religion, rather than official religion, is to the fore in comics. The turn to everyday life in comics and graphic novels since the late twentieth century is reflected in a more personal approach to religion, which also allows for humor and criticism. The religious comic has come of age.

The role that comics play in pilgrimage is particularly strong testimony to the fact that they are increasingly involved in religious practice "on the ground." All over the world, religious stories, symbols, and sites figure both in visual media such as films, games, and TV series, and in social media. In the Japanese examples MacWilliams provides, comics evolve from a guide to visiting existing sites to inducements to visit new sites. This phenomenon is far from restricted to the East. Comics take part in and influence lived religion. Lived religion is also living religion; it is open to transformation and innovation. Comics bring with them a tradition of humor, playfulness, and ambiguity.

This volume has presented some of the varieties of religious expression in comics. But both the production and the impact of comics deserve greater attention. How does production (Bourdieu 1996) work within the religious field? How are religious comics culturally produced, and how does the interplay between religious or secular publishers, authors, distribution companies, webhosts, and booksellers operate? Future empirical studies may also demonstrate tensions *within* religious fields between strategies directed toward safeguarding the status quo through instrumentalizing comics and strategies of renewal (Cadegan 2013).

Much can be learned from cultural sociology (Edgell 2012). In this volume, most authors have been interested in investigating the role of culture as a dependent variable: What is reflected in comics? Future research could also focus on culture as an independent variable: How do comics affect society and how does reading comics affect society? Such an approach would also enhance the visual literacy of academics.

Encountering Religion

In societies where religion is no longer, or never was, controlled by religious institutions, an important type of religious presence is that it is simply "out there" in society. Along with processes of mediatization, religion pops up in political campaigns, advertisements, documentaries, movies, games, and comics.

Graphic novels and comics such as *A Contract with God*, *Preacher*, *The Second Coming*, or *Habibi* are products of popular culture and happen to contain religious references. Their religious themes are not unimportant, but their production and reception are not determined by religious motives. These comics are made by artists who operate without any mandate from religious authorities, and they are published by commercial publishing houses. They are considered entertainment or art, not instruments for religious education or evangelization, although they are as likely to teach and inspire readers as they are to offend readers' beliefs or nourish their aversion toward faith. Whatever effect they have, they are important means of encountering the religious in contemporary culture, if only because of their wide popularity.

Often it is not quite clear whether the secular or the religious aspect is the predominant one, such as in Osamu Tezuka's manga *Buddha*. This series helps to disseminate the *dharma*, but is produced outside the religious realm and its readership is not confined to the Buddhist milieu. The *Amar Chitra Katha* series, including *Zarathustra* and *Krishna*, also contributes vastly to the presence of religion in popular culture outside the boundaries of religious communities, and it is appreciated as an attractive, if deficient introduction to the faith. Through comics, people—the secular, the religious as well as those on the boundary between the two—encounter "the religious," "the more diffuse articulations … [in which religion] is significantly transformed as it spreads throughout the surface of social life, disseminating signs yet having to accommodate to given formats" (Herbert 2012, 90; cf. Meyer and Moors 2006, 16–19).

The chapters in this volume have highlighted how the medium of comics influences the portrayal of religion. The format of traditional American-style comics promotes a focus on powerful problem-solving main characters who are preferably equipped with extraordinary powers. Gods become superheroes. The formats of the graphic novel and the *bande dessinée* seem to offer more space for the representation of everyday life. This permits the personal and social aspects of contemporary Judaism (*A Contract with God, Maus*) or Hinduism (the comics by Leka and Leka) to come to the fore.

Religion appears in comics as the object of ridicule or is portrayed in all its complexity—even to the extent of equaling a sociological approach (A *Contract with God)*—and this potentially in the same comic. It can be represented or criticized, it can inspire and appall. As the studies of the Lekas's comics, of *Preacher* and *Habibi* clarify, the way religion is portrayed says as much about what is represented as about the culture from which it springs. In this way, comics also confront readers with familiar cultural and religious elements that are implied in the representation of exotic religious universes: a Puritan ethic in *Preacher*'s parodic cosmology and liberal Protestantism in *Habibi*'s mystical Islam. Comics mirror culture, including religion.

Several religions are covered in this volume. Others have been discussed elsewhere and should be explored further. How do readers of comics come across new religious movements (Thomas 2012), new forms of spirituality (Locke 2012), esoterica (Knowles 2007), and religious themes such as messianism (Savramis 1985)? Underground comics, which are hardly covered in this volume, may throw light on specific subcultures associated with new spiritualities. Future research should also point out how readers, or, as in the case of *The Second Coming*, people who just catch glimpses of comics or only know about them by hearsay, experience, and evaluate these references. And how do these references influence people's perceptions of religion? There are promising avenues for research of comics as a part of networks in which artefacts, meanings, persons, and institutions interact.

Making Religion

Comics are not only a way of practicing preexisting religions and of encountering the religious, but they are also part of the production of something that is in some ways very much like religion. Comics are used for social functions that are often associated with religion: finding meaning, ritualization, sacralization, and imagining universes that somehow make sense and contribute to everyday life or extraordinary moments in life. Comics find readers, and the reading of comics may take on an existential dimension. Sometimes this happens in connection with religion, other times apart from it, and perhaps also in opposition to it.

According to Biano, a graphic novel such as *Maus* sacralizes the collective trauma of the Shoah. It contains explicitly religious elements from Judaism, but these become part of a symbolic universe that transcends traditional religious boundaries as it conveys something as fundamental as fidelity to trauma. It somehow makes sense of the incomprehensible. Religions are often said to do exactly this. Here, a graphic novel that can hardly be considered a religious comic in the traditional sense of the word, fulfills this function. In a much more mundane way, the Finnish comic book readers presented by Sjö have integrated reading comics into their worldviews and behavior patterns. Undheim has demonstrated how the complex layers of meaning in three Marvel and Disney productions playfully evoke awe. MacWilliams has shown how manga and anime can induce touristic pilgrimage—or tourism with ritual and sacred dimensions. Across the globe, people visit significant sites that connect them with the world of comics and animated films and share their presence through social media such as Instagram and Snapchat. The term "religion" does not seem to fit comfortably either the Japanese or the contemporary Western situation in which the boundaries between it and the secular, its opposite in the binary opposition, appear fluid. The separation of the religious and the secular may have been typical for a certain age (nineteenth and twentieth century) and area (Western societies) that also happens to be the birthplace of the modern study of religion.

As a playful medium, comics can contribute to sacralizing characters, sites, meanings—also if this sacred universe mocks established religion and even when the sacralization goes hand in hand with the realization that this is just fiction (also called "metamodernism"). The way people perceive and process comics is one subject that has not been researched enough yet. What varieties are there of the way these cultural artefacts are received by those who are not just consumers? The spectrum ranges from entertainment, art, economic investment, and fandom to fiction-based religion. And how do readers and producers interreact? Have there been attempts to influence their responses, either by promoting veneration, such as organizing events in the real world, or by "killing" or transforming a popular character? There are also material dimensions. What does the material appearance of a book tell us about the attitude it generates and receives (Kashtan 2018; Tinker 2007)? What does it signify that a rejected sketch for a *Tintin* book cover (*The Blue Lotus*) is able to fetch 2.6 million euros (January 14, 2021)? The study of what comics mean for readers and collectors could benefit from concepts and approaches developed in the study of believers and practitioners of religion.

Faith Imagined

With regard to the role of comics in the study of contemporary religion, it seems there are three ways in which comics are relevant, three ways that correspond with three categories in the population. Firstly, comics demonstrate how participants in religion practice the *imaginative* dimension of lived religion (Ammerman 2007): how they read the sacred stories, envision their gods and saints, and visit sacred places. Secondly, comics as cultural artefacts permit the general audience to encounter the visual imagery and textual traditions of various religions. Comics are part of artistic traditions in religions. Together with paintings, statues, tapestries, and calligraphic work they make up the world of material religion (Meyer 2012), or of *faith, imagined*. Thirdly, when people inside or outside existing religions learn about and imagine new symbolic universes, develop rituals, and create patterns of meaning in which they believe, for a while or more permanently, with strong or weak existential repercussions, comics may play a role in the *imagined faith* they share. Thus, new plausibility structures are formed, connecting and supporting people who are into comics. Comics, like literature, cinema, TV, music, concerts, festivals, and games, can be part of fiction-based religion (Cusack 2016; Davidsen 2014) in the making. There are all kinds of new territories to explore.

To be continued.

References

Ammerman, Nancy Tatom. (2007), *Everyday Religion Observing Modern Religious Lives*, Oxford: Oxford University Press.

Bourdieu, Pierre. (1996), *The Rules of Art: Genesis and Structure of the Literary Field*, Cambridge: Polity Press.

Cadegan, Una M. (2013), *All Good Books Are Catholic Books: Print Culture, Censorship, and Modernity in Twentieth-Century America*, Ithaca: Cornell University Press.

Cusack, Carole M. (2016), "Fiction into Religion: Imagination, Other Worlds, and Play in the Formation of Community." *Religion* 1–16. doi: 10.1080/0048721X.2016.1210390.

Davidsen, Markus Altena. (2014), *The Spiritual Tolkien Milieu: A Study of Fiction-Based Religion*, Doctoral Thesis, Leiden: Universiteit Leiden.

de Groot, Kees. (2018), *The Liquidation of the Church, Routledge New Critical Thinking in Religion, Theology and Biblical Studies*, London: Routledge.

Edgell, Penny. (2012), "A Cultural Sociology of Religion: New Directions," *Annual Review of Sociology* 38 (1): 247–65. doi: 10.1146/annurev-soc-071811-145424.

Herbert, David. (2012), "Why Has Religion Gone Public Again? Towards a Theory of Media and Religious Re-Publicization," in Gordon Lynch, Joylon Mitchell, and Anna Strhan (eds.), *Religion, Media and Culture: A Reader*, 89–97, London: Routledge.

Kashtan, Aaron. (2018), *Between Pen and Pixel: Comics, Materiality, and the Book of the Future, Studies in Comics and Cartoons*, Columbus: Ohio State University Press.

Knowles, Chris. (2007), *Our Gods Wear Spandex: The Secret History of Comic Book Heroes*, Newburyport: Red Wheel Weiser.

Locke, Simon. (2012), "Spirit(ualitie)s of Science in Words and Pictures: Syncretising Science and Religion in the Cosmologies of Two Comic Books," *Journal of Contemporary Religion* 27 (3):383–401. doi: 10.1080/13537903.2012.722028.

Meyer, Birgit. (2012), *Mediation and the Genesis of Presence. Towards a Material Approach to Religion (Oratie 19 Oktober 2012)*, Utrecht: Universiteit Utrecht.

Meyer, Birgit, and Annelies Moors (eds.) (2006), *Religion, Media, and the Public Sphere*, Bloomington: Indiana University Press.

Savramis, Demosthenes. (1985), *Tarzan & Superman Und Der Messias Religion Und Utopie in Den Comics*. 1. Aufl 1985 edn, Berlin: K. Kramer.

Thomas, Jolyon Baraka. (2012), "Horrific 'Cults' and Comic Religion: *Manga* after Aum," *Japanese Journal of Religious Studies* 39 (1): 127–51.

Tinker, Emma. (2007), "Manuscript in Print: The Materiality of Alternative Comics," *Literature Compass* 4 (4): 1169–82. doi: 10.1111/j.1741-4113.2007.00478.x.

van Asselt, Willem, Paul van Geest, Daniela Müller, and Theo Salemink. (eds.) (2007), *Iconoclasm and Iconoclash: Struggle for Religious Identity, Jewish and Christian Perspectives Series*, Boston: Brill.

Vermassen, Joris. (2018), *Heilige Tekst, Goddeloos Beeld: Een Gespannen Relatie*, Antwerpen: Uitgeverij Vrijdag.

Index

www.ingramcontent.com/pod-product-compliance
Lightning Source LLC
Chambersburg PA
CBHW071851270326
41929CB00013B/2186

* 9 7 8 1 3 5 0 3 2 1 6 2 5 *